PRAISE FOR THE
BESTSEL

# ANN RULE'S CRIME FILES

Seventeen must-read collections of "fascinating,
unsettling" (*Booklist*) true crime accounts!

"Chilling cases. . . . A frightening, fascinating rogue's
gallery of mercenary murderers."

—*Mystery Guild*

"The prolific and talented Rule brings to life a rich case."
—*Publishers Weekly* (starred review)

"Gripping. . . . Fans of true crime know they can rely on
Ann Rule to deliver the dead-level best."

—*The Hartford Courant*

"Rule leaves no stone unturned as she unravels the cases
from start to finish."

—*Night Owl Reviews*

"Among the very small group of top-notch true-crime
writers, Rule just may be the best of the bunch."

—*Booklist*

"Rule's ability to depict both criminals and victims as
believable human beings is perfectly embodied in this sad,
fascinating account."

—*Library Journal*

### TOO LATE TO SAY GOODBYE

"The quintessential true-crime story. . . . Mesmerizing. . . . Prepare yourself for a few late nights of reading."

*—Bookreporter*

### GREEN RIVER, RUNNING RED

"[Rule] conveys the emotional truth of the Green River case."

*—Los Angeles Times*

"Riveting. . . . Infused with a personally felt sense of urgency."

*—People*

Ann Rule worked the all-night shift at a suicide
hotline with a handsome, whip-smart psychology
major who became her close friend. Soon the world
would know him: Ted Bundy, one of the most
savage serial killers of our time. . . .

### THE STRANGER BESIDE ME
Now in an updated edition!

"Shattering . . . written with compassion but also with professional objectivity."

*—Seattle Times*

"Overwhelming!"

*—Houston Post*

"Ann Rule has an extraordinary angle [on] the most fascinating killer in modern American history. . . . As dramatic and chilling as a bedroom window shattering at midnight."

*—The New York Times*

## Books by Ann Rule

Practice to Deceive
In the Still of the Night
Too Late to Say Goodbye
Green River, Running Red
Every Breath You Take
. . . And Never Let Her Go
Bitter Harvest
Dead by Sunset
Everything She Ever Wanted
If You Really Loved Me
The Stranger Beside Me
Possession
Small Sacrifices
Heart Full of Lies

*Ann Rule's Crime Files:*

Without Pity: Ann Rule's Most Dangerous Killers

The I-5 Killer
The Want-Ad Killer
Lust Killer

# ANN RULE

# LYING IN WAIT

## AND OTHER TRUE CASES
### ANN RULE'S CRIME FILES:Vol.17

**POCKET BOOKS**

New York   London   Toronto   Sydney   New Delhi

Pocket Books
A Division of Simon & Schuster, Inc.
1230 Avenue of the Americas
New York, NY 10020

The names of some individuals have been changed. Such names are indicated by an asterisk (*) the first time each appears in the narrative.

First Pocket Books paperback edition December 2014

POCKET and colophon are registered trademarks of Simon & Schuster, Inc.

For information about special discounts for bulk purchases, please contact Simon & Schuster Special Sales at 1-866-506-1949 or business@simonandschuster.com.

The Simon & Schuster Speakers Bureau can bring authors to your live event. For more information or to book an event, contact the Simon & Schuster Speakers Bureau at 1-866-248-3049 or visit our website at www.simonspeakers.com.

Cover illustration by Tom Hallman
Cover lettering by James Wang

Manufactured in the United States of America

10  9  8  7  6  5  4  3  2  1

ISBN 978-1-4516-4829-4
ISBN 978-1-4516-4831-7 (ebook)

*For those who trusted too much—*
*and for those who still do*
*Beware*

# *Contents*

# *Introduction*

Readers often ask me if I get depressed writing about murder. Sometimes I do, of course. Man's inhumanity to man baffles me, and I wonder why murderers haven't chosen another path. Why on earth would anyone in an unhappy marriage pick murder instead of divorce? This bothers me particularly when there are children involved.

There may have been large insurance policies on the deceased. There may have been overwhelming rage. Or illicit lovers spurring on the actual killer. There are probably dozens of motives for murder, yet none of them seem reasonable to the minds of "ordinary" people.

So many of the victims in this book were kind people who cared about others, lived quiet lives with happy families, trusted in their God, and really did nothing at all to harm anyone.

There are three long vignettes and several shorter cases. And yes, writing them has made me depressed from time to time. The saving grace of what I do is that I've heard from many people who say that reading my books has, quite literally, saved their lives, that the stories of many innocent victims have been cautionary tales that kept them from trusting those who were too charming, too attractive, and told too many bizarre stories about their backgrounds to be believed. Others wrote that they realized someone they were about to marry had a veneer of good over the evil that lay just beneath.

Sometimes it's a simple matter of my warnings against hitchhiking, picking up hitchhikers, or meeting people on the Internet. Readers have told me that they recognized a dangerous sociopath for what he (or she) was, after reading my stories about charismatic killers with dark sides.

If my books can save just one life, it's all worth it.

The first case in *Lying in Wait* is "The Baby Seller." Initially, when a relative of a woman who allegedly killed new mothers called me, I was skeptical. The story she told me sounded too weird to be true, but it *was* true, and far more complex than I could have imagined. The deeper I dug into it, the more startling facts I excavated.

The next long story—"Secrets of the Amorous Pizza Man"—is a case that made me cry. Kathie Hill loved and trusted her husband and believed he felt the same way. Kathie, a brilliant meteorologist, found love "down on the ice" at the South Pole. Her life was ended by someone who planned her death with calculated cruelty.

"A Road Trip to Murder" tells the story of a modern-day Bonnie and Clyde, white supremacists who cut a bloody path from Oregon to Washington and then to Northern California. Heroes, too, play a part in these stories. In a strange coincidence, one of these heroes was once my neighbor. Terry Uhrich, the highway patrol officer who caught the killers in "A Road Trip to Murder," lived across the street from me when he was a boy. My daughter, Leslie, was his babysitter.

"Murderous Epitaph for the Beautiful Runaway" is the story of a free-spirited and trusting teen who did not recognize evil until it was too late.

During four bleak months in the winter of 1975, Seattle women were terrorized by an attacker so full of rage that detectives feared his next victim would die. "Tracks of a Serial Rapist" covers those dark days that finally ended when one victim refused to give in.

In "Take a Lifer Home to Dinner . . . with Murder for Dessert!" a pint-sized escape artist cannot be contained by law enforcement. Yet it is not his own cunning that brings disaster, but an overly optimistic government-sanctioned program.

# THE BABY SELLER

**When Dana Rose DiLillo\*** first contacted me in the spring of 2013, I almost put her in my "220" file—my file labeled with the term Washington State law officers use for someone who is mentally unstable. Her story was that far-fetched. It certainly wouldn't be the first time that someone has called or written me about a bizarre murder they have witnessed. Most of the time when I follow up on these cases, I find that they never really happened.

Those who tell me stories that would chill the blood aren't lying to me; their delusions are so entrenched that they actually *believe* they are true. Taken to ground level, some of my "informants" admit that the murder was something they had seen in a dream, or that they had not actually seen it themselves, but were relaying something that a psychic had told them about.

---

\* Asterisks indicate that a name has been changed to protect the individual's privacy.

It usually doesn't take me long to determine that there had been no unsolved cases in the locales they named. Their time sequences didn't fit and, sometimes, the "victim" was still alive and well, unaware of their alleged death.

In the corner of my office is a file stuffed with these "220" reports. I try to treat the people who send them with respect and kindness, and I feel sad for them; it must be a certain kind of hell to be haunted by unsolved homicides that never occurred.

I like to think that I've learned to spot people who are gullible, mistaken, obsessed, or just plain psychotic. I did, after all, write my first true crime article in 1969. Because I have covered thousands of criminal cases, I've had a front-row seat to the machinations of human behavior.

Generally, I have been able to winnow out the deluded and the liars early on.

But not always.

I could not make up my mind about Dana Rose. Had she really witnessed a murder—a murder committed by her *mother*?

We had spoken on the phone several times before Dana Rose told me that she had been committed to mental hospitals from time to time, and I wondered if my first impression of her had been right.

Dana Rose's claims were hard to believe, yet something told me I needed to take a closer look. And when I did, I was astonished to find her story turned out to be truth stranger than fiction.

*    *    *

Athens, Alabama, is one of the state's oldest incorporated towns. Founded in 1818, it is the county seat of Limestone County. It sits fifteen miles south of Tennessee, and its historic downtown is home to Athens State University— an institution of higher learning with roots that wend back nearly two centuries.

The crime rate in Athens is lower than the average for Alabama, and visitors would never guess the charming old town with its wide, clean streets and easygoing residents was the site of an afternoon of violence that cut deep and left an ugly scar that some say has never truly healed.

The story of the nightmare that struck Athens is reduced to a few paragraphs and engraved upon a historic marker that sits smack in the middle of the lawn of Limestone County's brick courthouse. It begins, "Athens Sacked and Plundered," and briefly describes that dark May 2 in 1862 when Colonel John Basil Turchin turned loose his brigade of Union soldiers.

The sign does not mention the fact that the Russian-born Turchin told his men that he would shut his eyes for two hours so that they could plunder and rape to their hearts' content.

Terrified citizens cowered in fear as the men ripped through the town, stealing anything of value that they could carry and destroying what they could not. Females were shoved and kicked and fondled, and when their husbands and fathers stepped forward to protect them, they were hauled off and arrested. The soldiers laughed at the hysterical girls and women, unmoved by their tears as they raped them.

When the shameful pillage was over, and authorities prepared to court-martial Colonel Turchin for encouraging the war crimes, his wife appealed to President Abraham Lincoln for help. Lincoln not only pardoned Turchin, he promoted him to brigadier general.

A pregnant woman was among the victims that spring day in Athens when evil came to town. The poor woman was so terrorized by the soldiers that she went into early labor. Both mother and baby died.

Over a century later, in January 1980, another young Athens mother would be subjected to that same, paralyzing terror. But this time, it wasn't an army of mad-dog soldiers that threatened to take away all that was dear, but a smiling woman who appeared so ordinary that anyone who passed her on the street would likely forget her immediately—if they noticed her at all.

She certainly didn't *appear* evil, or in any way threatening. If anything, the visitor at the door was simply an annoying interruption to Geneva Clemons, who had just settled down to watch her favorite TV show, her small daughter and infant son beside her.

But monsters come in all shapes and sizes, and the evil inside the frumpy, grinning woman was every bit as damaging as the cruelty of all of Turchin's soldiers combined.

\*     \*     \*

Geneva Clemons was happy that day as she cuddled her infant son. It was January 21, 1980, and five-year-old Tracy gazed proudly at her little brother. James was just sixteen days old. Tracy had waited a long time to become a sister, and she was so excited about finally having a sibling that she had wasted no time in donating her sippy cups to the wiggling infant. She was, after all, the big sister now, and she could drink out of a grown-up cup.

The baby stared at her so intently, it was as if he knew what she was thinking. She held out her finger and smiled as James grasped it in his tiny fist.

Though she had longed for a little sister or brother, Tracy had never been without a playmate. Her *mother* was her best friend and spent her days playing with her firstborn.

"She was a big kid at heart," Tracy remembers.

Sometimes Tracy's mother pushed her on the swing set in their big backyard, and sometimes they played hide-and-seek.

Geneva was always up for any game Tracy wanted to play, and Tracy remembers how she got down in the dirt with her to make mud pies. It didn't matter if they made a mess. Mother and daughter got lost in the moment, faces streaked with dirt as they giggled and "baked" their mud pies and then pretended to eat them.

Geneva's laugh was joyful, and all these years later,

Tracy can still close her eyes and hear her mother's laughter.

Geneva's kind hazel eyes were flecked with brown, and her silky black hair fell to her waist. She was striking, her Cherokee heritage obvious in her high cheekbones. Geneva's parents, Martha Louise Barnes, born in July 1925, and Henry Alvin Burgett, born in October 1918, both had Cherokee blood, and Geneva was three-quarters Cherokee.

Geneva was born on January 6, 1953, somewhere in the middle of a big, noisy brood of ten kids—four boys and six girls. The brothers and sisters all got along well and remained close over the years. They grew up in Tanner, Alabama, the family's Limestone County roots going back at least three generations.

Geneva Burgett met Larry Wayne Clemons when she was twenty. Larry, three years older than Geneva, was love struck from the moment he first saw her. She lived across the street from a friend's house in Tanner. At Larry's urging, the friend arranged for Geneva and Larry to double date with him and his girlfriend.

It wasn't long until Geneva and Larry were talking about a life together. Larry was in the service, and the plan was for him to support them while she stayed home with any children they might have.

The parents were thrilled when their first child, Tracy, was born in December 1974. A fiercely protective mother, Geneva worried when her infant daughter came down with colic.

Geneva sat in the rocking chair for hours, cradling her baby close and rocking so hard that the chair thudded against the wall. "My dad said she rocked me so much that she broke a few rocking chairs," says Tracy.

The Clemons family was happy. They didn't have a lot of money and couldn't afford to buy a house, but they had found a cozy place in the low-rent district of Athens. It was right next door to Larry's aunt and uncle, so family was always close by.

One sad thing had happened just a couple of weeks earlier, when Geneva was in the hospital giving birth to James. Her beloved pug, Poochie, was struck by a truck. Poochie was a ferocious guard dog. The Clemonses had had her since she was a puppy, and she was so protective of her family's turf that she chased a couple of Larry's aunts from the house when they stopped by to feed her.

"They were afraid of her," says Tracy. "She loved us, but she scared everyone else. If Poochie had been alive, no one would have bothered us."

Tracy missed Poochie, but she was excited to have a new little brother. The baby was with them as Tracy and her mother got ready for their favorite ritual. Every night they would snuggle on the couch and watch *Little House on the Prairie*.

Geneva favored Sun Drop soda, and right before *Little House* started, she would open a can and get a big bag of Funyuns to snack on. Geneva had just opened her soda, and they were getting ready to watch their show, when they heard someone at the door.

It was that lady from the contest again. Geneva had met her earlier that day at the supermarket. Geneva was grocery shopping, with baby James in her arms, when the magazine photographer—who said her name was Jackie—first approached her to suggest she enter James in a "beautiful baby contest." If James won, and his photo was chosen for an ad, then Geneva would get five hundred dollars.

The Clemons family was struggling financially and could really use the money. Geneva gave Jackie her address, then continued with her shopping.

Now, this was the third time that day that the lady photographer had approached Geneva. The new mother was a little put off by the woman's insistence. When she had come by earlier, she gushed about how perfect James was. She was so anxious to take the baby's photo for the contest.

Kathy and Wayne McMeans, Geneva's sister and brother-in-law, happened to be there earlier when the photographer popped in. Apparently not wanting to intrude while Geneva had company, she left. Now she was back. The sun had set, and dusk had melted into night, but the woman was insistent that Geneva and the children go with her so that she could photograph the baby.

Geneva was excited about the contest, but she hadn't had a chance to talk to Larry about it. She suggested that Jackie come back when her husband was home.

But the stranger with a camera was persistent, and said they should go with her now for a photo shoot.

Geneva was tired. She had given birth to James by cae-sarean section, and she was still sore. But she was nice to everyone, and she didn't want to be rude to the lady from the magazine who assured her that baby James was hand-some enough to win the contest.

She would get no argument from Geneva on that. She was proud of both her children, and she could understand why her visitor was so charmed by her infant son.

But it was 8 P.M.—getting close to Tracy's bedtime, and growing colder by the minute. It wasn't practical to scoop up her two small children and go riding off in a car with someone she barely knew. As nicely as she could, Geneva explained that she would not be going anywhere that night.

Not to be refused, the lady suggested that they all step outside and follow her to her car so she could take their picture. It would take just a moment, she explained, and there was a good chance that James would win the five hundred dollars.

While the photographer was a stranger, she hardly seemed threatening. She was, after all, a mother herself. In fact, her own daughter was with her, and she looked to be close to Tracy's age.

The woman didn't wait for an invitation, but brushed by Geneva as she stepped into the house. She quickly picked up the baby and handed him to her daughter, bend-ing to whisper something in the girl's ear.

Tracy and her mother followed the lady and her daughter outside. If Geneva thought something was amiss, Tracy wasn't aware of it.

A Chevy Malibu station wagon was backed into the driveway, and they headed toward the car so the photographer could get her camera. She explained that she wanted Geneva and her "adorable" daughter to pose for a picture before she took one of James.

Geneva and Tracy stood side by side, their backs to a tree beside the driveway as they posed for the camera. Then the woman raised her hands. She was holding something and pointing it at them. Tracy figured it was the camera.

"I heard a boom and a bang, and then I saw a flash," Tracy remembers. "I thought it was the flash on the camera."

*Boom! Bang! Flash!*

Geneva slowly slumped against the tree and then slid to the ground.

Confused, Tracy knelt beside her mother and looked into her anguished eyes. "Mama!" she cried. "What's wrong?"

Geneva gazed into her daughter's trusting eyes. Tracy was bewildered. She didn't know why her mama was on the ground or why she was staring at her with such sad eyes.

But there was no time for her mother to explain any of it to her. Geneva was dying; she could sense her life seeping away. She had only one last breath, only one last word to speak. Her voice was weak and gurgling as she whispered, *"Run!"*

Tracy didn't hesitate. She bolted into the shadows and was swallowed up by the dark edges of the yard.

"I remember it as if it happened last week," Tracy recalls some thirty-four years later.

The frozen leaves beneath her feet crackled as she moved toward the fence. It was so dark that she could not see where she was going, but fear and her mother's last words propelled her forward.

Tracy heard the sound of tires squealing as she scrambled over the fence and dropped into the yard next door where her daddy's aunt and uncle lived.

Ford and Ruby Tribble were horrified when they opened the door and found little Tracy standing there, covered with her mother's blood.

The traumatized child looked at them with wild eyes and cried, "Mama! Mama! Help! Help!"

She had no other words to describe what had happened. She was in deep shock, but she would remember the details of that terrible night forever.

As the Malibu roared away from the Clemonses' home, seven-year-old Dana Rose wailed in the backseat. She had just witnessed a woman killed, and the boom of the gun blast was as much of a shock to her as it was to the screaming baby in her arms—the *lady's* baby!

Dana Rose felt as if she were in a nightmare. Why had her mother shot the nice lady and taken her baby?

Dana Rose's little sister, Deanna,* was curled up on the seat beside her. She was asleep, but even if she had been awake, she would not have been able to understand what had just happened. Deanna was only four years old.

Harold Lee Schut, her stepfather, was behind the wheel of the Malibu, and he reached into the backseat and smacked Dana Rose across the face, telling her to "quit bawling." The blow bloodied her nose, and warm blood gushed down her face.

Her sobs diminished to soft sniffles as their car raced through the night.

The Tribbles rushed to the Clemonses' yard with Tracy behind them. When they saw Geneva on the ground, Tracy begged her aunt and uncle to help her, crying, "Get Mama up!"

The horror of the situation was just beginning to dawn on the middle-aged couple. Geneva was shot, and the baby was gone. The Tribbles hurried into the Clemonses' house to phone for help. "They took me inside with them," remembers Tracy.

Her eyes settled on the big, yellow bag of Funyuns and her mother's can of Sun Drop soda. "It was sitting there, still cold, but my mama never got to drink it."

The image of her mother's untouched soda was burned

forever into her memory—a reminder of how quickly things can change.

Just minutes before, Tracy had been cozy on the couch, excited to watch her favorite show with her mother, her baby brother safe beside them. Now, she was standing there numb with shock as the ambulance and police cars arrived with lights whirling.

Geneva Clemons had been shot with a .38-caliber pistol, struck twice, once in the abdomen and once near her shoulder, the force of one bullet dislodging her breast. She was taken away in the ambulance, but there was nothing more anyone could do for her.

The murder was so cruel, it shocked the small Athens police force. What kind of person would execute a mother in front of her child and then steal her newborn? And where was the baby? It hardly seemed likely that this was a kidnapping for ransom. The Clemonses lived in a modest home and were clearly not wealthy.

Investigators didn't know it yet, but the abductor hadn't kept the infant for long. Baby James had already been abandoned, left in a ditch by a field in Hartselle, Alabama, twenty-eight miles south of Athens. The baby was all alone, shivering in the cold, his cries unanswered.

Geneva's husband, Larry Clemons, was at his job at a co-op in Decatur, a few miles away, when his wife was killed. He was on a break when his sister-in-law called him. "She said my wife had been shot and my baby was kidnapped. I dropped the phone," he remembers.

Geneva was the love of his life, and Larry did not know what he would do without her. They had been so excited about the new baby, and now, both Geneva and the baby were gone. Larry was so shaken, he went into shock and was treated at the hospital.

It was a little before 10 P.M. when Clyde Reeves drove along Reeves Road, toward his Hartselle home. The farmer pulled into his driveway, and his headlights swept his field as he rounded a curve. For a split second, he saw something white caught in the beams of light, and he immediately thought of his cat. She was expecting kittens but had disappeared. Had she had her kittens in the ditch? Clyde was worried about the cat and was anxious to find the kittens. He parked the car and hurried to the house to get a flashlight.

"I think I found the cat," he told his wife, and he headed through the field toward the ditch. When he got close, the first thing he noticed was two tiny hands—*human hands!* He rushed back to the house and told his wife to phone the police.

Clyde Reeves had found baby James. The infant was wearing only a onesie and covered with a thin receiving blanket. He was barely alive, and he was rushed to the hospital. Gravely ill from his exposure to the cold, he soon developed double pneumonia. He had been left outside in near freezing temperatures for close to two hours. If another half hour had passed, the news would have been far more grim. It was a miracle baby James was found before it was too late.

"He had turned black and blue," Larry Clemons recalls. "My son had to be hospitalized for four weeks."

Authorities were stymied by the senseless killing. According to little Tracy, the shooter had been a woman with a daughter of her own. Was this a case of a woman unable to bear another child who was so desperate for a baby that she would commit murder? If so, why would she then reject the baby and leave him outside to die?

There was also the possibility that someone was so angry at Larry or Geneva that they attacked the family in an act of revenge. But the Clemonses had no enemies. There was no reason in the world for anyone to want to hurt them.

Larry could no longer live in the house where he had shared such happy times with his wife. The memories were too painful. "I told the landlord that I had to move," he says. "I couldn't live in a place where my wife had been killed in the driveway."

Larry could not bear to look at anything that reminded him of Geneva—and *everything* did. "I got rid of my car and my truck," he confesses.

The love of his life had ridden beside him in those vehicles, and every time he got behind the wheel, her absence cut deeper.

He asked his wife's sister to go through Geneva's belongings and take what she wanted. It hurt him too much to see her possessions.

Now, it was just Larry and the children. He loved them

dearly, and he vowed to be the best father he could to them. He thanked God the kids had two sets of grandparents to nurture them.

But Larry's grief was so overwhelming that it broke his spirit. He had a mental breakdown. "I was hospitalized for three or four months," he remembers.

Tracy, too, was anxiety ridden. She was so nervous that she jumped at sudden noises. Worst of all were the nightmares. She could not forget the face of the killer.

Even today, over three decades after the stranger destroyed their lives, Tracy still can't forget, and she says quietly, "I remember that monster."

Now the memory makes her sad, but as a child it terrified her. "That monster" came for the little girl in her dreams, and Tracy awoke in a cold sweat.

She felt so helpless when she saw her daddy crying. "I knew there was nothing I could do for him," she says, "but I did my best to try to make him smile."

As of this writing, thirty-four years have passed since Geneva was savagely taken from her family, and Larry admits he is still grieving. He married twice more, but those unions didn't work out. He accepts the fact that he will never again find the kind of love he had with Geneva.

"I miss her still," he says sadly.


One month after the Athens shooting, on Wednesday, February 20, 1980, Lori Vaughn,* age fifteen, of Oak Grove,

Louisiana, gave birth to a baby girl at University Medical Center in Jackson, Mississippi.

The baby was beautiful, and Lori named her Tina.* Just hours after Tina was born, the new mother noticed a chunky young woman hanging around the maternity ward.

Tired and sore, Lori was getting to know her newborn when she looked up to see the stranger enter her room. Lori wasn't alarmed. The woman was smiling and friendly, and she told her about her life as she admired the infant.

The visitor confided in the teen that she was depressed because she had recently given birth, but the baby had died. It made her very sad, she said wistfully, because she could not have any more children. She loved being around babies, she added, as she gazed adoringly at the infant.

Half a dozen times that day, the woman visited Lori's room, once changing Tina's diaper.

The next morning, around 10:30, the stranger showed up again. By now, Lori was comfortable with her, and she wasn't worried when the woman picked up Tina and said that she was going to take her to the nursery so that the doctor could check her umbilical cord. She assured Lori that this was part of the procedure, and that the baby could not be released from the hospital until the doctor checked her cord.

Long minutes ticked by, and the woman did not return with little Tina. When Lori asked the nurses about her daughter's whereabouts, they were alarmed. The baby wasn't in the nursery, and the doctor hadn't examined her cord.

Tina had been abducted!

Her teeth chattering with shock, Lori did her best to give police an accurate description of the stranger who had walked away with her new baby. The kidnapper was heavyset, about 160 pounds, and her hair was brown. She wore tennis shoes, jeans, and a red shirt with a blue jacket.

The FBI was called in, and they questioned the staff. One of the hospital employees remembered a woman who matched the description of the kidnapper. She had seen her use the telephone. The FBI checked phone records and were able to determine that the suspect had made a call to a woman named Rita Warner.*

They went to see Rita, and when they asked her about who had phoned her at the time in question, she told them that her daughter had. Mrs. Warner and her daughter, Bonnie Stevens,* hadn't been close in recent years, but Rita knew where she lived. She gave the FBI agents the address, and they arrested Bonnie at her home in Tallulah, Louisiana.

Baby Tina was returned to her mother at 10 P.M., eleven and a half hours after she had been taken. The doctor pronounced the infant healthy.

Kidnapper Bonnie Stevens was twenty-two years old, the mother of two children, and had been divorced for about a year and a half. She had recently been treated at the Tallulah Mental Health Clinic.

Bonnie wept as FBI agents accompanied her to the Jackson magistrate's office. She was in serious trouble. Not only did she face charges for kidnapping, she was a suspect in a murder!

It was the second time in four weeks that a stout, dark-haired woman had stolen an infant. While Lori Vaughn hadn't been harmed when her baby was abducted, there were too many similarities between the Vaughn case and the Clemons case to be ignored.

After facing charges for kidnapping Tina Vaughn, Bonnie was held for questioning in the Alabama case. Athens detectives were excited, hoping this would be the break they needed. They took Geneva's sister, Kathy, to identify the suspect. Could this be the woman she had seen hanging around the Clemons house on January 21?

But Kathy took one look at Bonnie Stevens and shook her head. This wasn't the woman she had seen. This was not the woman who killed her sister.


When the stranger complimented her baby, Cheryl Jones couldn't help feeling proud. Amanda *was* adorable, and she didn't doubt that her eight-week-old infant could win the beautiful baby contest that the woman had told her about.

The woman who introduced herself as Sally was short

and squat, with owlish glasses, and she repeatedly re-marked how pretty Amanda was.

It was March 6, 1980, and Cheryl, age twenty, was shopping at the PX on the naval station in the Algiers sec-tion of New Orleans, Louisiana. Her husband, Dennis, was in the navy. Cheryl missed him when he was on maneu-vers, but their baby kept her busy. Amanda Rae Jones was growing so fast, and Cheryl was excited about each new thing she did. She called or wrote letters to her mother, updating her on each little milestone.

Cheryl's mother, Margaret Pecore, would later tell a reporter how excited her daughter had been when she called her to report that baby Amanda had smiled for the first time.

Cheryl was *Margaret's* baby. Margaret and Alfred Pecore had six children—one boy and five girls. Cheryl, born in October 1959, was the youngest. They raised their family in Baldwinsville, New York, where Alfred worked as a machinist, and Margaret helped make ends meet by sewing and taking in ironing.

Margaret was a talented seamstress, and her daugh-ters, too, all learned how to sew at a young age. Cheryl picked up a needle and thread and started stitching pieces of fabric together before she was in kindergarten.

"Cheryl made all her own school clothes," says Cheryl's sister, Kathy Taylor, who was born two years before Cheryl. All the sisters sewed their own clothing, but Cheryl had a special knack for it.

"She made her prom dress," Kathy remembers. "And later on, I used it for my wedding dress!"

When she was a teen, Cheryl took a piece of pretty fabric and built an entire quilt around it, creating the design as she went. Even Mrs. Pecore was impressed by the lovely quilt her daughter created from nothing. "My mother was fascinated by it," Kathy says.

The Pecore house was small for a family of eight, and all five girls shared a bedroom. As the two youngest sisters, Kathy and Cheryl were very close.

Their home was in the country, and the sisters considered themselves "farm girls." They didn't live on a farm themselves, but they were right next door to a dairy farm. "It was owned by a man named MacDonald. That was *really* his name!" laughs Kathy, who remembers that they liked to go to MacDonald's farm for homemade ice cream.

Both Cheryl and Kathy were animal lovers, and they encouraged stray cats and dogs to follow them home. "Sometimes Cheryl would bring home a cat, and she would hide it from my parents for a few days," Kathy recalls. She would wait for their parents to be in a good mood, and then she would bring out the cat and act as if it had just wandered in. Margaret and Alfred likely saw through the scheme, but they just smiled and let most of the strays stay.

Cheryl had a wickedly silly sense of humor that sometimes got her in trouble with the teachers at school when she disrupted the class. She also liked to make Kathy laugh at inappropriate times.

Though Cheryl was intelligent, she had no plans for college—no lofty aspirations to become a career woman. Even as a young girl, when the other kids talked about what they wanted to be when they grew up, Cheryl had one dream. "She wanted to have a baby," says Kathy.

Cheryl met her soul mate at school when she was about thirteen. Dennis Jones was a year older than she was, and he fell for her as soon as he met her.

"Before he was old enough to have a real job, he mowed lawns all summer so he could buy her a ring," Kathy remembers. "His family was mad at him for spending all his money on that ring."

But both Dennis and Cheryl knew what they wanted. Cheryl was still in high school when they got married on December 30, 1977.

Dennis decided on a career in the navy, and when Cheryl graduated, they moved to Louisiana where he was stationed.

On Christmas Day, 1979, Cheryl gave birth to Amanda Rae. They joked that she was their Christmas present to each other—the only gift they gave each other that year.

It was Cheryl's dream come true. All she had ever wanted was a family of her own. Now, she had a kind husband who adored both her and their baby.

They planned to have more children one day and buy a house with a big backyard for the kids to play in. But for now, Cheryl was happy with their little apartment on the navy base where it was fun to play with Mandy and to cook meals for her husband—another thing she was good at. She especially liked to make breakfast.

Life was happy for the Jones family. It looked like they were headed down a charmed path—until Cheryl encountered evil. Initially, there was no reason to believe that the woman who said her name was Sally was anyone other than what she appeared to be—a rather dowdy woman on a photography assignment.

Sally took photos of baby Amanda in the parking lot of the PX. She told Cheryl that she thought there was a very good chance that the baby would win the beautiful baby contest, because she was so pretty.

If she should win, Sally warned Cheryl, then they would show up at her place early in the morning, and she would have to be prepared to leave immediately.

The very next morning at around seven o'clock, Sally was at Cheryl's door. She had good news and bad news. The bad news was that Amanda hadn't won first prize. But the good news was that she *did* win a shopping spree in Houston.

If the photographer had been a man, Cheryl probably wouldn't have gone with him. But there was nothing threatening about Sally. She appeared to be middle-aged, though she was actually only twenty-seven.

And Amanda was so beautiful, the young mother didn't even question the news that she had won a prize.

Sally seemed happy for them that Amanda had been a finalist.

Cheryl packed up the baby and the diaper bag and all of the other things she would need for a long day trip to Houston.

Cheryl may not have been aware of the man until she climbed into the car. He was a small man—short and skinny, with a wispy mustache. He was apparently married to Sally.

It was about a five-hour drive to Houston, a long time to be in a car with people she did not know well.

No one knows exactly what was in Cheryl's head as she got farther and farther from the cozy little apartment she shared with Dennis, but investigators believe that the young mother began to get nervous.

Before long, Cheryl realized that her journey was no longer voluntary. There was no beautiful baby contest, and Sally was no photographer.

The woman had only pretended to take pictures, and the camera probably didn't even have film in it, according to Houston detective Gil Schultz. "If any were ever taken, we never located them," he says.

Sally had been so friendly in the beginning, but that was an act. Cheryl didn't know it, but she was trapped in the car with a woman so sadistic that her crimes would shock even seasoned detectives.

Cheryl's captors wanted to calm her down, but not because they cared about her feelings. They simply could not have the young mother's hysteria foil their plans.

At some point, perhaps before they arrived at the swanky hotel in Houston, the couple drugged Cheryl. That probably wasn't necessary; even if Cheryl saw an opportunity to run away, she wouldn't have tried, because she would never risk putting Amanda in danger.

There is no doubt that Sally used Cheryl's love for Amanda against her. If she should try to get away or to signal anyone she was in trouble, she was afraid they would harm her baby.

When Cheryl was pregnant with Amanda, she had written to a friend, telling her that she already loved her baby so much that she knew she would give up her own life for her. Now, those words turned out to be prophetically tragic.

Once in the hotel room, Sally forced Cheryl to write a suicide note. Sally dictated ugly things—thoughts so foul that when the FBI handwriting experts finally examined the letter years later, they would determine that the note was hatched in the mind of a "sexually deviant female." The FBI could also tell by the pinched handwriting that though it came from Cheryl's hand, she had been coerced into writing it.

The gist of the note was that Cheryl was killing herself because she had run off with another man and he had abandoned her. She regretted that she had betrayed Dennis, and the other man didn't want her.

"I have nothing to live for," the fake suicide note ended.

Sally and her companion slipped drugs into a soda and forced Cheryl to drink it until she overdosed.

It was a bad ending to a good life.

"She died trying to save me," says Amanda Jones, who is now thirty-four and a mother herself.

Cheryl's friends and family agree that she would have done anything to save her baby. Cheryl's death was senseless. If her captors were so eager to have Mandy, then why didn't they keep her?

Later that day, a taxi driver in New Orleans rolled up to a hotel to pick up a passenger who had called for a ride. A woman walked out to the car and set a baby down in the front seat. She handed the driver an address and a twenty-dollar bill, and instructed him to take the baby to her father, who was in the navy.

The taxi driver told the woman that he couldn't take a baby by itself, and that she would have to come along, too.

"Okay," said the woman, coolly. "Let me just get my luggage." She turned and walked back into the hotel. When she didn't come back out, the driver went into the lobby to look for her.

The front desk employees told him that she wasn't a guest at the hotel—just someone who had asked to use the phone to call a cab. She had walked in one door and out the other. Now she was long gone.

The taxi driver decided to just go ahead and take the

baby to the address the woman had given him. He didn't have a car seat, so he strapped the infant to the seat beside him as best he could, and he drove her to the naval base.

The next day, a maid found Cheryl dead in the Houston hotel. The medical examiner noted that Cheryl's left wrist was cut but hadn't bled. She had died from an overdose of Tuinal, a type of barbiturate. The ME ruled her death a suicide.

Homicide detectives Paul Motard and Gil Schultz did not believe it. And neither did Cheryl's family.

It would be five years before the manner of Cheryl's death was changed to murder.


Months rolled by, and Geneva's killer was still on the loose. Tracy's sleep continued to be riddled with nightmares. What if the killer returned and tried to hurt her? The idea frightened her. And it worried her family, too. As the only witness to the murder of her mother, she was in a dangerous spot.

If police were ever to capture the killer, Tracy would be able to identify her. A woman so evil that she could kill a mother as she stood by her five-year-old could be capable of eliminating a witness—no matter how young.

She had, after all, left baby James for dead. If Clyde Reeves hadn't found him when he did, the infant would surely have died.

"I was scared when I started school," Tracy confides.

Not only did she feel the sorrow of her mother not being there to pick out her dress for the first day of kindergarten and to brush her shiny brown hair, she struggled with the fear that the bad lady could appear at any moment and shoot her. "I had a nightmare that she came to school and got me and took me away with her."

Though her teachers were protective of her, and the school administrators tightened security, the child was aware of how quickly bad things could happen.

Both sets of Tracy's grandparents rallied around and helped Larry care for the children. Tracy's aunts and uncles helped, too.

They all did their best to go on with life without Geneva, but everyone would have felt so much safer if only the police could find the killer.

The anxiety-ridden days and the sleepless nights dragged on for five years. James turned five—the same age his sister had been when he was kidnapped. Tracy was ten. She had now spent half her life as a motherless child.

The murderer could be anywhere. For all Larry Clemons knew, the woman who had stolen his joy could be living just blocks away, and she could appear at any moment and try to hurt them again.

But there were no new leads in the case. Everyone feared that the killer would never be caught.

Though Athens detectives could never have guessed it, the answers were two thousand miles away in Yakima, Washington. Geneva's killer was happily going about her life, enjoying shopping sprees during the day and playing bingo and partying at night.

Her story began on October 7, 1952—the same day that sports headlines were dominated by the news that the New York Yankees had won the World Series for the fourth time in a row. Theaters across the country were showing the movie *The Winning Team,* starring Doris Day and Ronald Reagan. *American Bandstand* made its debut on a Philadelphia TV station.

And in Yakima, Washington, a killer was born.

Jackie Sue Gardenhire was a bit of a shock to her parents. George and Gladys were not exactly thrilled when they learned they were going to be parents again. They had four grown kids from former marriages, and they thought they were done raising children.

The Gardenhire and the Cornelison familes had strong Cherokee roots, and in the early 1900s, they lived on tribal land, including reservations in Muskogee, Oklahoma; Tahlequa, Oklahoma; and Siloam Springs, Arkansas.

George Gardenhire, who was born in Sequoyah, Oklahoma, on October 9, 1911, was charmed by the Cornelison sisters, Gladys and Ruth.

Gladys, the older of the sisters, was born in Arkansas and was the same age as George. She was very young the first time she got married—only seventeen when she and Rodney Stowe* were wed in Washington County, Arkansas, in March 1928. Ten and a half months later, they welcomed their first child, Luke,* born in 1929. Their daughter, Rosemary,* was born about three years later.

Ruth Cornelison, born in Arkansas in 1915, wed four years after her sister. At age eighteen, she married George Gardenhire in Siloam Springs. They soon had two little girls, Clara,* born in 1934, and Anita,* in 1935.

Sadly, poor Ruth died at age twenty-four in 1939, leaving George a widower with two small girls.

George and the girls lived for a while with his uncle, Steve Gardenhire, and his family, in their home in Greenland, Arkansas, in the Ozarks. George contributed to the household with his income from pumping gas at a filling station.

Though Gladys was still married, she realized after her sister died that she and George felt a strong attraction for each other. Her feelings for her husband had changed from the time she was a teenage bride. The love she had once had for Rodney was overpowered by the feelings she had for George.

Their families didn't approve, but George and Gladys knew they were meant to be together. It was painful, but Gladys broke it off with Rodney. Though now commonplace, divorce was scandalous in the 1940s—particularly when it was motivated by a love triangle.

When Gladys married George, her nieces became her stepdaughters. She vowed to be a wonderful mother to all four of the kids.

George and Gladys moved to Yakima, Washington, to escape the disapproval that their union inspired and to start a new life.

George's uncle Steve and other close relatives also moved to Yakima, and soon there were a number of people from both the Cornelison and Gardenhire families settled there.

The years rolled by, and one by one, the kids grew up and started families of their own. Gladys and George had finally raised their brood, and now they were looking forward to their golden years.

But suddenly, in early 1952, they found themselves rearranging their lives to make room for a new baby. They hadn't planned for it, but they decided to make the best of it.

At the same time Gladys Gardenhire was carrying her baby, Martha Burgett was pregnant with Geneva. Both women carried baby girls with Cherokee blood, and both women had nothing but hope for the new lives growing inside them.

They lived on opposite sides of the country, and though neither Martha nor Gladys was aware of each other's existence, they had more in common than their Cherokee heritage. They shared a tragic future.

The daughters they carried would one day cross paths in a moment so violent it would break the hearts of both Martha and Gladys.

But violence was the furthest thing from Gladys's

mind as she busied herself getting the nursery ready for the new baby.

As it turned out, there would be *two* new babies in the Gardenhire family. George's second daughter was pregnant, too. Anita was a young mother at seventeen, while Gladys was at the other end of the age spectrum. Though it's not unusual today, few women over forty gave birth back in the 1950s.

Anita was too old to be a playmate for Jackie, but her baby daughter, Sandra, would be just the right age, and everyone looked forward to watching Sandy play with her soon-to-be-born aunt Jackie.

But in the middle of a hot summer, as Gladys grew big and round in her seventh month, the Gardenhires suffered a heartbreak. On August 6, baby Sandra died shortly after she was born.

The loss rocked the family.

Sandy would have been like a sister to Jackie, but now Jackie would grow up without her. Even though Jackie had four siblings, she might as well have been an only child, for they were all old enough to be her parents. Her four half siblings—two of them also her first cousins— adored Jackie, and they were grateful that she was healthy.

The family spoiled her rotten, according to Ellen Turner,* a retired teacher who once lived down the road from the Gardenhires.

It's easy to see how a family that had tragically lost an infant might be tempted to overcompensate. If the baby so much as whimpered in her sleep, Gladys rushed to make sure she was okay.

Jackie learned early on that her needs came first. "Whatever Jackie wanted, she got," Ellen explains. "She never heard the word *no*. It got worse as she got older."

Kelly Gilmore,* a girl a couple of years older than Jackie, played with her a few times when Jackie was about six. She remembers that Jackie was a cute little girl. "I had a birth defect, and other kids made fun of me, but Jackie never did," says Kelly.

Though she never saw Jackie be mean, she did notice that she was a little bit bossy when they played, and that she got whatever she wanted. "She'd run to her mom and ask for a cookie, and Gladys *always* gave it to her," says Kelly. "I thought she was spoiled, but I never thought she was evil. When I read about her in the paper, I was shocked. I couldn't believe it."

Jackie may have been a cute kid, but she was a handful—more than her aging parents could handle. The Gardenhires had a reputation as nice people. One acquaintance remembers that George was distant and hard to get to know, but he was always polite. Gladys was very warm and friendly, and "never had an unkind thing to say about anyone."

The minute a visitor stepped into her home, Gladys would offer them a glass of iced tea and either cake or cookies she had baked. She made everyone feel welcome.

Neighbors say she was a nice woman, and not the kind

of person who liked to see people hurt. She *wanted* to do the right thing. She and George certainly not did not set out to spoil Jackie. If they'd had a crystal ball and could have seen the future for their overindulged child, they would have been shocked.

Unfortunately, there was no way for the Gardenhires to see what their daughter would become. She would one day break their hearts, but they could not have known that then.

As Jackie got older, she became more defiant. She stayed out past her curfew, drove too fast, and mouthed off to teachers at school. "She had no respect for authority," remembers Ellen.

But despite her bad traits, Jackie was fiercely loyal to her parents. She would not stand for anyone saying anything unkind about George and Gladys.

Some people remember Jackie as a normal kid who was generally happy, but her mood could turn quickly if she didn't get her way.

Ellen describes Jackie as "too smart for her own good," adding, "She could have gone far in life if she wasn't so impatient to have everything she wanted right away. Other kids had to do chores for an allowance, but not Jackie."

According to Ellen, Jackie was once hired to babysit for a friend of hers, Nancy Osbourne,* who had five little girls, the youngest still in diapers.

The Gardenhire home was on Rosenkranz Road in Tieton, Washington, a small town in Yakima County about fourteen miles northwest of the city of Yakima. Jackie was a teenager at the time, and the Osbourne family lived only a few blocks from the Gardenhire home.

"Jackie loved to eat baby food," remembers Ellen. "But she was afraid she would get in trouble for eating the little one's food, so she made all the older kids eat the baby food, too. She figured if they all did it that the kids would get the blame."

The girls did not care for their babysitter, and they told their mother that Jackie had ordered them around and treated them as if she were the queen, and they were her servants.

The Osbourne family was struggling financially, while Jackie's family was better off. Even the children sensed that the teenager looked down upon them because she had nicer things than they did.

Worst of all, she had neglected to change the baby's diaper—which was desperately in need of changing. Nancy came home to find a garbage can full of empty baby-food jars and her baby waddling around in a heavy, drooping diaper.

Nancy was livid. "She marched over to the Gardenhire home and told Gladys what Jackie had done," recalls Ellen.

Gladys was obviously embarrassed, but she was gracious as always. She told Nancy that she could certainly understand why she was angry and that she should not pay Jackie. She was never again asked to babysit for the

Osbourne children, and whenever she saw them, she was rude.

In March 1971, Jackie got married in Yakima. The groom, Blake Simons,* was only seventeen, and Jackie was eighteen—one year and nine months older than he was. Seven and a half months later, in October 1971, she had a son, Buddy,* who was born in the Modesto, California, area.

Though online Stanislaus County, California, records indicate the baby was born in October, later records give his birthdate as November. Which of these dates is correct, and whether or not the discrepancy is a clerical error or deliberate, is unknown.

Jackie claimed she married and divorced at least four different men over the next decade. She told an acquaintance that one of these marriages ended dramatically when she walked in on her husband in bed with a man.

Most of Jackie's husbands were in her life so fleetingly that some of her family members don't remember even meeting them.

One of her relatives remembers that Harold Lee Schut appeared on the scene in the early 1970s, and he stayed around longer than any of the others. He went by "Lee" and was about eight years older than she was. At some point, they, too, divorced, but it is unclear exactly when that happened.

Some people wondered if her marriages were all legal

or if maybe, at times, they overlapped—though there is no proof that Jackie is a bigamist.

Margaret Jacobs,* a woman who was friendly with Jackie in the 1980s, describes her as plump, with a perpetual bad perm. She didn't take much care with her appearance, wore no makeup, and her upper lip needed a waxing. Her mustache was clearly visible in bright light. Few people were rude enough to mention it to her, so maybe she thought they didn't notice.

Her clothing—though casual—was of the highest quality. She usually dressed in jeans with T-shirts and sweatshirts from the best stores.

By 1980, Jackie was twenty-seven years old and claimed she had given birth to three children: Buddy, Dana Rose, and Deanna. Deanna was born in 1976, when Jackie was allegedly married to her third husband, Rick Morely.* Buddy and Dana Rose went by the last name of Simons, and Deanna went by Morely.

Dana Rose was told she was born in 1973, and that Jackie's first husband is her father, but she has doubts about this.

"I'm not sure who I am," she admits. "I don't look like anyone in my family."

Is it possible that Jackie did not give birth to Dana Rose, and that she stole her from her real mother, as Dana Rose suspects? Or is this just wishful thinking on Dana Rose's part?

When Dana Rose first told me about her life, I was

shocked to hear of the unimaginable ways that she was betrayed by the person who should have loved and cared for her more than anyone else. I can understand that it would be a relief for her to learn that Jackie is not, in fact, her biological mother, and that somewhere out there her real mother is still looking for her. But as of this writing, no DNA tests have been done to verify Dana Rose's relationship to Jackie.

Jackie's friend Margaret says the lack of resemblance between Jackie and the girls was so noticeable that she had once commented on it. "I told the girls, 'You guys must look like your dad because you don't look anything like your mom.'"

With the grab bag of genetics, of course, there is no telling what a child is going to look like. Sometimes kids look nothing like their biological parents.

Margaret was a casual acquaintance who met Jackie in a bar, and she had occasion to visit Jackie's home a few times. It was a small rental on North 24th Street in Yakima.

Margaret remembers that whenever she saw Dana Rose and Deanna, they were dirty, and their clothing was rumpled and their hair uncombed. "They didn't have many toys, and the ones they had were the cheap kind that break easily," says Margaret.

Though the carpet was stained, the house was pretty well kept and filled with the expensive items Jackie bought for herself. Margaret assumed Jackie was divorced, because she never saw a husband or heard her speak of one. At that time, Jackie went by the last name Morely—Deanna's father's last name. At least, that's the name that Jackie gave to Margaret. Jackie didn't have a job but managed to travel quite a bit, and Margaret wondered how she could afford it.

She also loved to play bingo, and she played it every chance she got. Sometimes she had people over to play poker and drink, and Dana Rose remembers seeing stacks of plastic chips on the kitchen table.

"Jackie liked to party, and she brought people she met in bars back to the house," Margaret recalls.

Dana Rose and Deanna appeared very uncomfortable whenever Jackie brought strangers home. They hung back, afraid to make eye contact or speak to visitors.

Though Jackie was approaching thirty, she liked to hang out with teens, and she invited them to the house and gave them alcohol. "It was kind of like Jackie was stuck, like she was still a teenager herself," says Margaret. "And sometimes Dana Rose seemed more mature than Jackie."

Dana Rose was very protective of her little sister, and she was cooking meals before she turned ten.

One day Margaret found herself alone in the kitchen with Dana Rose. The little girl looked at her sadly and said, "I don't like my mom."

Margaret could understand that, because from what she'd witnessed, Jackie was not very nice to the girls. "She was cold and distant, and she had a bad temper."

One night the girls forgot to clean up the kitchen after a meal, and Jackie blew up. "She was scary," Margaret says with a shudder. "Her eyes bulged, her face turned red, she threw things, and she yelled. I knew that the kids were going to get in big trouble after I left."

When she wasn't angry at the kids, Jackie seemed oblivious to them. Margaret describes her as being in her own little bubble. She appeared to have other things on her mind, and one night as they were having drinks, she startled Margaret by asking her, "Would you ever kill someone?"

"No!" Margaret replied.

"I have," said Jackie. "But it was necessary."

Margaret stared at her, taken aback by the casual way Jackie had brought up such a dark topic.

Jackie did not appear emotional about it. It was as if she was genuinely curious about whether or not Margaret was capable of killing—as if she was wondering if it was a normal thing to do.

Margaret was too stunned to ask for details about what Jackie had just confessed to, and the conversation drifted to another subject. Years later, when Margaret read about Jackie in the news, she thought back to that strange conversation and Jackie's offhand confession.

Margaret had not hesitated to say "no" when Jackie asked her if she would kill. And Jackie had not seemed ashamed when she admitted that she had.

\*     \*     \*

It is particularly painful for victims and their families when violence goes unpunished. While Colonel Turchin was not punished for the hate he unleashed upon Athens in 1862, the proverbial wheels of justice were just beginning to spin in the Clemons case—though in the spring of 1984, no one knew it yet.

Bernard Dale Oldham, a career criminal whose crimes never made the front page, would soon bust the investigation wide open. Whether or not he leaked information to save his own skin or because he had a hint of conscience is a moot point.

The probe would cover horrific crimes that involved at least five states, left at least three children motherless, and wreaked immeasurable heartbreak.

Oldham was never implicated in the murder of Geneva Clemons. But he *knew* something. If he had not come forward and shared information with Yakima detective Bob Regimbal, events would have unfolded very differently.

Bernard Oldham was no Boy Scout. Far from it. He was a criminal with a lengthy rap sheet.

Bernard was born in Tulare, California, on September 19, 1939, to Nellie and Ordie Oldham. His mother, who was Nellie Marie Creekmore before she married Ordie, was eighteen when Bernard was born.

Baby Bernard suffered a terrible loss when he was nine months old: Nellie died. She was just nineteen years old. While infants don't know much, they *do* know who their mothers are, and the sudden absence of her loving arms must have impacted the baby boy. His mama was suddenly gone, and she no longer held him close when he wailed for her.

He might have taken a different path if he'd had a mother to guide him, though a mother's love is not necessarily a deterrent to a life of crime. There are any number of criminals who grew up with nurturing mothers, and plenty of law-abiding citizens who were orphans.

For whatever reason, Bernard Oldham started breaking the law at a young age. On August 15, 1959, the *Centralia Daily Chronicle* reported that a state patrolman, Charles Werner, arrested Bernard in a stolen car. The Yakima teen was with two other juveniles who were out joyriding after stealing the car from Portland, Oregon.

At the time, Bernard was also wanted for forgery, and Officer Werner apprehended him shortly before midnight in the Centralia, Washington, area on that Friday night and deposited him in the Lewis County Jail.

About three years later, on November 12, 1962, the *Seattle Daily News* reported that three fugitives, all from Yakima County, had escaped from the Washington State Reformatory prison "honor farm" and were apprehended in Salt Lake City, Utah. Bernard Dale Oldham and his two accomplices were captured by police responding to a burglar alarm at a building-supply firm.

In December 1966, *The Oregonian* reported that "transient" Bernard Oldham pled guilty to receiving and concealing stolen property. (He had earlier been charged with

44

burglary in the same incident.) He was given eighteen months in the Oregon State Pen.

Oldham's small-time crimes usually warranted just a half-inch column, tucked in somewhere between the funny pages and the classified ads of the daily news. In truth, he had connections to dangerous criminals, but he had somehow escaped serious scrutiny by law enforcement. It may be that he had no blood on his hands, or perhaps he was crafty at avoiding detection. Bernard Oldham seemed to always be on the periphery of the headline crimes.

On May 30, 1974, *The Seattle Times* reported that thirty-four-year-old Bernard Oldham had been arrested for lewd conduct for his behavior at the Bear Cave tavern, a sleazy topless bar frequented by bikers on Seattle's East Marginal Way. Oldham was the Bear Cave's bartender/manager, and the bar was regularly raided by police, resulting in multiple arrests and violations on several occasions.

The Bear Cave tavern is at the center of one of Seattle's most complex cold cases. Bar owner Frank L. Hinkley, age forty-five, and his girlfriend, Barbara Rosenfield, forty-two, were found shot to death in the bar at 2 A.M. on November 3, 1975. The two had gone to high school together and had recently reunited. Each had children, and when their romance ignited, the couple and their kids moved into a posh home with a swimming pool—a rare luxury in the state of Washington.

The Bear Cave had recently lost its liquor license, and

detectives found evidence that at least three people had been sitting together and drinking sodas when the violence erupted.

The bar had been locked from the outside, and investigators concluded the killer was likely someone close to the victims who had access to the Bear Cave's keys. Allegedly only two other people besides Hinkley had sets of keys, and Hinkley's keys were still in his pocket.

At least seven others associated with Hinkley died under suspicious circumstances in a four-year span—including a twenty-two-year-old dancer, Linda Faye Nickles, a nice girl who had gotten on the wrong path. She had a family who loved her, and she tried to hide her lifestyle from her mother, who was devastated when Linda vanished from the Bear Cave in May 1975 while taking a break. Linda was last seen walking out of the bar with a man in his forties, who was balding but let his white hair grow long in the back.

Linda's remains were found beneath tree roots at Blewett Pass the following May. Investigators suspect the hapless girl had seen something she shouldn't have, and she was killed as a result.

In 2006, detectives finally arrested a suspect in the Hinkley and Rosenfield murders. James B. Braman, like Bernard Oldham, was a manager at the Bear Cave and had a set of keys. Not only that, Braman's former roommate claimed he had confessed the murders to him many years earlier.

To the great relief of Hinkley's and Rosenfield's families, it looked like there would finally be answers to the decades-old murder mystery.

But before he could be tried for the double homicide, Braman died from a methadone overdose. Braman had been released on a half million dollars' bail, two weeks after his arrest, and four days later, he was dead. He was taking methadone for liver cancer, and some say the fatal dose was suicide, while others think it was coerced by someone else involved in the crimes.

When pressured to confess, Braman, age fifty-six, had allegedly told detectives others were involved and cried, "They'll kill me!"

Many of those entangled in the murders and suspicious accidents associated with the Bear Cave are long dead. The building itself was long ago demolished.

Detectives and suspects alike are now dust in the wind, and the answers to the long-ago questions are as elusive as last summer's dandelion fluff.

Investigators have tried to find a connection between the Bear Cave tavern murders and the September 6, 1975, murder of the owner of the Wagon Wheel restaurant near Yakima, Washington—which happens to be Bernard Oldham's hometown, though there is no proof he was in any way involved in that homicide.

Everett "Fritz" Fretland was found shot to death, with five bullets in his back, inside the Wagon Wheel only two months before the Bear Cave shootings. Fretland, who owned three restaurants in the Yakima area, was the father of a young son.

More than three decades later, a former Wagon Wheel employee, Gary Isaacs, was found guilty of first-degree murder in November 2007. He insisted he was innocent, and when asked about the victim, Isaacs told reporters, he was devastated because "I loved that guy!"

Detectives suspected the murder was a hired hit, masterminded by another Wagon Wheel employee, Richard Sanders, who is unable to defend himself because *he* was murdered in 1989.

Whether or not Bernard Oldham was in any way involved in the murders at the Bear Cave or the Wagon Wheel is unknown.

The Bear Cave was implicated in counterfeiting, prostitution, and drug dealing—and one close associate had ties in the car sales industry, an industry that Bernard moved on to not long after he finished his stint at the Bear Cave.

In fact, Oldham would use this car dealership as the front for a Yakima prostitution ring—one that catered to the lowest of the low: *pedophiles*.

Bernard Oldham's friend and partner in crime looked like a typical dowdy housewife. At first glance, no one would suspect she was dangerous. But the mother of three was, in fact, far more dangerous than Bernard.

By the time Bernard met her, Jackie was married to Harold Lee Schut. Bernard was a dozen years older than

Jackie, but they had things in common. The three Yakima residents were interested in making money, and they were not picky about *how* they made it as long as it didn't involve hard, honest work.

Neither Bernard nor the Schuts cared if children were damaged by their get-rich-quick schemes. In fact, Jackie sacrificed her own little girls, Dana Rose and Deanna. She often left them with "Uncle Bernie" so that he could babysit while she went to play bingo.

Bernard parked a large metal shipping container behind the dealership. It was about the size of a small trailer, windowless, and furnished with a filthy mattress.

Dirty old men paid a fee to watch Dana Rose and Deanna put on shows in the cold, dimly lit metal box.

When I talked with Dana Rose about these nightmarish memories from her childhood, she told me it felt as if she were talking about someone else's life rather than her own. Though she remembers parts of her past in excruciating detail, she has distanced herself from the emotion that went along with being a sexually abused child. It's not easy for her to revisit these memories, but she hopes that by telling her story, it will help children who were trapped the way she once was.

When she speaks of Bernard Oldham, she refers to him as "that old man." He wasn't really that old. He was in his forties, but that must have seemed quite elderly to a little girl. In her child's mind, she probably heard his name, Oldham, as "old man."

Because she was so young when the abuse started, some of the details of the shows Dana Rose performed in are hazy.

"At first," she recalls, "we put on our shows in the back room of the old man's business. I remember that we had to do something with toothbrushes that Jackie taught us. We were just supposed to do sexy little dances and be nice to the men who paid to see our show."

Dana Rose remembers that "Uncle Bernie" was "very rich," and she thought he owned the car dealership where she and her sister were forced to perform. Sometimes, she recalls, "that old man" got a cheap motel room where the little girls were forced to entertain the customers.

There were other girls about Dana Rose's age that also performed in the shows. Melody* and Krista* were the daughters of Frank* and Ginger Wynters,* and Dana Rose often saw them in the trailer behind the car lot where the perverts gathered.

The children were told that they had to do a good job, because there were important people watching them. If they did well, their parents would make lots of money and the girls would be rewarded.

"Bernie rewarded me with cigarettes," says Dana Rose. "He taught me to smoke when I was eight."

The child's addiction to nicotine was just one more thing that Bernie could use to control her.

Bernie was sadistic, and "he liked to hurt little girls," says Dana Rose. Sometimes he violated her with objects, and once when she was about eight years old, he used a glass soda bottle with a long neck. "It broke inside of me," she remembers.

When Dana Rose shrieked with pain, Bernie told her that was her punishment for not cleaning her room.

Jackie, too, violated Dana Rose with objects. "She sometimes used a hairbrush, and she would set up cameras first to take photos of it—both stills and videos."

Once, while the Schuts lived in a trailer park, one of Jackie's pals from the pedophile ring crawled through the window of Dana Rose's room. "He held a knife to my throat," says Dana Rose. He forced the little girl to perform a sex act as he threatened her life.

Dana Rose suspected that Jackie knew about the assault, and had even encouraged it. It was a twisted game, and the child's terror gratified her attacker.

The damage to her body from the sexual abuse was so severe that years later a gynecologist would tell her that she would never be able to carry a child. "But they were wrong," says Dana Rose. "I had three children. As a mom, I can't understand how anyone would could hurt their children the way Jackie hurt me. It's one of the reasons I've always thought that she isn't my biological mother."

Most of the sexual abuse was directed at Dana Rose. "They usually chose me, because I was older," she says. "Lots of times Deanna would be in the room when it was happening, but nothing would be done to her."

But Deanna did not escape unscathed, and the sisters

would often hold on to each other in the night. Dana Rose recalls, "I did my best to protect her. Deanna and I would sit in the bed and hold each other and rock back forth. I told her we'd be okay, as long as we had each other."

Dana Rose had been Deanna's protector as far back as she could remember. Dana Rose was just three when she started fixing her little sister's bottles and changing her diapers.

Buddy, Dana Rose, and Deanna lived for long periods at the elder Gardenhires' home, but whenever Jackie applied for welfare, she claimed the kids lived with her.

Dana Rose remembers that she and her siblings had been staying with Gladys and George when Jackie brought her and Deanna and to live with her. Jackie left her son behind, but she needed the girls for the pedophile shows.

Dana Rose craved Jackie's approval. The little girl wanted Jackie and Lee to care about her. There was a time when Dana Rose wanted so badly to connect with her "parents" that she was glad when Lee allowed her and her siblings to use the Schut name at school. She wanted them to be a normal family, and she thought that having Lee's name would make her feel as if she belonged.

Abused children typically blame themselves, and Dana Rose was no exception. If something went wrong, then it had to be her fault. And because things always seemed to be going wrong, Dana Rose suffered from guilt.

She was an intelligent girl, so in her logical mind, she

knew she did not deserve the way she was treated. But on an emotional level, she felt like a bad person.

Lee punished the children by making them bend over and hold their ankles. "Then he would hit us with a belt," she remembers.

Lee and Jackie were affectionate with each other, and Dana Rose sometimes saw them kissing. "I thought they loved each other," she says.

But Jackie had no affection for Dana. If Jackie had simply ignored her, that would have been bad enough, but Dana Rose was frequently the recipient of Jackie's rage.

The woman was terribly frightening when she got angry—which she often did. "She would roll her eyes back so that only the whites of her eyes showed, and she would look like she was demonically possessed," Dana Rose confides. After a few minutes of yelling and throwing things, Jackie would suddenly snap out of it. "She'd get up and go to the bathroom or something, and come out and act like nothing had happened."

When Dana Rose was under the age of eleven, her grandparents, George and Gladys Gardenhire, treated her well. "My grandma and I had a bond, and my grandpa was always nice to me," she says. But when it comes to her recollection of Jackie, Dana Rose says, "I don't have one memory of any affection—any kindness shown to me by her. Not one moment."

Still, Dana Rose continued to seek approval from Jackie. When she was about ten, she won a blue ribbon at school for a sculpture she'd made from pieces of wood. "I was so proud and so excited to show it to her," Dana Rose remembers. "I got off of the school bus, and she was standing outside smoking. I ran up to her and showed her the ribbon and the sculpture, and she grabbed it out of my hands and threw it down on the asphalt. It broke into pieces."

"That's nothing! That's just garbage!" Jackie screamed, and Dana Rose ran away in tears.

*You are ugly. You are fat. You're nothing and you're always going to be nothing. You are worthless.*

Jackie belittled Dana Rose every chance she got, and the cruel words burned holes into her soul.


Sarah Moore,* who is now a grandmother and still lives in Yakima, was just thirteen when she met Bernard Oldham.

Though Sarah managed to get away before Bernard could physically harm her, the memories of that time are so dark that just sharing the details with me has given her nightmares. "I've been waking up in the morning with anxiety attacks," she says. "I'm talking about it to you because I think it is healing for me. My sister told me that if I let the dark out, there will be room for the light to come in."

Sarah recalls that Bernie took her and her friend, Brenda Rowe,* to a sleazy motel—the same motel where Bernard had taken other children.

"I was naïve," Sarah admits. "I didn't really understand what was going on." What Sarah *did* know was that she did not want Bernie touching her.

"Bernie was short and fat, and he had body odor," she remembers. He tried to cover up the fact that he'd skipped a shower by dousing himself with cheap cologne, but that just made the smell worse.

His hair was silver, and it not only grew from his head, but sprouted profusely from his ears and nose. "His hands were always dirty," Sarah adds. "He had grease under his fingernails—probably because he worked with cars at the dealership."

Brenda was a beautiful fifteen-year-old brunette with bright blue eyes and a voluptuous body. She let Bernie make out with her in the motel while Sarah watched TV.

"She did it because her boyfriend wanted her to," Sarah explains. "Tom* was nineteen and he worked at the dealership with Bernie. Brenda was madly in love with Tom and she would do anything for him. He encouraged her to do things with Bernie because he wanted the money."

Though Brenda probably did not look at it that way, Tom was her pimp. He had introduced her to Bernie for the sole purpose of extracting cash from him in exchange for sex with the underage girl.

Sarah was careful to keep her eyes trained on the TV while her friend wrestled on the bed with the old married guy. She was not sure exactly what they were doing, and she did not want to know.

Several times, Sarah went with Brenda to hang out with Bernie. He drove the girls around and told them stories about all the important people he knew. He claimed to be pals with a man known in Yakima for his connections to organized crime, and Sarah got the feeling that he was trying to intimidate her by dropping the name of the dangerous character.

"I found out later that he didn't even know the guy," she recalls. Bernie put a lot of energy into trying to impress the young teens by bragging about his friends and entertaining them with dumb jokes. "He goofed around a lot," says Sarah.

Bernie was annoying, but hanging out with him proved to be profitable. "He stuck twenty-dollar bills down my bra, and I would say, 'Don't expect me to do anything.'"

And Bernie replied, "I'm just trying to help you out because I know you need the money."

A twenty-dollar bill was a windfall for a thirteen-year-old in 1984. Sarah refused to let Bernie touch her, but she kept the cash. She didn't realize that the dirty old man was grooming her and probably expected that he would eventually have his way with her. She was constantly dodging him as he tried to put his arm around her or smacked her on her backside.

Sarah and Brenda were not the only teens that hung out with Bernie. There were about half a dozen other girls from Sarah's school who dropped in at the car lot.

"We knew that when we needed money, we could go

see Bernie," says Sarah. One of her friends told her that Bernie had a business in Seattle and had promised her that if she went to work for him there, she could make a lot of money.

Many of the girls who spent time with Bernie were from low-income families, and they were dazzled by the pedophile's promises of riches.

Sarah does not know if any of the other girls from the group let Bernie touch them, but there was no question about Brenda. Sarah had been there when Brenda and Bernard were intimate.

She could not understand how her friend put up with it. One afternoon after a session with Bernie, Sarah told Brenda in disgust, "You're a moron!"

But Brenda seemed to think she had hit the big time, and that she was on her way to becoming rich and famous. One day she took Sarah behind the dealership and proudly showed her the trailer.

Sarah cautiously peered into the cavernous metal box at the mattress surrounded by lights and movie cameras.

*"This,"* said Brenda triumphantly, "is where the magic happens. *This* is where stars are made."

Bernie had apparently convinced Brenda that he was as well connected as a Hollywood director and that she was going to be a movie star.

Bernie was making movies, but they wouldn't be winning any Academy Awards.

While Brenda was enthusiastic about the moviemaking

in Bernie's trailer, Dana Rose and Deanna were terrified of it.

On a summer day when temperatures were creeping into the 90s, the neighbor, Ellen, had legitimate business at the car dealership, and she pulled into a parking space there right next to Jackie, who also happened to be just pulling up.

As Jackie got out of the car, she chatted with Ellen and explained that she was picking something up at the dealership.

Ellen noticed Deanna and Dana Rose in the backseat and asked Jackie's permission to take the girls next door to a fast-food stand for a soda.

"It was the oddest thing," Ellen confides. "The girls didn't want to get out of the car. It was really hot, but the girls looked scared and refused to get out to go with me. I couldn't understand why they were so afraid, and it wasn't until years later that I understood why."

Sarah, too, now understands what Bernie was up to when he asked Brenda to bring her along for visits at the motel all those years ago. "I just recently learned that Bernie was paying Brenda a hundred bucks for every girl she brought to the motel," says Sarah. "I thought she was my friend, but she betrayed me."

The proprietors of the Yakima pedophile prostitution ring were trying to build their stable of young females. Prepubescent girls were in high demand, and they were also easy to manipulate.

Sarah was lucky. As Bernard was working to draw her into the fold, news of his degrading activities was beginning to circulate. Bernard's empire was about to fall.

No one knows how many other children were harmed by Bernard Oldham and the Schuts. The "work" the girls were asked to do damaged body, mind, and soul. They were exposed to ugly, dehumanizing things, and no one ever worried about their emotional *or* physical health.

There were no nutritious meals at Jackie's house, and the girls were often sleep deprived, because as "stars" of Bernie's shows, they were kept up until very late. Dana Rose did her best to take care of her little sister.

Why would a mother allow her children to be subjected to such sleazy and degrading abuse? Jackie Schut not only allowed it, she *encouraged* it.

This is my thirty-fourth true crime book, featuring the horrific acts of sociopaths. When I first began to write about crime, it was hard to wrap my mind around the fact that some people do not possess consciences. And schooled as I am in the dynamics of evil, I still cannot understand it on an emotional level. But when I boil it down to the hard facts, it's clear that Jackie Schut has no conscience.

While Jackie appeared to have no moral compass, Dana Rose *did*. When I asked her about her very earliest childhood memory, she described how Jackie and Lee had shared pornography with her. "I was about three when they called me into a room, and they showed me pictures in dirty magazines. I remember them telling me that this was something fun to do."

Even as a small child, Dana Rose somehow knew that what the people in the magazines were doing was wrong. She was confused and repulsed.

Jackie was the only mother that Dana Rose ever knew— or at least, the only mother she *remembered*. The child grew up with abuse, yet she herself was kind. And in all the chaos, she figured out that the world she lived in was not right. She sensed that there could be a better life for her.

Dana Rose remembers a moment when she thought she was going to be rescued. Jackie had taken her to a doctor, and it turned out that the little girl had a sexually transmitted infection. Dana Rose overheard the grown-ups talking about it and hoped that now someone was going to realize what was going on and help her.

But Jackie took her aside and whispered, "Tell them we take baths together."

Dana Rose did as she was told, and the doctor believed the lie. He bought the story that the child had contracted the infection from the shared baths with her mother.

Sometimes Dana Rose wondered what would happen if she told someone what was happening to her. But she was afraid to defy Jackie. At least ten strange men violated Dana Rose and other children in the metal container behind the dealership or in the sleazy motel rooms Bernard rented.

Dana Rose was exploited by Bernard Oldham for years. She was ten when someone finally came to her rescue.

Bob Regimbal had never considered a career in law enforcement until he happened to run into an acquaintance who was a Yakima sheriff. It was 1967, and he was twenty-five years old.

Bob was looking for work, and when the sheriff suggested he go down to the station and fill out an application, he figured he had nothing to lose.

Shortly after applying at the police station, he was offered a job delivering magazines in Ellensburg, Washington. It was not particularly exciting work, but it paid the bills.

Bob was surprised when he got a call from the sheriff's office. There was an opening, and he could have the job if he could start that night at midnight.

Working for the sheriff would be a step up from delivering magazines, but he did not want to leave his boss in a bind. "I was taught that you don't quit a job without giving notice," he says.

Luckily, when Bob talked to his boss, he encouraged him to take the new job. "I never shorted a man for trying to get ahead," Bob's boss told him. "We'll find someone to take your route."

Bob showed up at the Yakima County Sheriff's Office

at midnight, and that was the beginning of a career in law enforcement that would last twenty-nine years.

He began as a deputy sheriff and also served as the jailer. After two years, he was sent out on patrol.

When he was young, Bob also worked in the narcotics division for a while. When he let his hair grow, it was easy for him to blend in and bust drug dealers.

Later, he worked investigating burglaries, and he found that detective work came naturally to him. At one point he was promoted to chief criminal deputy, but he found his five years in that management position unsatisfying. "That was the worst five years of my career," he says. "I wanted to be outside working."

Bob, who was "in two shoot-outs and lived to tell you about it," says he never understood why some of his cop friends quit because they couldn't take the stress.

He loved his work in law enforcement, though the darkest part of his career was the year he spent working sex crimes, beginning in 1984. "It's very difficult to work sex crimes. Especially kid related," he confides. As a father, his protective instinct kicked in whenever he came across a case of an abused child.

The abuse that went on behind the car dealership could not be kept secret forever. Detective Regimbal and Detective Mike Amos were assigned to investigate.

The detectives worked with Children Protection Services and with Robyn Light, senior investigator and victim witness manager for the prosecutor's office.

They suspected that in addition to being exploited by Bernard Oldham, Dana Rose was also being sexually abused by her mother and stepfather, Harold Lee Schut.

The detectives interviewed countless people and began building a case. Though the evidence was stacking up, they did not yet have enough proof to make arrests.

Then Regimbal got a phone call that spurred him into action. Word was that Jackie and Bernie were making plans to check the girls out of their school in Selah, Washington, and whisk them away on a trip.

"Knowing that these kids were possibly being abused by their mother, stepfather, and Bernard Oldham, we couldn't let them take them," Regimbal explains. "In order to protect them, we went to the school and said we were taking the girls and putting them into protective custody."

The detectives were shocked by the abuse of Dana Rose and her little sister. "Dana Rose was older, and she got the brunt of it," says Regimbal. "She was abused so badly, I don't know how she survived."

At the time the children were put into protective custody, Regimbal and Amos believed they were investigating a case of multiple sexual abuse of minors and pornography distribution. That was bad enough. But they had barely penetrated the surface of something even darker that lay beneath.

With Dana Rose and Deanna safe—at least for the moment—Bob Regimbal found Harold Lee Schut, but he couldn't find Bernard Oldham. "I got Lee in custody, and I interviewed him," Regimbal remembers. "And it's a funny thing. Lee seemed to be kind of a nice guy, except for, of course, his participation in the crimes that Jackie and Bernie drew him into. He was willing to talk to me, and he was almost repentant for what he'd been doing."

Detective Regimbal knew that Bernard was the orchestrator of the pedophile prostitution ring, and he needed to apprehend him as soon as possible.

"I made a deal with Lee, and I regretted it," Regimbal admits. "I had a warrant for Lee on the statutory rape charges, but I told him I'd let him loose if he located Bernie for me. I had the squeeze on him, so I sat on the warrant."

Lee Schut agreed to the deal.

"Lee booked on me," the Yakima detective says ruefully. "He didn't try to find Bernie for me."

In addition to exploiting children, Jackie and Bernard had a legitimate gig, hauling cars between the Yakima dealership and one in Portland, Oregon. After checking around, Regimbal learned that the pair was off "fetching cars" someplace near Portland. When they returned, he served a warrant on Jackie Schut for sexually abusing her daughters.

Jackie went to jail. Unlike her ex-husband, she was sullen and angry, reluctant to talk to law enforcement officers.

Bernie got word that Jackie was in jail and that the detective was looking for him. He hired an attorney and then he turned himself in.

Shortly after Bernie was incarcerated, he sent word that he wanted to talk to Detective Regimbal.

Regimbal was interested to hear what he had to tell him, and Bernie was escorted from his cell to a meeting with the detective.

"He wasn't too concerned about what was going on," remembers Regimbal. "I think he realized he'd been caught, but he said, 'I just wanted to share something about what happened with me and Jackie on a road trip.'"

Regimbal watched him closely, wondering what he was up to, as Bernie insisted, "I'm not looking for any favors. I'm not looking for anything. I just wanna share this with you."

According to Bernie, it was during one of their trips hauling cars that the peculiar event unfolded.

Sometime after 1980, he and Jackie were riding together on the stretch of freeway between Yakima and Portland, as sheets of rain fell so furiously the windshield wipers groaned with the weight of the water they wiped away.

They noticed a hitchhiker getting drenched as she held out her thumb. If they had chosen to pass her by, things would have turned out very differently. But they pulled over, and the grateful woman climbed in.

The trio stopped at an International House of Pancakes

restaurant for something to eat. Bernard took a place at the counter, while Jackie and the hitchhiker settled into a booth. A little later he glanced over at them and was startled to see that Jackie was crying.

The other woman appeared to be listening intently as Jackie talked, telling a story so sad that tears seeped from her eyes as she spoke.

*Ah, women!* thought Bernard, shaking his head as he dismissed the emotional scene.

When Jackie got up to go to the ladies' room, the hitchhiker cautiously approached Bernard. "How well do you know that woman?" she asked.

Bernard shrugged and fibbed, "Not well."

"She just told me that she killed a baby in Athens, Alabama, in 1980!" blurted the hitchhiker.

Bernie digested the information, filing it away. He didn't know if it was true, but he had never seen his partner in crime become so emotional.

They say there is no honor among thieves, but somehow, the producer of pedophile porn had a flash of conscience and was compelled to share the story with Detective Regimbal.

On the surface, it seemed that that was what happened—that Bernie told on Jackie because it was the right thing to do. But Regimbal was not taking anything for granted. He knew it was possible that Bernard Oldham deliberately shifted the focus of the investigation onto Jackie Schut, to take the spotlight off himself.

Yet Bernard did not strike the detective as being very bright, and Regimbal doubted he was clever enough to manipulate the situation. He claimed he had nothing to do with the alleged murder, and that he had never been to Alabama. "I didn't even know Jackie in 1980," he added.

It seemed to the Yakima detective that nothing Bernard had told him really fit. Regimbal had never heard of Athens, Alabama, and Jackie Schut was a small-time child molester. Why on earth would she have killed a baby in Alabama?

He picked up the phone and called Information and said he was trying to reach the police department in Athens, Alabama. There *was* such a place! He called the number Information gave him.

When someone at the faraway police department answered, Bob Regimbal explained that he was a detective in Yakima County, from the state of Washington, who was working on a sex crimes case there.

"I need to ask you a question," he began. "Do you have the death of a child—a baby—in Athens in 1980?"

Without missing a beat, the officer on the other end of the line startled Bob with his quick reply: "No, the baby didn't die. The *mother* did!"

The Athens officer was referring to the tragic unsolved murder of Geneva Clemons—the case that was never far from the thoughts of law enforcement there. He heard the words *death, baby,* and *Athens,* and his mind immediately flew to the night that the newborn was abducted as his mother lay dying.

*"The baby didn't die—the mother did!"*

Suddenly, one of the most despicable crimes in recent history came to light.

Regimbal and the Alabama investigators filled one another in on what they knew. The file from Athens soon arrived, and Chief Faulk wasted no time in reserving plane tickets for a flight to Yakima.

Bob Regimbal pored over the file, soaking in the shocking details of the Clemons murder. It soon became clear that if Bernie's story was to be believed, Jackie thought that baby James Clemons had perished—she assumed that the helpless infant had not survived being deserted on that icy night. Indeed he would *not* have, had he not been miraculously discovered.

Had Bernie *really* seen Jackie crying about the baby? It's hard to believe that a killer capable of shooting a mother in cold blood in front of terrified children could then turn around and be so remorseful.

There was no way to prove or disprove the hitchhiker story.

If Bernard was involved or knew more than he said, and he wanted law enforcement to focus on Jackie, it was awfully convenient that an anonymous hitchhiker was the one who spilled the beans. No one knew her name, and it would be impossible for the long gone hitchhiker to validate or contradict Bernard's story.

Did the hitchhiker ever exist, or did Bernard concoct her from thin air as a means to alert detectives to Jackie's involvement in the Athens murder?

Though he certainly could not consciously remember losing his own mother, and it's hard to imagine that the sadistic Oldham could have compassion for anyone, maybe the murder struck a nerve—maybe some small part of Bernard Oldham was moved by the tragedy of a baby ripped from its mother's arms, and it prompted him to come forward.

Detective Regimbal had not expected to find himself in the middle of a murder investigation, but he was horrified by the cruelty of the homicide, and he was determined to do what he could to help get justice for Geneva Clemons.

Regimbal contacted Dana Rose. She had been placed with Blake Simons in Rancho Mirage, California. According to Jackie, Blake was Dana Rose's father, but the girl had never felt any real connection with the man. He was nice enough to her, but she never felt he was her father.

"His mother wasn't interested in me, either," Dana Rose says now. "She didn't treat me like I was her grandchild. I think she knew that I wasn't really related to her."

But Blake welcomed Dana Rose into his home, sheltering her while authorities tried to sort out the Yakima pedophile ring mess. Detective Regimbal called and explained to Blake that he needed to talk with Dana Rose.

"Tell her she's not in any trouble," said Regimbal. "But I need to talk to her."

Regimbal made small talk with Dana Rose for a few minutes, and then he said, "Dana, I'm investigating something, and I need to ask you some questions."

Prompted by his inquiries, Dana Rose told him about a long trip that she and Deanna had taken with Lee and Jackie in 1980. Her memory was fuzzy on some details, but she knew they had taken the Malibu. And she remembered something about harvesting peas. (Geneva had been shot in January, and it is not unusual for peas to be harvested in Alabama at that time, though pickings are better later in the year.)

Dana Rose also remembered going to a house where there was a lady with a baby, and a girl about her age.

At some point in the conversation, Regimbal asked who shot the lady. "You're not in any trouble," he assured her again.

There was a very long silence. And then Dana Rose replied, "My mom did. My mom shot the lady."


Richard Hollis Faulk was a highly regarded police chief in Athens, Alabama. Born in Athens in 1926, he was a World War II veteran who started his career in the police force as a patrolman, and then studied at the police academy. Shortly after graduating from the academy, he was promoted to assistant chief.

The father of four was known for his integrity and the fact that he truly cared about people. Tracy Clemons remembers how kind Chief Faulk was to her after her mother was murdered. He often came to the Clemonses' home to check on them and bring toys for the kids. "He gave me a baby doll with a bald head," Tracy recalls.

The police chief took it personally whenever someone in his community was victimized. He was especially disturbed by the Clemons case, and it bothered him that they had not yet caught the killer. He was a diligent investigator and had explored every angle he could think of, but had not come up with any good leads.

It wasn't because of lack of ability. Faulk was known for his crime-solving skills. In 1977 he had been credited with breaking one of the largest burglary rings in the nation's history. The ring of thieves operated in multiple states and was responsible for up to ten million dollars in stolen goods.

Chief Faulk's involvement in that case started when Athens resident Martha Clay Smith's home was burglarized while she was at work. The thieves got away with thirty thousand dollars' worth of jewelry and silver.

Faulk had traveled to four states in that investigation, interviewing witnesses and recovering stolen merchandise. The suspects were arrested and convicted and were serving their time, and now, Faulk was about to take another trip.

He and Bobby Smith, the chief investigator for the

Limestone County's district attorney's office, were soon on their way to Yakima.

Regimbal did not want to tip off their suspect, so he held off interviewing Jackie until the Athens team arrived.

As Detective Regimbal and Chief Faulk sat across the table from Jackie Sue Schut, she stared back at them coolly. She listened, seemingly with little interest, as the men explained to her that they suspected she was involved in a murder. She did not appear angry or even indignant that they should accuse her of such a horrible thing.

Her responses to their questions were clipped, and she admitted to nothing. Her eyes simmered with the same controlled fury that they always did whenever Bob had encountered her. It was obvious to him that Jackie despised him.

He glanced at Faulk and wondered if his laid-back southern charm could coax Jackie to open up to him.

"Chief Faulk was a nice old guy," remembers Bob. "He was grandfatherly."

It occurred to Regimbal that Faulk would have much better luck extracting a confession if he questioned her alone. In a strategic move, Regimbal excused himself.

There was no two-way glass here, no cameras rolling— no way to witness the conversation between Faulk and the suspect. Regimbal waited in the other room, hoping their suspect would admit something to Chief Faulk.

Regimbal's hunch was right. Jackie *was* more comfortable with Richard Faulk, and he got further with her than the other investigators had. Soothed by Faulk's easygoing manner and slow Alabama drawl, she tiptoed dangerously close to the truth. At one point, Jackie ventured, "What if it was an accident?"

"Well, we know it wasn't an accident," Faulk replied.

Jackie tried again. "What if it was self-defense?" she asked.

"Well, we know it wasn't self-defense," said Faulk.

Jackie tensed up. "I've never been to Alabama," she said firmly.

When Faulk later relayed the conversation to Regimbal, the Yakima detective winced. Jackie had come so close to admitting she was involved in the murder, but the chief had not given her an inch. While known in Limestone County for his interviewing skills, Chief Faulk's hard-line tactics had not worked on Jackie Sue Schut.

Regimbal wished Faulk had allowed Jackie to explore the possibilities she had suggested. If he could have gotten her to admit to pulling the trigger—even in an accident or self-defense—they could have at least placed her at the scene of the crime with some culpability.

But now, Jackie would not admit to *ever* setting foot in Alabama—let alone confess to her presence at the scene of the crime with a smoking gun in her hand on January 21.

Jackie was forever after steadfast in her denials. *She had never been to Alabama.* She would not budge on that point. Her jaw set, her eyes clear, cold, and calculating behind her large, round Sally Jessy Raphael–style glasses, she shook her head. If she had never been to Alabama, then she was not guilty of the crimes she was accused of.

As it turned out, the murder case would hinge upon proving Jackie's whereabouts on that tragic January day.

Jackie Schut had a number of friends and relatives with remarkable recall who could remember exactly what they were doing four years earlier on January 21. They were positive that they had seen Jackie on the day of the Athens murder, and she had been in Yakima.

Jackie's army of loyal supporters would stand by her, and that wall of defiance would be just one of the many obstacles law enforcement would need to break through to prove her guilt.

While Jackie continued to deny she had ever been to Alabama, her ex-husband, Harold Lee Schut, *had* been to Alabama. The woman who raised him, Ruby Bates, was one of the most famous yet controversial characters ever associated with Limestone County, Alabama.

Ruby was at the center of the "Scottsboro Boys" case—a case involving false allegations of rape that would dominate headlines for years.

In 1931, Ruby Bates and a friend, Victoria Price, accused nine black males of raping them. It was a lie that would destroy the lives of many, and inspire the courtroom scenes in Harper Lee's *To Kill a Mockingbird*.

In Harper Lee's novel, the character Atticus Finch defends a black man falsely accused of rape by an ignorant white woman named Mayella Ewell, who is loosely based upon Ruby Bates—a seventeen-year-old millworker who lived in a poor neighborhood in Huntsville, Alabama.

Ruby, who had once been arrested for hugging a black man in public, hopped a Southern Railroad freight train with Victoria on March 25, 1931, in Chattanooga, Tennessee. Dressed like males in coveralls and caps, they mingled with the rowdy young men who filled the car. A fight broke out between the white men and the black men. Shortly thereafter, Victoria cooked up the story of the gang rape. The youngest of the accused was only thirteen.

When the train reached Paint Rock, Alabama, the nine were arrested and sent to the Scottsboro jail.

Victoria was twenty-one, four years older than Ruby, and she was also the more outspoken of the two. Ruby was not very bright, and she quietly went along with everything that Victoria said.

Years of courtroom conflict followed, but in the spring of 1933, Ruby had a fit of conscience and retracted her statements. She confessed that it had all been made up. It was not the end of the legal wranglings, however, because Victoria stuck to her guns and accused Ruby of lying about lying.

A notable moment in the drama took place in Athens, Alabama, at the Limestone County Courthouse on June 22, 1933, when Judge James Edward Horton Jr. risked his career by standing up for what he knew was right.

"Scottsboro Boy" Haywood Paterson had been found

guilty of the rape and sentenced to death. But Horton set aside the verdict, detailing why he found Victoria Price's testimony to be contradictory and unreliable.

It was a brave stance to take in the Deep South in the 1930s. Judge Horton later lost his bid for reelection because he had ruled in favor of a black man. But it was more important to him to keep his integrity intact.

The Limestone County courthouse would one day be the stage for the drama involving Harold Lee Schut. Some say he is the son of Ruby, while others insist he is her nephew. At any rate, she raised him.

In May 1976, Ruby Bates Schut filed a $2.5 million libel and slander suit against NBC for airing the made-for-TV movie *Judge Horton and the Scottsboro Boys*.

Ruby and Victoria were angry because the movie gave the impression that they had both died in 1961. In addition, Ruby felt that the movie, which depicted her as a prostitute, had been an invasion of privacy, and she sought an injunction, barring its repeat airing.

Ruby had married Elmer Schut in 1943, and had lived a quiet life in Yakima County ever since. The suit said that she was respected in her community until the movie aired, and that it had exposed her to "hatred, shame, contempt, ridicule, aversion, degradation, or disgrace" by falsely accusing her of "committing perjury, false swearing, falsely imputing to plaintiff a want of chastity, being sexually promiscuous and of loose character, being of bad character, being dead."

In October 1976, Elmer and Ruby died within days of each other before the lawsuit made it to court.

One of the accused, Clarence Norris, finally received a full pardon from the state of Alabama, two days before Ruby died. He was sixty-four years old and was believed to be the last living "Scottsboro Boy."

Because Ruby had resurfaced in 1976 to file a lawsuit, the Schut family was no longer unknown. No one had realized that Ruby—who went by the name Lucille Schut— was the scandalous character in the NBC movie until she called it to everyone's attention by suing. According to the movie, she was *dead*.

Ruby had complained that her reputation was ruined by the movie, but *she* put herself in the spotlight. And because her suit had attracted attention to her family, there was no way that Harold Lee Schut could deny he had ever been to Limestone County.

Limestone County played a prominent role in the Schut family history, yet the Schuts had chosen that very location to kidnap an infant. Had they chosen a place where they had no ties, it might have been easier for them to cover their tracks.

Dana Rose had met Ruby and Elmer Schut just once. "We went to their trailer, and they told us they were our grandparents," she says. "They gave us some snacks— some kind of beef jerky. As I was eating it, I glanced at the package and saw that they were *dog* treats! I stopped eating right then."

Buddy continued to munch on the treats, oblivious to Dana Rose's discovery. Dana Rose nudged him and tried to get him to stop eating, but Buddy ignored her.

Dana Rose glanced around and noted that the Schuts appeared to be dirt poor. While Dana Rose had lived in trailers, as well as little houses and cramped apartments, they were mansions compared to Elmer and Ruby's place!

With his obvious connection to the widely publicized Ruby Bates, there was no way Harold Lee Schut could deny his connection to Limestone County. He could not take the same stubborn stance that Jackie had taken and claim he'd never set foot in the state of Alabama.

But he *did* deny involvement in the Athens homicide.

Investigators found Lee near Reno, Nevada, where he had been working for the Circus Circus Hotel and Casino, and they took him into custody. Regimbal and polygraph examiner Ron Gidge flew to Reno, where they met Chief Faulk and Bobby Smith.

When Lee was escorted into a room at police headquarters to meet with Regimbal, he sheepishly hung his head.

"I think he was ashamed because he'd run after he gave me his word he wouldn't," says Regimbal. "He felt bad about that."

Regimbal thought he had a pretty good sense of who Lee was. The man obviously felt guilty whenever he was caught doing something wrong. Unlike Jackie, he seemed to have a conscience.

But Lee was no genius, and he was certainly not the brains of this operation. Lee seemed to be easily influenced by others. He denied any involvement in the murder of Geneva Clemons or the kidnapping of her infant.

"Will you take a polygraph?" asked Regimbal.

"Sure," Lee agreed amicably. He took the test, and he "blew ink all over the walls." The test showed he was lying.

Regimbal told him, "Lee, you didn't do real well on the polygraph."

"Well, I didn't do it," Lee said. "But if I *had* done it, this is how I *would* have done it." And then he proceeded to describe the murder to the detective.

"He gave me details about the crime scene that only someone who was there could have known," explains Regimbal.

Lee wanted to draw the layout of the house and yard so that he could demonstrate where he *would* have parked the Chevy Malibu if he had been there. Regimbal gave him a pen and a piece of paper.

Lee knew just where the driveway was, and he added it to his diagram. Regimbal watched, fascinated, as Lee drew an accurate image, complete with trees surrounding the house.

Lee's illustration showed the car backed into the driveway.

"Why did you back in?" asked Regimbal, deliberately dropping the pretense that they were talking about a hypothetical situation.

"Well, you know," replied Lee, "if you need to make a fast getaway, it's better to back in."

Harold Lee Schut had used a ploy implemented by any number of killers—including Ted Bundy—to distance themselves from the murder while feeding details to investigators.

The roundabout "confession," coupled with his failure of the lie detector test, was enough for Alabama to get a warrant for Lee's arrest.

"I still had the rape warrant for Lee," explains Regimbal. "But I told them, 'If Lee will waive extradition, take him with you.'"

Soon Lee was in handcuffs, on his way back to Limestone County, Alabama.

What was the motivation for the murder of Geneva Clemons? What could possibly compel the Schuts to travel two thousand miles to murder a young mother and kidnap her newborn—only to abandon him in a ditch?

There was no evidence that the Schuts knew the Clemons family, so they certainly could not have held a grudge against them. The Clemonses were not a wealthy family, so obviously ransom was not the motive.

But money *was*.

While the Clemonses did not have a stack of cash to pay to get their baby back, there were childless couples who *did* have money and were willing to pay hefty fees for healthy babies to adopt.

Though it took a while to pry the information from Harold Lee Schut, he and other witnesses eventually told detectives enough for them to build a case that was based on the premise that the Schuts were involved in a kidnapping ring. At the center of the ring was an unidentified doctor who paid two thousand dollars for each baby that was brought to him—no questions asked.

If the doctor was paying thugs two grand a head for each infant, it followed that he earned much more than that in the "adoption fees" he charged to infertile couples who were desperate for babies.

But why did the kidnappers abandon James Clemons by the side of the road? According to Lee, they had heard sirens and thought the police were in hot pursuit. Panicked, they had dumped the kid.

As cold as that sounds, Tracy suspects that the Schuts abandoned her brother for another even more callous reason.

*Buyers' remorse.*

"My brother had a clubfoot," says Tracy. "They wanted a perfect baby they could sell." She suspects that once the Schuts got the baby in the car, they examined him and were not pleased when they saw the infant's left foot, curled and turned inward.

Children with this birth defect typically require medical treatment so that they can walk normally, though it often results in uneven shoe sizes, with one foot requiring a shoe up to one and a half sizes larger than the other. The child's mobility could also be limited.

If untreated, arthritis will likely develop, the curled foot can result in an odd gait, and there could also be muscle development problems. As it turned out, James was lucky. His defect eventually corrected itself, and he grew into a strong man.

But Jackie could not see the future, of course, and if she noticed the curled foot, it could have triggered her temper. She had been angry when Geneva foiled her plans and refused to go away with them in the car. Lee told detectives that nobody was supposed to have gotten hurt, and that he had been shocked when he heard the gun go off.

Jackie did not like being told no, but Geneva had refused to follow the plan. Jackie was so infuriated that she had *killed* her.

Jackie had been fed up after spending days in the Malibu, with Lee and the girls getting on her nerves for hundreds of miles. She had put a lot of thought and energy into her kidnapping plan. And she had had to go back to that house *two times*, and still, Geneva had not cooperated with her.

She blamed the baby's mother for being so stubborn— for forcing her to do something that she could go to prison for. And after all that, when Jackie looked closely at the baby, she saw that he was flawed.

This may have been the last straw for Jackie. She may have even blamed Geneva for deceiving her. Why hadn't she mentioned the kid had a clubfoot when Jackie told her that she was looking for a perfect baby for the contest?

How was she supposed to sell the kid now? The baby was a burden—a noisy burden that needed its diaper changed.

Enraged by the final insult of discovering the kid's clubfoot, it would not have been out of character for Jackie to discard him in a ditch out of spite.

In Harold Lee Schut's version, they had heard sirens screaming and believed the police were catching up to them. But they had already driven thirty miles and were a safe distance from the crime scene.

According to Limestone County prosecutor James Fry, investigators checked police records that night, and they found no indication there were any cars in the vicinity that activated their sirens.

Fry agrees with Tracy Clemons. "Most likely," says Fry, "they didn't discover the baby had a clubfoot until they were in the car. When they unwrapped the baby blanket, they saw the foot and said, 'We can't sell *this* baby.' And then they dumped him in the field."

Whatever the reason for leaving James behind, one would hope there would be a shred of humanity between

Jackie and Lee—*just a tiny drop of compassion*—that would compel them to find a phone booth and make an anonymous call. They could have told someone where the baby was.

But they didn't.


After hearing Harold Lee Schut's hypothetical confession, Detective Regimbal flew to Palm Springs, California, to meet with Dana Rose.

The eleven-year-old was a witness to murder. She had been there when Jackie shot Geneva Clemons. She remembered how Jackie had barged into the Clemons home, scooped up the baby, and handed him to her. "Take him to the car," she had whispered.

Dana Rose had been terrified, but she did as she was told. She was in the backseat, crouched on the floor, when she heard the deafening blasts of the gun. The poor baby was screaming his head off, and Dana Rose started screaming, too.

She would never forget how Lee had reached back and hit her so hard that blood gushed from her nose. "I was bleeding, and they didn't care," she remembers.

Dana Rose's description of the crime matched the hypothetical scenario that Lee had described.

Dana Rose was given a polygraph test, and she passed.

Meanwhile, Jackie Sue Schut had lawyered up, and she was sticking to her story that she had never been to

Alabama. The Gardenhires hired Yakima attorneys Adam Moore and Tim Ford to represent her.

Athens prosecutor Jimmy Fry was ready for a fight. The murder of Geneva Clemons had disturbed him more than most homicide cases he handled. What could be crueler than shooting a mother in front of her child, and then leaving her baby in a field to die?

Whoever did this was diabolical.

It bothered Fry even more because he *knew* the victim's husband. In fact, he had known Larry Clemons since they had gone to grade school together.

"I've tried hundreds of cases," says Fry. "But the Schut case was meaningful to me." Serendipity, he points out, played a role in the arrest and prosecution of the Schuts. "So many pieces had to come together in order to prosecute the case," he says. And "so much could have gone wrong," but it didn't. "We were lucky to make our case."

Fry was relieved when he heard that the Schuts were apprehended, and he wasted no time in getting to work building a case against them.

In January 1985, a Limestone County grand jury indicted Lee and Jackie on capital murder and kidnapping charges. Lee had taken back his confession, and now he said he was innocent.

Jackie was well aware that Alabama had the death penalty, and she was nervous—especially after hearing the comments by "Electric Chair Charlie."

Judge Charles Graddick, attorney general for the state

of Alabama from 1978 to 1987, had been dubbed Electric Chair Charlie because of his enthusiasm for the death penalty. During his campaign in 1978, Graddick had said that when it came to murderers, he'd like to "fry 'em till their eyes pop out, and blue and yellow smoke pours from their ears."

Graddick's graphic description of the electrocution process must have been more than Jackie could bear, for she made a calculated move to avoid extradition to Alabama. She pled guilty to the child molestation charges in the case involving her young daughters—the case she had originally been arrested for. She was given a ten-year prison sentence in Yakima, Washington.

Limestone County prosecutor Jimmy Fry told reporters that he was outraged that Jackie Schut had found a way to sidestep extradition. "I was so mad I could have blown the roof off the courthouse," Fry said.

If Alabama had to wait ten years before they could try Jackie Schut, it would make it difficult to prosecute her for the murder of Geneva Clemons.

Fry was also frustrated by the fact that he had followed Washington authorities' directions for filing extradition papers for Jackie Schut, but was stonewalled when he was told the papers were not properly prepared.

"The lack of cooperation frightens us," he told a reporter for the Associated Press. "We want to make sure that Mrs. Schut is not released from prison under a work release program until she stands trial here."

Fry's concerns were well grounded.

Washington State did indeed have a disturbing record for releasing violent offenders into work-release programs. In the 1960s and 1970s, I was the Northwest stringer for several true crime detective magazines, and I covered over one thousand crimes.

It was not unusual for me to report on a case of rape or murder, only to find that the offender had already been released from prison by the time my story was published six months later. Sometimes they were put on work release programs, and sometimes they were sent to the Honor Farm in Monroe, Washington, where security was so relaxed it was easy to escape. Almost invariably, they offended again.

Jackie Schut dug in her heels and refused to face the Alabama charges, but Fry would not let it drop. He requested that the Alabama Department of Corrections direct Washington State officials to put a detainer on the defendant so she would be forced to face the capital murder charges.

It was challenging enough to prosecute a murder case without the added burden of an evasive defendant. Fry and Regimbal and their teams worked together, building the case against the Schuts, so that they would be ready when legal arguments about Jackie's extradition were settled.

In an April 1985 press conference, Electric Chair Charlie made a prediction about the impending prosecution of Lee and Jackie Schut. Charles Graddick told reporters, "The evidence will be overwhelming," and "If found guilty here, they should be electrocuted."

Jackie's attorneys took issue with Graddick's comments. They asked Washington State governor Booth Gardner to refuse to extradite their client on the grounds that Graddick's remarks would make it impossible for her to get a fair trial. The Alabama public had been "poisoned" by Graddick's remarks, her attorneys argued.

Prosecutor Jimmy Fry insisted that there was no lynch-mob mentality in Athens, and that it would not be difficult to find unbiased jurors in Limestone County because many residents had never even heard of the Schut case.

Jackie's legal team presented Governor Gardner with documents that they said would prove that she had not been to Alabama that January 1980. There was no way, her lawyers maintained, that she could be involved in the Clemons homicide.

Governor Gardner weighed the argument, and in mid-June 1985, his attorney, Terry Sebring, gave a written statement to Jackie's attorneys saying that Gardner had decided not to "intervene on behalf of your client to delay or prevent her return to the state of Alabama. Only in an adversarial proceeding, such as a criminal trial, could the truth of Ms. Schut's contentions regarding her whereabouts be adequately tested.

"Granting asylum to Ms. Schut is not an appropriate

remedy to curb alleged misconduct in the state of Alabama. These matters could only be resolved through either direct contact with Alabama officials or judicial action in Alabama."

Even as Gardner refused to block Jackie Schut's extradition, her attorneys were looking for more ways to prevent her from facing Alabama charges.

Jimmy Fry knew it was detrimental to Geneva's family and to the case itself to let the tug-of-war drag on. The Clemonses needed justice so that they could go on with their lives. Fry offered a compromise. He would take the death penalty off the table if Jackie would stop fighting the extradition.

Her attorneys found that acceptable, so Fry flew to Washington, and he went to the Purdy Correctional Facility in Gig Harbor, Washington, to claim his suspect and personally escort her back to Limestone County.

She didn't say much to him on their journey back to Alabama. Asked to describe Jackie, Fry says, "She's really a troll-like figure, but because I am a southern gentleman, I will say that she is singularly unattractive."

One week before Christmas, at midnight on Wednesday, December 17, 1986, Jackie Sue Schut arrived at the Athens City Jail to await trial.

Washington authorities had been reluctant to let her go, and they would call Fry repeatedly over the next months to ask for her return so that she could face additional charges there for her sex crimes. "They didn't seem to grasp the gravity of the crimes committed in Alabama and Texas," Fry explains.

Fry was angry. The pencil pushers in Washington had made it impossible for him to pursue the death penalty for the murderer who had destroyed so many lives—and would certainly continue to hurt others if she were ever freed.

Finally fed up with the constant requests for him to return Jackie Schut to Washington, Fry told them in his charming southern drawl that he planned to make sure that she died in prison and *then* they could have her back. "I'll send her dead, rotten corpse back to you in a box," he said.

That was the last time Washington requested her return.

Six years and eleven months after Geneva Clemons's murder, the defendant was finally in place and waiting to be prosecuted.

It had been a tough fight just getting her there. The defendant and her family had not only made it difficult to prosecute the case, they also made it difficult to investigate it.

Simply interviewing witnesses had turned out to be a monumental task. Jackie's big brother, Luke, blocked Detective Regimbal's access to two of the most important potential witnesses.

"Luke would not let me talk to George and Gladys," says Regimbal. "He ran the family."

Luke, a pastor at a Pentecostal church, was in his fifties when Jackie was indicted in the Clemons case, while the elder Gardenhires were in their seventies and growing frail with age. Perhaps Luke wanted to protect them from the fallout of what he apparently believed was a witch hunt. He was Jackie's staunchest supporter, and he seemed convinced that his baby sister could do no wrong.

It was frustrating for the detective to be banned from speaking to two people who could very well have the answers. Could it be that Luke feared that the elder Gardenhires had information that could hurt Jackie's case? Regimbal suspected that, but he never got the chance to ask them anything.

Regimbal was a little surprised that Luke allowed him to talk to Buddy. Jackie's son was about thirteen when he sat down with the detective. Buddy knew nothing about a trip to Alabama, but he did reveal something that shed light on Jackie's character.

"He told me he was with his mother when she robbed somebody," says Regimbal.

Jackie, according to her son, had once pointed a gun at a man and demanded cash. Buddy could not remember (or would not say) the name of the victim or where and when the alleged incident occurred.

Regimbal believed the kid when he said he didn't know anything about his mom taking a trip to Alabama. Buddy was given a polygraph test, and he passed. That was the one and only time that Luke allowed Regimbal to interview the boy.

The Chevy Malibu was another key factor in the case, but Regimbal could not find the car. Harold Lee Schut had described driving the Malibu in his hypothetical journey to kidnap a baby, and Dana Rose had remembered riding in it on the long trip she had taken with her mother and Lee that January.

Luke scoffed when he heard about the Malibu. It was just one more hole in the investigators' ridiculous case against his sister—one more thing that proved Dana Rose was lying.

"The Malibu didn't even run!" he said, pounding his fist on the detective's desk for emphasis. "It didn't run, and it was stuck in a snowbank that time of year. She's *not* guilty!"

The question of the Malibu worried Regimbal. He tried to keep an open mind, and he checked himself to be sure he was not forcing pieces to fit into a puzzle where they did not belong.

A lot of time, energy, and money—not to mention emotion—was being poured into the case, and it had all begun with Regimbal. What if he were wrong? In the beginning, he worried that maybe he *was* wrong, that he was accusing the wrong person of murder.

Jackie Sue Schut was certainly not going to win the award for mother of the year, but did that make her a killer?

Athens detectives had found no physical evidence at the scene of the crime—no hairs or fingerprints that could be matched to Jackie. And no murder weapon had been located. If they *had* found a gun, or even spent bullets and cartridges in Jackie's possession, comparisons could have been made to the spent bullets extracted from the victim's body.

Investigators had eyewitness accounts from Geneva's sister and brother-in-law who had briefly seen the suspect at the house shortly before the murder. And they had Tracy, an actual eyewitness to the murder, but she was only five when she saw her mother shot. After six years would she remember? And if she did, would a jury believe her? They would certainly feel sorry for a child who had seen her mother gunned down, but that did not mean they would find her to be a reliable witness.

There was Lee's hypothetical account, and Dana Rose's statements. But Dana Rose was an abused child, and she'd been treated at a psychiatric ward. The girl had—understandably—suffered a mental breakdown after all she had been through, but the defense would likely use that against them and question her credibility.

Regimbal had his work cut out for him, and the responsibility weighed on him heavily. The biggest question was Jackie's whereabouts on January 21, 1980. If the defense could prove that she was in Washington on the day of the murder, then a jury could not possibly find her guilty.

Jackie's attorneys had a pile of documents that they

said would prove that she was in Yakima on January 21, 1980. These were the same alibis that the defense had tried to foist upon Governor Booth Gardner, who had wisely decided it was not up to him to make a judgment about her guilt.

Regimbal worked to shred Jackie Schut's so-called alibis. The question of the Malibu was one of the first obstacles. If the car were dead in a snowbank in January 1980, as Luke claimed, that would not be good for the prosecution.

The Schut story was big news in Yakima, and the local newspaper published an article informing the public that detectives were trying to prove that the now missing Malibu was running in January 1980.

Shortly after the article appeared, Regimbal heard from a surprising source—a temporary resident at the Department of Corrections. Hank Rhoades* was in jail in Yakima when he phoned the detective to set up a meeting.

As Rhoades sat across from Regimbal, he said, "I just want to share this information I have about the Malibu."

He told Regimbal that he knew that the Schuts's Malibu was running in January 1980. "I know that that car ran because I'm the one who fixed it for them so they could go on a trip," he said. He explained that when he had done mechanical work on the blue Malibu, he had been impressed with it, and that was why he remembered it so well. "I told them I wanted that car," said Rhoades. "It was a hot car."

Regimbal wondered if the inmate wanted a favor in return for the information, but he asked for nothing.

"Crooks are people, too," says Regimbal. "People in prison have kids, and they don't like to see children abused."

Regimbal's point is well taken. The news that children were sexually abused at the hands of Bernard Oldham and the Schuts sickened most Yakima residents—even those behind bars. Convicted pedophiles are considered the lowest form of life in prison, and are, not surprisingly, targeted by child avengers.

And now that the Schuts had been accused of murdering mothers to steal their infants, their status sunk even lower.

When Detective Regimbal finally tracked down the Malibu, it was crunched up in a wrecking yard, disposed of years earlier.

On another occasion, Luke pointed out to the detective that the investigators had made a big mistake when they calculated the time it would take to travel by car from Yakima to Athens. He claimed it would have been impossible for the Schuts to drive that distance in the time allotted.

Regimbal did the math, and it was obvious to him that Luke was wrong. If two drivers took turns behind the wheel, chose the most direct route, and drove day and night, they *could* make a round-trip between Yakima and Athens in a week.

"To prove it couldn't be done, Brother Luke and his entourage drove from Yakima to Alabama to attend the trial," Regimbal says. "He never mentioned it again. I think they realized that it *can* be done."

When the Houston detectives got a call from Athens police chief Richard Faulk, they were elated to hear that there had been an arrest in the murder of Geneva Clemons.

They had compared notes on their cases years earlier, and Faulk had agreed with them that Cheryl Jones had not committed suicide. Detective Gil Schultz, who was partnered with Detective Paul Motard for over a decade, says, "We knew somebody else had to be there in the room with Cheryl Jones, because that baby did not get back to New Orleans on its own."

In 1980, when Schultz and Motard first began investigating Cheryl's death, they were able to quickly clear Dennis Jones as a suspect. His alibi was solid. He had been working when Cheryl died.

"The toxicology report showed that Cheryl had a lethal amount of drugs in her system," says Schultz. "We went to her husband and asked him if she ever used drugs. He told us she didn't."

The whole thing was hinky.

The baby did not walk out of the hotel room. A woman had given the child to a taxi driver. Who was that woman? And someone had ordered cocktails from room service.

The room service charges were applied to the credit card of Dr. Taylor,* who lived in Orange, Texas. Who was *he* and what was he doing in that room?

There was another thing that the detectives found to be very odd. There were baby clothes left in the room, but all of the labels had been ripped out.

Despite the fact that the ME ruled the death a suicide, Motard and Schultz did not stop investigating it as a murder. Now, with the call from Chief Faulk, it looked like the case would finally be solved.

When the Houston detectives questioned Harold Lee Schut, he gave them the same kind of roundabout confession he had given to Bob Regimbal in the Athens case.

"I didn't do it, but if I had, I would have done it this way . . ."

Lee described the murder to the detectives in detail. "He told us things that no one could have known unless they'd been there," says Schultz.

To the great relief of Cheryl's family, the ME changed the manner of death to homicide. They had known in their hearts that Cheryl was murdered, and now they hoped that her killers would be prosecuted.

Dr. Joseph Jachimcyk, the Harris County medical examiner, told reporters, "This case had all the earmarks of a textbook suicide. But after reviewing the new evidence, it is apparent that it was a homicide."

While Cheryl's wrist had had only superficial cuts on it, it was still strange that it had not bled—an indication that the cuts were made after her heart stopped beating. She could not have made the cuts herself.

Though the cause of death was officially changed to homicide, public records still list Cheryl Ann Jones's death as a suicide—a fact that troubles her sister. "I've tried to have it changed many times," says Kathy. But she has always gotten the runaround.

Detectives eventually were told by Lee that Amanda Jones was supposed to be adopted on the black market, and that the Schuts had expected to earn two thousand dollars for kidnapping her.

Then why was the baby sent back to her father?

According to Lee, they had panicked when Cheryl died.

Detective Shultz said that the Schuts "were so dumb, they thought if they gave her these drugs that she wouldn't remember anything."

Lee told the detective he expected the drugs to "erase her memory." He said he had not expected the young mother to die.

He was either dumb or *playing* dumb.

If they hadn't expected Cheryl to die, then why was she forced to write a suicide note?


On May 4, 1987, the Limestone County courthouse was packed with media and spectators crammed into the long wooden benches. Circuit Judge Henry Blizzard presided, and a jury of five women and seven men had been chosen to decide the fate of Jackie Sue Schut.

Jackie's family had hired Athens attorney Jerry Barksdale to defend her. Unbeknownst to the jury, some of the key players in the case were connected. Judge Blizzard and Jerry Barksdale had once been in private practice together.

In 1968, the then young attorneys had paid sixty bucks a month to rent two rooms in what had previously been Booth's Pool Hall on North Marion Street in Athens. They hung out their shingle, and the old pool hall became the law firm of Barksdale & Blizzard.

The prosecutor, the defense attorney, *and* the victim's husband had all gone to Athens High School, though Barksdale had graduated a few years earlier than the others.

While the attorneys and the judge often crossed paths and had chosen careers rife with drama, Larry Clemons hadn't, but he was inextricably caught up in it—forever part of the tragic story he wished had never happened.

Detective Bob Regimbal had flown from Yakima to serve as a consultant for the prosecution. He knew the case so well, and he sat at the State's table, prepared to offer his insights.

Fry, who had once been a high school football star, was an imposing figure, and Larry Clemons was glad he was on the side of the good guys. Husky, with a booming voice, Fry always got his point across, and in his opening statement, he pulled no punches. "This is a case of clear, cold-blooded murder!" he announced.

The defendant sat quietly by her attorney, betraying no emotion as Fry explained to the jury what he would prove. "The evidence, we believe, is strong," he told them. "We'll put two people on the stand who will tell you that less than an hour before the victim was killed, they saw a woman that we believe was Jackie Schut at the Clemons house, begging to take the baby's picture to put in a beautiful baby contest."

That baby was now seven years old, and he was perched beside his grandfather on one of the hard benches, appearing a little dazed.

Barksdale assured the jury that his client was no killer. She was the victim of shoddy police work. The *real* killer was still on the loose. The injustice of it angered Barksdale, and he explained, "The killer has not been arrested. The police, acting under pressure to make an arrest, took the words of scum and criminals to hatch up a false claim against Jackie Schut."

Barksdale said he didn't know who shot Geneva Clemons, but he was certain it wasn't Jackie. She was in Yakima that day, and he would prove it. For one thing, he had evidence that Jackie had telephoned her mother from her apartment.

"It has to have been a case of mistaken identity, because the 'witnesses' fingered the wrong person. It was a shame that the real killer hadn't been caught, but that wasn't the fault of the defendant. She wasn't even in Alabama in January 1980.

"We will present evidence of this!" Barksdale promised. "The very day that the State says Jackie Sue Schut was here in Athens, killing and kidnapping, she was in Yakima, Washington, filing a welfare claim."

Barksdale didn't realize it, but Detective Regimbal had already destroyed the welfare claim alibi. Admittedly, Regimbal had been concerned when he first heard about the existence of a signed and dated legal form that could positively place Jackie in Yakima on the day of the murder. "I thought, 'Oh, well that throws a wrench in things,'" he remembers.

Regimbal had gone down to the welfare office in Yakima to check out the validity of the welfare form alibi. A rather rude clerk wasn't eager to answer the detective's questions. "She wasn't a very friendly person," he says with a grin. "She acted like I was putting her out. I was investigating a murder, but she didn't want to be bothered!"

With a little persistence, Regimbal was able to pry loose the answers he needed. As it turned out, the form could be mailed to the welfare office, and the people who filed the forms were often not present when clerks stamped the time upon the documents. The stamped date in no way proved that Jackie was at the welfare office on that date.

Before Barksdale even got to the point of presenting his welfare claim "evidence," Fry took the wind out of his sails, telling the jury that the alibi was useless. "We'll show that the caseworker does not remember Jackie Schut being in the office that day," he said, explaining that the claim was probably mailed, and then it wasn't processed until the day of the murder.

As for the phone records that Barksdale said would prove Jackie had called her mother from her Yakima apartment, they did not carry much weight. The prosecution alleged it was Buddy who used the phone that day, and the eight-year-old had called his grandparents to come get him because his mother wasn't there.

Fry was eager to demolish Barksdale's opening-statement allegation that cops had "hatched up" the case against the Schuts. His voice booming, the prosecutor told the jury that Barksdale "is not telling you the truth when he says the police officers hatched all of this up."

But Barksdale would not let it go. He went after everyone he could. He attacked investigators, and at one point during the trial Detective Regimbal became the target of his wrath. The *Yakima Herald-Republic* had done a story on Regimbal and his work on the case. Regimbal hadn't asked for the publicity, but he did not turn away reporters when they questioned him.

The Yakima public was hungry for details about the Schut story. The article praised Regimbal for his work in cracking the case. The detective hadn't sought out the limelight, but now, Jackie's attorney used the article against him.

When Regimbal was on the stand, Barksdale waved the newspaper at him and loudly accused him of "grandstanding."

Barksdale was trying to give the impression that Regimbal had implicated the Schuts to make himself look good—to get his picture in the paper. Poor Jackie Schut was being railroaded to feed a detective's ego!

The best defense, they say, is offense. It's a cliché, and it might not always be true, but it *was* the strategy used by Jackie Schut's attorneys in their attempt to shred the State's case. The defense's best defense was clearly *offense*.

When Barksdale attacked him, Regimbal found it unsettling, and after nearly thirty years, the memory still disturbs him. If a seasoned detective was rattled by Barksdale's accusations, imagine what it would do to two little girls.

Tracy Clemons was now twelve, and Dana Rose Simons was fourteen. The daughters of a killer and her victim were the State's star witnesses.

They were children, and Jackie Schut had hurt them both tremendously. Seven years earlier, the two girls had met on a tragic night that neither one would ever forget.

Tracy could not forget the night she was splattered with her mother's blood. Dana Rose could not forget that night, either, nor could she forget the unbelievable cruelty she had suffered at the hands of the one person who was supposed to care for her.

Now, these two girls were expected to face the monster. The burden would have been too much for most adults. But each was determined to do what she must. And Barksdale was determined to break them.

It was, after all, his job to discredit the girls. "I don't know what Dana Rose is going to tell you," he said to the jury, "but we will prove by her school attendance records that she was in school that day."

When Fry had first heard of the existence of that alleged evidence, he was a little concerned. The school secretary had, in fact, marked Dana Rose as present during the period of January 16 to 24.

But just as the welfare form alibi had turned out to be a dud, so did the attendance record "proof."

The prosecution played a videotape of Yakima County school administrator Richard Sippola, who explained that the secretary could have easily made a mistake because the record of those particular days were on a separate page from the rest of the month.

"It is possible that she entered her record on the wrong line," Sippola said, and then he pointed out that the name of the girl on the line below Dana's was marked as absent on those days.

When investigators checked with the parents of the girl who was marked absent, they stated that their daughter *was* in school on those days. It looked as if the secretary had accidentally transposed the names.

Indignant, Fry told the jury, "Dana should know

whether or not she was in school during that period, and she says she was not."

Dana Rose was petrified when she was called to testify. She hadn't seen Jackie in over a year, and she dreaded walking into the courtroom to face her. Though she knew that Jackie had done wrong, Dana Rose at times felt crippled by guilt for going against her.

It seemed her entire family was on Jackie's side: All of Dana Rose's aunts, and her uncle Luke. Dana's beloved grandparents—Gladys and George. Even her brother Buddy! They had all traveled to Limestone County to support Jackie.

Dana Rose hadn't had much communication with her family, but in the few exchanges they did have, they made it clear to the girl that they did not approve of the stance she was taking. She was forcing them to choose sides, and they chose Jackie.

Poor Jackie, they moaned. How dare Dana Rose do this to her? How dare she try to hurt Jackie like this?

Dana Rose was bewildered. The grown-ups in her family had seen the proof that Jackie had sexually abused her—seen the photographs of the twisted things that her alleged mother had done to her. The detectives had *shown* them the evidence!

And Jackie had, after all, pled guilty to the crime. According to Dana Rose, not a single relative had reached out to tell her they were sorry for what she had gone through. They didn't seem to care.

"They swept that under the rug," Dana Rose says. "It was as if it didn't even happen."

Gladys and George had taken Dana to the Pentecostal church with them many times over the years. They had told her about God—taught her about right and wrong. Brother Luke was the pastor there, and Dana Rose had listened very carefully when he preached.

And she had *believed* her uncle. She had believed what her grandparents and Luke had told her about God. They said that if she was good, she would go to Heaven when she died. And if she wasn't, she would go to Hell.

When she was trying to gather the courage to testify against Jackie, Dana Rose imagined what it would be like to meet God. "I thought about how someday I would have to face God," she explains. She wondered what she would tell Him if she *didn't* try to stop Jackie. How could she stand before God and say that she hadn't had the courage to stand up against evil?

"I knew in my heart that I had to do the right thing," says Dana Rose. "I couldn't allow another little person to be hurt."

Dana Rose also knew that if she did not stand up to her now, Jackie would probably kill her. If she was released from prison, Dana Rose was as good as dead.

In the eyes of the Gardenhire family, Jackie was the victim, and Dana Rose was a liar who was determined to destroy them.

Detective Regimbal shakes his head as he remembers

how Dana Rose's family abandoned her. "They just threw her to the wolves," he says.

Dana Rose felt alone that day in the Athens courtroom. On shaky legs, she approached the stand and took her seat. She stole a glance at her family. They sat together, stone-faced, all in a row on one of the long wooden benches.

Dana Rose did not want to look at Jackie. And she managed to avoid the defendant's eyes when prosecutor James Fry questioned her. He was on her side, of course, and Dana Rose knew him and was comfortable with him.

Detective Regimbal was there, too. He had rescued her and Deanna—he'd taken them out of school that day, and no one had touched her since. It was reassuring to know that he was there.

The courtroom was hushed as Dana Rose described the trip they had taken in the blue Malibu, the thousands of miles they had driven that ended in murder.

"I remember my mother taking the baby from her," said Dana Rose. "My mother told me to get in the car . . . Then I heard two shots."

At one point in her testimony, Dana Rose said something that shocked the entire courtroom. She confided that the Clemons murder wasn't the only homicide she had witnessed.

Jackie had shot *another* mother and abducted her infant, too.

Barksdale objected but was overruled. Dana Rose's memory was vague about this other murder, and details of the case were not forthcoming.

Dana braced herself for cross-examination. She'd been warned that Jerry Barksdale would try to unnerve her, and he did. "He badgered me and badgered me and badgered me," she said. "It was horrible."

Worse, Barksdale made a point of standing next to Jackie while he questioned Dana Rose. The girl was forced to look in his direction—forced to meet Jackie's icy glare.

The attorney had positioned himself intentionally to rattle Dana Rose, and it worked. As Dana Rose answered Barksdale's questions, Jackie communicated with her through angry eyes. "It was like she was saying, 'You just wait. You're going to get it later!'"

But Dana told the truth. "I knew it was the right thing to do," she confides. "I knew I had to make sure that she couldn't hurt anyone else."

As far as Barksdale was concerned, her testimony was fiction. It seemed to Dana Rose that the defense attorney pestered her for hours. She thought he sounded sarcastic and angry, and he continued to hover over Jackie, so that when the girl answered his questions she saw both their unfriendly faces staring back at her. But she stood up to him as he tried to break her down. Every so often, Judge Blizzard interrupted to offer Dana Rose a break and a drink of water.

Finally, it was over. Dana Rose stepped down from the stand, exhausted and mentally drained.

Tracy, too, was nervous about facing her mother's killer. "I was scared," she remembers. "But I was also relieved because it was finally coming to an end."

When Tracy glanced at Jackie, she was startled to see how blasé she appeared. Jackie showed no more emotion than you would expect from a person waiting for a bus.

James Fry asked Tracy the questions she had been expecting, and she sat up straight as she answered him in her polite southern drawl. She pointed at Jackie and said, "That is the woman that killed my mother. I wasn't but five years old at the time, but I saw her kill my mom. I can never forget it."

Tracy described how the predator had come to their home two times that day, and how she had promised to give them cash if she could take pictures of the baby.

Then it was Barksdale's turn. Tracy's heart quickened as he approached. Barksdale was well aware that he had to tread lightly with this girl. Any jury would be sympathetic to a child who saw her mother murdered. If he took too hard a stance, he would alienate them.

Still, he had to discredit the witness. He would do that as gently as possible. Barksdale decided to poke holes in her memory. He tried to get the girl to admit that she didn't remember the day her mother was killed, because she was too young.

She was amazingly calm and firm as she stood up to

him. "I remember it well," she insisted as she held her head high. "I didn't talk about it at first, but I can never forget it. I know I was just five, but I remember."

Larry Clemons was extra proud of his daughter that day. He wished her mother could see what a brave girl their daughter had grown into.

At the end of the day that Dana Rose had testified against her, Jackie asked to see her. It hurt Dana Rose to see the woman she called mother in chains. The girl asked the guard if he could remove them for a moment. He complied, but kept a watchful eye.

"Jackie put her arms around me," Dana says. "I kind of melted into her, as kids do when their parents hug them." Though she had never found warmth in Jackie's embrace, she found herself still hoping for affection.

But the woman was as cold as she had always been as she stiffly held her. Her mouth close to the girl's ear, Jackie said, "I forgive you."

The words were as cold as the hug, and Dana Rose felt a chill.

Throughout the five days of the trial, a number of witnesses took the stand, including Geneva's sister and brother-in-law, who placed the suspect at the scene of the crime. Kathy and Wayne McMeans identified Jackie Sue Schut as the woman they had seen at the Clemons home a short while before the murder. They testified that the defendant had been trying to persuade Geneva to allow her to photograph James for the beautiful baby contest.

Seven of Jackie's loyal supporters had traveled two thousand miles to swear that she could not have been in Alabama on the day of the homicide.

A middle-aged Yakima couple, Will and Carla Stemm,* said that they had seen Jackie at a restaurant in Washington on January 21, 1980.

Jackie's son, Buddy, who was now fifteen, took the stand to say he had no memory of his mother leaving the state of Washington during January 1980. "I guess you could say I was a mama's boy," he said. "Wherever she went, I'd have to go . . . I don't recall her ever going away for a night."

On cross-examination, Frý fished for a possible motive for Buddy to lie, and the boy admitted that he loved his mom, "and I don't want her in prison in Alabama. I want her back home."

Fry asked Buddy if he had ever seen his mother with a gun.

"No sir," said the teen. Asked about his admission to Regimbal about seeing his mother hold up a man, Buddy denied he had ever said such a thing.

Buddy's testimony was in direct contradiction to his sister's earlier testimony. Dana Rose had stated that Buddy was left behind when they took the trip to Athens, Alabama. She also said that Marcy* and Earl Small* had been living with the Schuts, and that they had stayed with Buddy while the rest of the family was gone on the trip.

Earl Small took the stand, and his version of events matched Dana Rose's.

Jackie's sister, Anita, also supplied her with an alibi, insisting that the night before the Athens murder, Jackie had visited her apartment in Yakima.

"Jackie came to our apartment and told my husband about a job," Anita said. She was quite sure of the date, even though seven years had now passed.

When Fry questioned Anita, she confessed that she would "do anything to get my sister out of this and back home."

It wasn't the answer Jackie's attorneys would have liked to hear, but it was honest.

When Gladys Gardenhire took the stand, she said that Jackie "depended on us for everything," and she would certainly have noticed if her daughter was gone for any significant period of time.

It was true that Jackie leaned on her family. Dana Rose remembers that George, Gladys, and Luke were constantly rescuing Jackie—bringing her groceries when the cupboards were empty, paying the electric bill when the power was turned off, or driving her to the hospital when she got one of her frequent migraines.

The jury wasn't privy to all of the evidence investigators had gathered—including the results of polygraph tests taken by both Jackie and Dana Rose.

# THE BABY SELLER

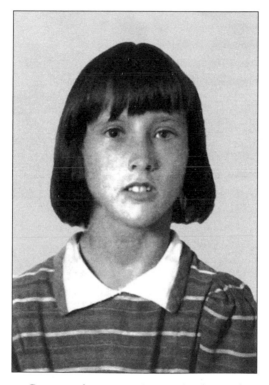

Geneva at about age twelve. Her brothers and sisters remember that even as a child, she was considerate of others' feelings. (*Tracy Clemons*)

Larry and Geneva Clemons with their first child, Tracy.
Geneva loved being a mother. (*Tracy Clemons*)

Geneva grew up in
Tanner, Alabama.
Her family had
been in Limestone
County for at least
three generations.
(*Tracy Clemons*)

Larry and Geneva Clemons were happy with the simple things in life. They loved children and hoped to have many. (*Tracy Clemons*)

Geneva and Larry, relaxing at home. The first time Larry Clemons saw Geneva Burgett, it was love at first sight.

Tracy Clemons in December 1979. She was a happy five-year-old. One month after this picture was taken, she saw something that would give her nightmares for the rest of her life. (*Tracy Clemons*)

Dennis Jones and Cheryl Pecore met when they were young teens. From the beginning, they knew they were meant to be together. (*Amanda Jones*)

Pictured here in high school, Cheryl Pecore expected to live a long and happy life with Dennis. (*Amanda Jones*)

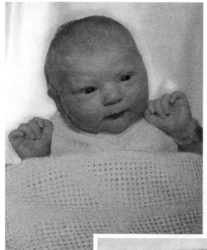

Newborn Amanda, in the hospital, posing for her first picture. When Cheryl was pregnant, she told a friend that she already loved her baby so much that she knew she would give her life for her. Her words were prophetically tragic. (*Amanda Jones*)

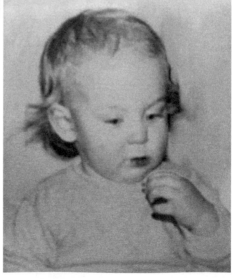

Amanda was a beautiful baby with golden curls and bright blue eyes. Though she did not consciously remember her mother, she missed her profoundly. (*Amanda Jones*)

Amanda Jones and her boyfriend, Joe Bell, at her senior prom in 1996. The two fell in love as teens, and then went their separate ways. They never forgot each other, and when their paths crossed again, they realized they were meant to be together. (*Amanda Jones*)

Amanda is happy today, pictured here with Joe, the love of her life. (*Amanda Jones*)

Detective Bob Regimbal was credited with cracking a cold case so strange that it shocked the nation. Pictured here in the spring of 2014 with one of his rescued horses, on his ranch in Selah, Washington. (*Leslie Rule*)

Richard Faulk was a highly respected police chief in Athens, Alabama. Pictured here in the 1970s, he cared about the people in his community, and he vowed to catch the monster who killed the young mother. (*Author's collection*)

Jackie Schut outside the courtroom in 1986, with her big brother, Luke,* who believed she could do no wrong. (*Heritage Images*)

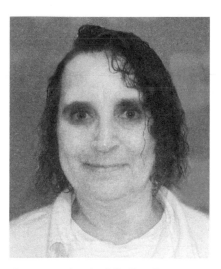

Incarcerated at the Julia Tutwiler Prison for Women in Wetumpka, Alabama, Jackie Schut is a sickly shade of prison pallor. (*Tutwiler Prison Photo*)

Harold Lee Schut (left) used a photography ruse to abduct babies. A "Photographer" in the police sketch (right) abducted an Inglewood, California, baby. Investigators suspect the cases are connected. (*Mug shot and police sketch*)

Ruby Bates dominated headlines in 1931 when she made false accusations of rape. Pictured here in 1976, Ruby and her husband, Elmer Schut, sit on the steps of their Yakima County home. Soon after this photo was taken, their son, Harold Lee Schut made headlines of his own. (*Author's collection*)

When a young mother was murdered in Limestone County, Alabama, in 1980, no one guessed there was a connection to the infamous Ruby Bates, who had made news there decades earlier in the "Scottsboro Boys" trials. Ruby, pictured here in court in the early 1930s, would later move to Washington State and raise a killer. (*Author's collection*)

Tracy Clemons (middle) first crossed paths with Dana Rose Schut (right) when they were terrified children on a cold, dark night. They met again a quarter of a century later and vowed to be friends forever. Larry Clemons (left) also reached out to Dana Rose, and told her they didn't blame her for his wife's death. (*Tracy Clemons*)

Limestone County, Alabama, Prosecutor Jimmy Fry knew the Clemons family, and he was determined to put Geneva's killer away. (*Jimmy Fry*)

# SECRETS OF
# THE AMOROUS PIZZA MAN

Kathie Hill as a senior in high school. She always looked for the good in people. (*Hill family*)

Kathie Hill, after graduating with a master's in software engineering in 2010. (*Hill family*)

Kathie Hill was happy and still in love with her husband, Al Baker. She had no idea he did not feel the same. (*Hill family*)

The Baker residence was on Silver Cloud Lane in the Greenbank community on Whidbey Island. Neighbors were shocked when the home became a crime scene. (*Author's collection*)

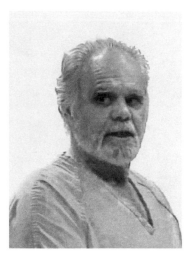

Robert "Al" Baker was not an attractive man, but Kathie was devoted to him. She had no idea about his dark past or the evil in his heart. (*Author's collection*)

Al and Kathie in happier times. They were very affectionate with each other, and most people who knew them believed they were in love. (*Lori Snider*)

No one watching Al Baker and Kathie Hill could predict
their grim future. They enjoyed all kinds of activities,
including boating, as pictured here. (*Lori Snider*)

Kathie Hill loved animals, and her dogs
were family to her. (*Lori Snider*)

Kathie Hill's smile was infectious. Her family always felt better when she was around. (*Lori Snider*)

Detective Mark Plumberg sensed something was wrong from the moment he arrived at the Silver Cloud Lane home. He was part of a team of investigators that were shocked by what they discovered. (*Leslie Rule*)

Polygraphs are not always accurate, and some detractors claim that 28 percent of the time the tests give false results. Because they are unreliable, polygraphs are usually not admissible in court. Jackie had failed her test, but Dana Rose had passed hers.

The State wanted the jury to know about the test results and tried to slip in the information in a roundabout way. When Chief Faulk was on the stand, Fry asked him what steps he had taken to determine that Dana Rose was truthful.

Faulk replied, "We made arrangements with the local police department there to have their polygraph examiner give Dana Rose a polygraph examination."

Barksdale was on his feet. "Your Honor," he said, "I'm going to move that that be excluded as not being responsive to the question and that the jury be instructed to disregard it."

Judge Blizzard said, "All right. I'll strike it. I don't think it's an issue. The jury can disregard it."

The question of the so-called confessions was another issue. Barksdale told reporters he would like to put Jackie on the stand, but that he would do so only if Judge Blizzard suppressed statements she had made to Chief Faulk.

Barksdale was worried about the conversation she had had with Faulk—the conversation when she suggested that "self-defense" or "an accident" could be factors in Geneva Clemons's death. Fry, of course, was eager to ask her about the comments she'd made, but he could not if the judge blocked those questions.

In the end, Jackie did not take the stand—much to the disappointment of spectators, who were dying to hear from the overweight, plain woman from Yakima who had been accused of doing such monstrous things.

The jury would not get to hear about Jackie's conversation with Faulk, nor would they hear about Lee's hypothetical confession to Regimbal.

Court watchers were also hoping to see Harold Lee Schut on the stand. Lee, represented by a court-appointed attorney, Limestone County public defender Dan Totten, listened to Judge Blizzard's advice as he stood before him on Friday afternoon. "Harold Lee," said the judge, "I want to explain the law to you. You are a co-defendant in this case, but will be tried at a later date. The State has agreed to give you immunity, but you do not have to testify. I want you to know that. The law gives you the right to decide whether to testify or not."

Lee replied, "After talking to my attorney, I've decided that I do not want to testify, Your Honor."

Lee was to be the last witness, and because he'd chosen not to take the stand, final arguments began.

"Somebody in Yakima, Washington, knew about this case in Athens, Alabama," Fry told the jury. "The Yakima police didn't dream it up." The killer, he said, was "Jackie Sue Schut. She pulled the trigger to the gun that killed Geneva Clemons. She kidnapped that baby."

Fry reminded the jury that they had heard from four eyewitnesses that put Jackie Schut at the scene of the crime. "Two of them saw her kill Mrs. Clemons. We also presented two witnesses from Yakima who told you that Jackie Sue and Harold Schut left for a trip four days before the murder and kidnapping."

When Barksdale addressed the jury for the last time, he said, "It is a sad thing that Geneva Clemons was killed. But the killer is still out there. Jackie Schut did not kill Geneva Clemons. I just hope you, the jury, can see that."

Barksdale added that some of the witnesses for the State had out-and-out lied. While some had lied, others, he said, were confused. "Some of Mrs. Clemons's relatives said Jackie killed her, but I think they were just mistaken. It has been a long time."

The jury retired at 4:20 on May 8, Friday afternoon. They deliberated for four hours and then sent out for sandwiches. Late that Friday night, they were still at work, when an anxious Jackie was overheard complaining to her attorney. "I can't stand this," she said. "This is worse than being in jail!"

It was 11 P.M. when the jury came back. It had taken them six and a half hours to find Jackie Sue Schut guilty of murder, and kidnapping in the second degree.

When she heard the verdict, Jackie cried, "Oh God! Not this!"

Gladys wept and exclaimed, "This is wrong—all wrong! My daughter wasn't in Alabama!" Jackie's mother was heartbroken. She had probably convinced herself that her daughter was innocent of the horrendous things of which she'd been convicted. What mother wants to think she has given birth to a monster?

Dana Rose was in a motel with a victim's advocate, and her eyes were glued to the TV screen when the news broke.

The news camera zoomed in on George Gardenhire's face. The old man was weeping. Dana Rose felt sick. "I'd never seen my grandfather cry before," she says.

The girl was torn apart. She had tried to do what she felt was right, but it had hurt people—hurt the only family she had ever known.

Reporters crowded around Larry Clemons and asked how he felt now that his wife's killer had been found guilty. "This has been seven years—seven long years that have been a nightmare," he said. "I felt all along that she was guilty. Now this proves it. We can get a little sleep tonight."

District Attorney Jimmy Fry told reporters the verdict was a "blessing for justice. If ever anyone needed convicting, this woman did. In my opinion, she did the most vicious crime that there is."

Fry also made a point to single out Detective Regimbal for praise, and added, "If it hadn't been for Regimbal, we could not have been able to solve the case here."

When reporters asked Jerry Barksdale to comment, he said, "It's been a long day, and I just don't know what we'll do, but I'd say we are leaning toward an appeal."

Jackie's attorney would later tell reporters that the case

against her was "one of the biggest miscarriages of justice that I have ever seen. This case is going to be in court a long time."

Jackie Schut lost her appeal for a new trial. She was sentenced to life (*with* the possibility of parole) for the murder of Geneva Clemons, and two years (to be served consecutively) for the kidnapping of James. She is currently incarcerated at the Julia Tutwiler Prison for Women in Wetumpka, Alabama. Women who have been there say it is truly "hard time."

Jackie denies any connection with the death of Geneva Clemons and has not yet been charged in the death of Cheryl Ann Jones. She was denied parole in 2014 and her next review will be on May 1, 2017.

Lee Schut pled guilty in both the Clemons case and the Jones case. He is currently incarcerated at the Ellis Unit in Huntsville, Texas. He was recently denied parole and his next parole review will be in January 2017.

Because my books are about real life, the stories I write never truly end. The victims' families, the detectives who worked so diligently for justice, and even the killers—who, fortunately, usually continue their stories behind bars—all have lives beyond the endings of my books.

Usually there are questions left unanswered. In some

cases, victims are never found, their bodies hidden forever in vast waterways or hidden beneath slabs of concrete or paved roadways. Their families are forced to wonder and worry for the rest of their days.

And then there are the killers who still insist they are innocent and continue to profess that, even after decades in prison. Some of them manage to make news from behind bars, filing legal motions, picking fights, and sometimes even escaping.

Many of the murderers I've written about serve their time and are set free among the rest of us without fanfare. Drama usually follows them, but unless they are caught breaking the law again, we seldom hear about it. Still, their stories go on.

The case of the "Baby Seller" has more unanswered questions than any of my other books.

What about that other murder that Dana Rose testified she had seen Jackie commit? Did she *really* see it, or was it a bad dream that blended with the reality of her nightmare life?

Detective Bob Regimbal was shocked when he rescued Dana Rose and her little sister from the Schuts and Bernie Oldham. The abuse Dana suffered stunned him, and he was amazed that the child managed to survive.

She made it to adulthood, but her life has not been easy. The only family she ever knew gave her the cold shoulder after she testified against Jackie. Dana Rose grew up in foster homes, many of them abusive.

She was a teen when she gave birth to a daughter who brought love and light into her life. "She was my angel," says Dana Rose. But she had a serious heart condition and died in 2004 at age fourteen.

Although Dana Rose is now stable and happily married to a supportive husband, she admits that she attempted suicide many times over the years. "It's a miracle I'm still here. I've been close to death many times, and I've often wondered why I survived," she tells me. "It makes me think there is a reason I'm here—that there is something I'm supposed to do to help others."

Dana Rose *has* helped others. When she gathered the courage to testify against Jackie Schut, she prevented her from hurting more people. Few souls could have stood up against evil the way Dana did.

In my opinion, Dana Rose is a hero. But she is also an enigma—one more mystery in this strange case.

She herself recognizes this, and she wants the answers more than anyone. The biggest question for her is her identity.

Dana Rose would be thrilled to discover that she is not the biological daughter of Jackie Schut, and that somewhere out there, her real family still searches for her.

"I don't look like anyone in my family," she points out. "And I've never seen a picture of myself under the age of three."

When she was a little girl, going through boxes of family photos at the Gardenhires' house, she asked why there were no baby pictures of her. "There were photos of everyone else from the time they were born," says Dana Rose. "But not me."

Gladys told her that none had been taken. I find that very odd. But *Jackie* is odd, and she neglected Dana Rose in so many ways, it would not be out of character for her to neglect to take her baby's picture.

Dana Rose has seen her own birth certificate, but she questions its authenticity, because there are *two* birth certificates for Deanna. One states that she was born in Yakima, Washington, and the other in California. If Deanna's birth certificate was forged, maybe Dana Rose's was, too.

Dana Rose would like a DNA test to answer the question of her identity. The wheels are in motion to make that happen. If Dana Rose finds she *is* the biological daughter of Jackie Sue Schut, I hope she is not too disappointed. Even if they *are* genetically connected, Jackie's actions do not reflect upon Dana Rose, who is a good person. I've gotten to know her while writing this book, and I'm proud to call her my friend.

Jackie Sue Schut swept across the country like a tornado, sucking up those who got in her way, their destroyed lives trapped in her vortex of peculiar evil.

Much of what Jackie Schut did made no sense. She has yet to explain any of it. She has yet to admit to any guilt in the deaths of Geneva Clemons and Cheryl Jones. She has yet to admit to kidnapping babies.

If, by some miracle, Jackie *did* speak out and tell all, it could answer questions that torment countless people. As I wrote this frightening story and watched it unfold on my computer screen, I found myself shaking my head at all the dark secrets I uncovered.

## What About the Other Babies?

More than one investigator was quoted saying that they believed that the Schut case was related to at least half a dozen other infant abductions. Robyn Light, the victim witness manager who interviewed Dana Rose in the 1980s, says "I got the impression that she had witnessed Jackie sell many babies."

Prosecutor James Fry always believed there was much more to this case than anyone could guess. When he reflects on it today, he says, "I'm convinced the Schuts were operating a kidnapping ring. My hunch is that these are not isolated cases."

When she testified against Jackie in 1987, Dana Rose said she had seen Jackie murder another woman and sell her baby. But nearly three decades later, the details evade her. She has a vague recollection of a baby, and of columns— like those on the porch of a southern mansion. And she has an eerie feeling. But she remembers nothing more.

Dana Rose *does* recall that during the January 1980 trip to Athens, Alabama, they stopped by hospitals so often that it became a tedious routine. Jackie would go in, and they would wait in the car for her to come out.

She was possibly shopping for infants to abduct. Larry

Clemons remembered seeing a strange woman staring a little too intently at James in the hospital nursery. Whether or not this was Jackie, I don't know. Jackie approached Geneva at the grocery store, but she—or perhaps someone else in the ring—could have been tracking the Clemons family for a while.

At the time Jackie Schut was committing her crimes, hospitals were one of the most common locations for infant abductions.

In recent years, most hospitals have tightened the security in their nurseries, but in the 1980s, they were often wide open to any stranger who happened by. The kidnapper typically donned a nurse's outfit, and mothers calmly handed their babies over to strangers. They believed, of course, that the smiling women in uniform were who they said they were, and that their babies were going to be tested or fed.

In many of these cases, the abductors were infertile and desperate to have babies, often because they were trying to keep restless boyfriends or husbands from leaving them. More often than not, the fathers were clueless, accepting the abducted infants as their own without question.

In most of these cases, the mother was not harmed—if you don't count the searing agony that slices a mother's heart in half when her child is missing. The women were not *physically* harmed in the majority of these instances, but that does not rule out the Schuts as suspects.

In the most horrific cases, kidnappers strike while a baby is still in utero—literally cutting a baby out of its womb and sacrificing the mother.

The deaths of Geneva Clemons and Cheryl Jones may very well have been inconsistencies. Maybe, as Lee Schut claimed, no one was supposed to be killed. Maybe the Schuts had stolen other babies whose mothers are still alive and searching for them.

There are numerous cases of babies abducted in the 1970s and 1980s—some with similar MOs to that of the Schuts. In December 1984, two-month-old Donel Jacoby Minor was abducted in Inglewood, California, by a man posing as a photographer. Harold Lee Schut was living in neighboring Nevada around that time, and the composite sketch of the abductor resembles him. "The Inglewood case could have been a Schut kidnapping," says Prosecutor Jimmy Fry. "It is too similar to be ignored."

If Donel Jacoby Minor is still alive, he would now be thirty years old.

Chances are, we won't connect the Schuts to the Minor case or find the answers about Dana Rose's true heritage before this book goes to press, but I will be sure to post updates on my webpage.

Dana Rose and Tracy first met each other on that horrible day in 1980, never suspecting that they would one day appear on television together. A quarter of a century later, in 2005, they met again—this time on the stage of the *Montel Williams Show*.

Larry Clemons was there, too, and he said that Dana Rose had arranged the on-the-air meeting because she "wanted to know if we're mad at her. We're not."

Tracy looked Dana Rose in the eye and told her, "We both lost our mothers. I don't have a sister. If you ever need a sister, I'll be your sister."

Prosecutor James Fry, who was also a guest on the show, said, "There was not a dry eye in the place."

Tracy and her father travel to Wetumpka to testify each time Jackie Schut is considered for parole.

If Jackie Sue Schut *is* ever paroled, Cheryl Jones's family will fight to make sure she is finally charged with her murder. Amanda has recently started a blog, called *My Journey for Justice,* where she shares her struggles to find justice for the mother she does not remember yet misses profoundly.

Amanda's life has not been easy. Her stepmother seemed to be threatened by the fact that Cheryl had been the love of Dennis's life, and she would not allow her name to be mentioned in their home. Though she was close to her father, Amanda experienced little warmth from her stepmother. Dennis eventually divorced, and he dated a wonderful woman with a generous heart who encouraged him to talk about Cheryl. Sadly, Dennis drowned in Cayuga Lake, one of central New York's glacial finger lakes, in August 2009 at the age of fifty.

Both Detective Bob Regimbal and Prosecutor Jimmy Fry are involved in charitable work. After an illustrious career that included a position as a judge on the Alabama Court of Criminal Appeals, Fry is now the executive director of Legal Services Alabama, a nonprofit organization that provides free legal services to low-income Alabamians.

Bob and his wife, Kerrie Regimbal, rescue horses and bring them to live on their ranch in Selah, Washington. For nearly a decade, they have saved dozens of horses—some starving and others headed toward the slaughterhouse. Their nonprofit organization, Kidz N Horses, pairs neglected horses with children with low self-esteem.

# SECRETS OF
# THE AMOROUS
# PIZZA MAN

**"Things are seldom** what they seem," Gilbert and Sullivan wrote in their musical *H.M.S. Pinafore.* "Skim milk masquerades as cream . . ."

All people hide things, but rarely do they have secrets as dark and dangerous as those of Robert Alan "Al" Baker. At first glance, Baker does not appear threatening. He is a short man who resembles a concrete garden gnome with wisps of white hair curling around his face, and deep-set eyes that can be alternately glaring and seductive. Far from attractive, he has somehow managed to captivate his share of females—including a few very smart women, impressing them by exaggerating his academic achievements.

While Baker earned a modest undergraduate degree from California's Sonoma State University, and worked as a cryogenics technician for the Raytheon Polar Services Corporation (RPSC), he is not the brilliant scientist he claims to be.

*Who is he?*

His name is so common that he can easily camouflage his identity, altering it a bit as needed by changing spellings. At this time he is "R. Allen Baker." His friends call him "Al."

He was "Robert Baker" at his graduation from Sonoma State University, where, clean shaven, he stood smiling for the camera in his cap and gown, eyes strangely obscured by reflective sunglasses. In one of his run-ins with the law, his attorney claimed that he was an "internationally known expert in cryogenics," a field within physics that explores the behavior of matter in extreme cold.

In actuality, Baker *did* work at a basic level in the cryogenics field. In 2002, he gave a brief presentation at a National Science Foundation meeting, explaining how to purchase the difficult to procure liquid helium used as a coolant for the advanced telescopes used in astrophysics research in freezing temperatures. But his "expertise" does not extend far. An article self-published by Baker and posted on the web was apparently intended to impress but resulted in a serious teasing from science bloggers—one of whom compared it to an elementary school science project.

Most women wouldn't be drawn to him, and yet he has never failed to attract those females who had something about them that *he* wanted. He was charismatic and interesting, and he regaled prospective lovers with his stories of his fascinating past.

When Al Baker met Kathie Ann Sharp, née Hill, in the RPSC Denver offices in the mid-1990s, they were both employed there full-time. They were nearing middle age—she was approaching forty, and he was a decade older. The two had something in common. They were not afraid of the cold, and were, in fact, *drawn* to it.

In his role as a physicist in the art of cryogenics, Baker studied the minutiae retrieved in experiments in Antarctica. Kathie was a genius with advanced science degrees, including a master's in meteorology. In 1993, she became the twenty-ninth woman to winter at the South Pole, and she was the first female to spend an entire winter there as a meteorologist.

Kathie Ann Hill was born in Fairbanks, Alaska, on July 24, 1958. Her parents, David and Barbara Hill, raised her and her three brothers, David, Richard, and James, in Boulder, Colorado. A happy child, Kathie always tried to see the bright side.

The Hills were a musical family, and Kathie's brothers Jim and Dave were members of the "Mary Jane Bann'd." Iconic on a local level in the Colorado music scene in the 1960s and '70s, they had a huge following with frequent gigs in Boulder and Aspen. Jim played the drums, and Dave played the guitar and wrote songs. Kathie wasn't as musically talented as her brothers, but she loved watching and listening to them.

She was very young when she married her first husband, Thomas*. Her dreams were dashed when the

131

marriage ended badly. It left her so emotionally fragile that she guarded her heart carefully after that. She dated infrequently, and was content to be with her close-knit family.

Kathie was sensitive and kind, and so up-front herself that she expected the same honesty from others. Despite the fact she had been badly hurt, she looked for the good in people. When she met Al Baker, she probably had no inkling that his charming personality hid a manipulative mind.

When Al was assigned to organize teams of scientists and their assistants and deploy them through the several stations of the Polar Program, he became a puppeteer, placing people where he wanted them—attractive women near his station, and men, whom he wanted to isolate for his own reasons, farther away.

Antarctica, which contains the geographical South Pole, lies at the southernmost tip of the world. Hardly a tourist spot, it is the coldest, driest, and windiest continent, buffeted by fierce winds that can knock down a grown man.

The few women brave enough to spend the coldest months "on the ice" have to be strong—both mentally and physically. To make their way from the central lodge to their living quarters or to laboratories, all "Poleys" have to snap a carabiner to a strong line strung between the buildings. Without it, people could literally blow away in the sudden gusts.

Kathie didn't mind the arduous trips between the hunkered-down buildings.

She was a tough lady, but tender, too.

To reach the South Pole, employees must take a boat to New Zealand and pass customs there, before continuing the journey to Antarctica. One year, Kathie was on a boat out of New Zealand when a violent storm whipped up rough seas. She fell down iced-over metal steps and broke several bones. Their ship was in the midst of nowhere, and it would be two weeks before they reached a spot where her bones could be set properly. She was sedated to ease her pain for the long voyage to land.

Unfortunately for Kathie in this instance, she was a fast healer. Her bones had begun to set before she reached a hospital. They had to be rebroken and set correctly.

The pain never really went away, but Kathie kept her job at the South Pole. She was so enthusiastic about her career that she started a foundation to encourage high school girls to study science. Her favorite part of her day in Antarctica was when she released the weather balloons that sent back information.

The pay was good, but few would choose to travel so far from home to work in a dark and frigid world. The icy realm became a romantic place for Kathie and Al in the seemingly endless months they spent there, working on Raytheon's Polar Program.

Kathie was flattered by the attention of the articulate man who appeared to have vast knowledge in several scientific areas.

There weren't very many Raytheon employees on the

ice at any given time, so the crews bonded and became close as they sought surcease from the icy winds and bitter cold.

Employees congregated in the central lodge, where movies were shown, or they could visit others' rooms for more intimate gatherings.

Al Baker, several times divorced, was drawn to Kathie, but when she wasn't looking, he also flirted with bush pilot Trudi Gerhart. The trio spent their free time together during the dark days when the sun was elusive.

Kathie and Trudi were adventuresses—brave enough to face the challenges of life at the bottom of the world. Both women were buxom, their blond hair shot with gray. Al focused his attention on Kathie, who was taller than Trudi, and also a few years younger. He treated her like a princess, and it seemed every time she turned around, he gave her a romantic card.

Al eventually proposed to Kathie. But there was a problem: he was already married. He told Kathie that his marriage to Mary was an unhappy one and that they planned to divorce. Kathie was flattered by Al's attention, but she was firm when she told him that she simply would not date a married man.

Her life was complete. She wasn't looking for another husband, but she did enjoy the cards and flowers that Al Baker sent her. Al always had a stack of romantic greeting cards handy, but he had to go to great lengths to find flowers for the object of his desire.

It was a Victorian romance in an alien landscape, with Al showering Kathie with gifts. Suspiciously, a government audit revealed that taxpayers footed the bill for a number of questionable luxuries purchased by an unnamed Raytheon manager: a tower of chocolates from Harry & David, expensive soaps from Venus Bath and Body. The audit does not provide concrete evidence that any of the questionable purchases can be traced to Al Baker, but it underscored the lax oversight that allowed a scoundrel free rein for romance in the icy realm.

Eyebrows were raised and chuckles were heard around the globe when 16,500 condoms were shipped to Antarctica just before winter fell in 2008. One would hope that with a winter population of fewer than three hundred folks, the quantity sufficed for those cold, lonely souls on the ice.

Condoms or not, Kathie was not about to rush into anything. On one occasion, when she was back home, Kathie and her niece Jami Hill were sipping margaritas and discussing men. Kathie was torn about what she should do about Al Baker.

"One thing," Kathie said with a laugh, "I know what I had to go through to be cleared by security for my job. They not only checked me out—but the rest of our family, too. Al can't have any secrets now. You have to be clean as a whistle to qualify for the Polar Program, and have the proper identity to pass customs in New Zealand to get there!"

Kathie had never expected to be married again; she

was happy with her extended family. And they needed her; she was the matriarch of the Hill family, the shoulder to cry on, the one who would always listen, and offer good advice. The Hills were a very close group of relatives whose home base was in Colorado. They all cherished Kathie.

The Hills had gone through so much in recent years. Kathie's older brother Jim (Jami's father) died young. Kathie's mother, Barbara, fell victim to Alzheimer's disease and sight-stealing macular degeneration. She was nearly blind because of the latter ailment. Where she had always been gentle and sweet, Barbara's personality changed as the diseases moved on inexorably. She became mean and used obscenities she'd never used before. It was Kathie who cared for her mother. She couldn't go to Antarctica those years because she stayed with her mother until the end—even after Barbara Hill had to be moved to an assisted living facility. She wanted to be sure her mother had the best of care.

The Hill family losses did not end there. Kathie's brother David had been happily married to his wife, Jeanette, for many years. Sadly, she contracted breast cancer. Although she fought hard, she lost her battle.

Al never gave up on Kathie. Throughout the tragedies that stalked the Hill family, he was always there, attending funerals, memorial services, and weddings, comforting Kathie or celebrating happy times with her. In the end, his persistent courtship both charmed Kathie and wore her down. In 2007, they were married in Colorado in front of her family. Kathie was forty-nine, and Al was fifty-eight.

Kathie's decision to marry Al Baker had come rather suddenly and her relatives were surprised, but she was clearly so happy that not one of them dared to rain on her parade. Behind Al's back, some of her family called Al "The Troll," which he did resemble—with his long white hair in a ponytail and his voluminous white beard. Still, the Hill family welcomed him to their gatherings. To his face, they called him "Alan," a name he preferred. They thought he was a little odd, but they never dreamed he would hurt Kathie. He seemed to dote on her.

Kathie had far more assets than Al did: a lovely home in Aurora, Colorado; savings; and investments. She was scrupulous about keeping records and managing her own finances.

Al was the idea man, freewheeling, with dreams of making a fortune. As yet, he hadn't done that. Opposites *do* attract, and they were as different as night and day.

Kathie Hill Baker could juggle her marriage, her job at Raytheon, and the needs of her extended family. Kathie refused to let her family fall apart despite too many losses in too short a time. Through her efforts, she kept them together, supporting one another.

So it was wrenching for Kathie to acquiesce to Al's plans to settle on Whidbey Island, Washington. It was such a long way from the Hill family and the house Kathie owned in Colorado.

Still, Kathie loved her husband and was prepared to follow him wherever he would be happiest. That was her nature—to take care of those she loved. During most of the time they were married, she continued to work for Raytheon, where she was highly respected. It meant doing much of her work via the Internet and phone, and with quarterly visits back to Raytheon headquarters in Colorado.

Al also continued to work for Raytheon, and was sometimes also employed by the National Science Foundation. The Bakers bought a house on Silver Cloud Lane in Greenbank, Washington, on Whidbey Island. It was a home with a lot of potential, and Al had a number of DIY projects he wanted to accomplish.

Al Baker always seemed to choose isolated corners of the planet, perhaps with a sort of animal instinct, places where he might easily obscure his being. While Whidbey Island is certainly no parallel in its remoteness to the South Pole, it is accessible only by ferry and a two-lane bridge at its northern point, spanning, in a bleak coincidence, the waters of Deception Pass.

The island where the Bakers made their home was off the beaten path and as lush as Antarctica was barren.

Life was peaceful in the town of Greenbank, named for the historical Greenbank Farm—legendary for its onetime fields of sweet berries, it is now a hiker's paradise.

While balmy in comparison to the frigid South Pole, the waters of Puget Sound average a crisp fifty-three degrees in July. Whale watchers gather here in hopes of glimpsing a magnificent orca. Though commonly called killer whales, the enormous black-and-white beasts are actually members of the dolphin family.

Kathie missed Colorado, but she was enchanted with the beauty of Whidbey Island. Several years after they moved to Greenbank, the Bakers bought Madistone's pizza restaurant and renamed it Harbor Pizzeria. Kathie managed the pizza shop while Al was working in Antarctica.

"I think she made only one pizza there," her niece Jami recalls. "She handled the counter and the cash register."

The rest of the year, Kathie and Al worked side by side.

"She was the rock of our family," one niece recalled.

"There were so many secrets we didn't know," Jami Hill recalls. "It was like peeling an onion. You think you've come to the last layer—but there's always something more lying beneath."


June 2012 marked exactly two hundred and two years since Joseph Whidbey had first mapped Deception Pass, as he explored the island as part of Captain Vancouver's expedition.

June 7 was a typical spring day in the temperate climate. At dawn, a gray mist shrouded the island, yet fronds of shimmering green plant life embroidered its terrain, bringing promise of summer.

The pastoral quiet was broken by an ominous phone call to the Island County Sheriff's Office.

The caller said he was in Colorado, stationed at a Raytheon office there. Bill Sloan was a security officer and had grown concerned when he had been unable to reach one of their most reliable employees. She had never before ignored her coworkers' calls.

Bill had been trying for a week to get ahold of her. He requested a well-being check on Kathie Hill Baker.

"This isn't like her," Sloan explained. "We usually hear from her several times a week. She telecommutes from her home, but we can't even get her on her cell phone—our calls go directly to her voice mail."

Patrol lieutenant Evan Tingstad and Deputy Leif Haugen were two of the first sheriff's men to arrive at the Baker home on Silver Cloud Lane. Haugen drove all the way to the house as Tingstad stopped to check the name on the mailbox. As he did, a red pickup with a male driver turned onto Silver Cloud and approached him slowly. Tingstad walked over to the truck.

"Are you Mr. Baker?" the patrol lieutenant asked.

"Yes," the white-haired man said.

Asked if his wife was home, Baker shook his head. "She flew to Denver a couple of days ago—for her job. I haven't talked to her or gotten any messages from her since."

Tingstad noted that the pale-faced Baker appeared unusually nervous. One would think he was dreading some bad news about his wife—but he didn't ask any questions about Kathie or show any outward concern about her.

"Can we talk with you?" asked Tingstad.

"C'mon up to the house."

Once there, Tingstad glanced up at a window on the second story of the home. A buxom woman in a hoodie stood peering out at him. He noted the ash-colored hair, and he thought that she matched the description of Kathie Baker.

Puzzled, he asked, "Is there anyone else in your house?"

"A friend," Baker answered. He sounded calm now, and he explained that he had taken Kathie to Sea-Tac Airport on June 3 to catch her flight to Denver for one of her regularly scheduled meetings at Raytheon. After Kathie entered the departures level, he had picked up a mutual friend of theirs.

The woman that Lieutenant Tingstad saw at the window was, Baker said, Trudi Gerhart, whom both he and Kathie had befriended while they were all working down on the ice in Antarctica. Without any prodding, he assured the detectives that Kathie knew Trudi was coming for a visit, and didn't mind at all.

While the circumstances seemed a bit peculiar, there was no reason for Tingstad and Haugen to linger. But later, when Haugen spoke with Bill Sloan, he learned that Kathie still had not contacted her employers. Nor had she been scheduled for any training or other site work at any Raytheon facility.

"She hasn't used her corporate credit card, either," Sloan said.

Kathie's relatives were contacted, and not a one of them had heard from her with news of a sudden trip to Colorado. Worried sick, they offered to do anything they could to help find her.

By the next day, when there was still no word from Kathie, Whidbey Island investigators rallied. Joining Patrol Lieutenant Evan Tingstad and Deputy Leif Haugen in the probe into Kathie Baker's whereabouts were Island County detectives Mark Plumberg and Laura Price. The case had ominous rumblings and the team suspected that the outcome would be grim.

"Baker's given us improbable stories about the whereabouts of his wife," Tingstad briefed Plumberg and Price when they arrived at the Silver Cloud Lane residence. "And now he's stopped answering our questions."

The gnome-like Baker had given them permission to search the house, and fortunately, he had yet to rescind it. As soon as Mark Plumberg crossed the threshold, he noted a vivid dark stain splotching the light-colored carpet in the living room. It was long and consistent with something having been dragged over the carpet.

Leif Haugen stood on an upstairs landing, and from there, he noted that the stain on the carpet continued across the kitchen floor tile, and then down a small flight of stairs to the garage door.

"They also located what appeared to be blood on the

inside of the garage door," Plumberg recalls. "And I could see that dirt on the garage floor next to the reddish stain looked like something had been dragged through it to the rear, exterior, garage door."

Tingstad pointed out a small, dried pool of blood on the master bedroom carpet. It was partially covered with a pillow. Mark Plumberg wondered why no apparent attempt had been made to hide a virtual abattoir's worth of blood in Baker's house.

There had been plenty of time for Baker to clean up the mess since the investigators visited the day before. Was Al Baker so confident that he believed that the detectives accepted his story about dropping Kathie off at the airport? Was he so sure of himself that it didn't even occur to him that they might ask to search his house?

Or was Al a candidate for "Dumbest Criminals of 2012"?

There was also the possibility that there was an innocent explanation for the bloodred stains. Detective Plumberg tried to keep an open mind, but his gut told him that it did not look good for the missing woman.

The investigators asked for access to the Bakers' computers, so they could see if there had been any activity in Kathie's accounts. Red-haired Detective Laura Price was tall and fit, and she towered over the short, bearded suspect as he typed in the various passwords to his missing wife's email and banking accounts.

Meanwhile, Deputy Leif Haugen was scrutinizing the

stained carpet. He did a double take when a woman suddenly walked down the steps from the upper part of the house. Was this some kind of a macabre joke? At first glance, the detectives thought that Kathie herself had appeared.

But on closer inspection they saw that she was heavier and somewhat older than the photos of Al Baker's missing wife. Asked to identify herself, the blond woman held out her Alaska driver's license.

She was Trudi C. Gerhart, sixty-one, and she said she'd come down from Alaska to visit Al. She had known both the Bakers for several years, she explained. They had all been Poleys—a term the Raytheon employees who worked at the South Pole called one another—although she hadn't seen Kathie for quite some time. Deputy Haugen asked if she would step out on the deck. She agreed.

Leif Haugen asked her if Al Baker seemed concerned about his wife, and Ms. Gerhart said she felt that "he does now."

Trudi recalled that in February 2012, Al had written to her with upsetting news. He and Kathie were having troubles in their marriage.

"All he would say was it was 'heavy stuff, but we're working through it. It's heartbreaking but necessary. I just wanted you to know . . .'"

Trudi said she had commiserated with Baker about that news. "I told him I was sad to hear it—but sometimes things will be what they will be and everyone must adjust."

Whether she really felt that way, since she and Al seemed to be living in an intimate situation, was moot. Trudi may have been glad that Al would soon be a single man.

As she talked to Leif Haugen, a light suddenly seemed to come on in Trudi's brain. Maybe the deputy didn't know the whole story.

"You realize, don't you," she asked, "that Kathie doesn't live here? Right?"

Haugen was momentarily nonplussed.

"Right?" Trudi asked with more emphasis. "Kathie's been living in Colorado for a long time. She doesn't live here anymore."

Trudi had her own doubts. She commented that she thought it strange that Kathie had left her two corgi dogs—one more than a dozen years old—at the house on Silver Cloud Lane. "Those dogs are like her children. Kathie's life was work and those two dogs. She never would have left without them."

Trudi said she had arrived from Alaska on June 3 in the late afternoon, and Al had picked her up at Sea-Tac Airport, south of Seattle. She said she was hoping that Kathie would be at the house, that things might be better in their marriage. Perhaps.

But Kathie wasn't there when they arrived in Greenbank.

"Al soon made it clear," Trudi said, "that he wanted a romantic relationship with me. He didn't say anything about Kathie or their marriage."

Trudi said that Al had visited her in Alaska twice that spring; his March visit was close to two weeks long. He had sent her the ticket she'd just used to fly to Seattle for an extended visit. He told her Kathie had left him months before, and he was for all intents and purposes a single man. He did *not* tell Trudi about his taking Kathie to the airport only a few hours before he picked *her* up.

Kathie likely had no idea where her husband really was in March 2012, or who he was with. She had sounded like her usual peppy self when she emailed her brother David Hill in March saying how happy she was for him and his bride, Melody. Knowing that David had grieved terribly for his late wife, Jeanette, Kathie was relieved that he was now able to love again.

The plan was that David and Melody—who had met when they owned mobile homes next door to each other—would come to live with Kathie and Al until they found their own place on Whidbey Island. Al had assured Kathie that would be fine with him.

Kathie wrote:

*Wow! What an awesome picture!!!! I can see you're happy even in the dark and with you looking away from the camera.*

*Funny, you've been on my mind so much today! I almost called you but then I got called away. I'm in Colorado now. Alan is in Washington, D.C.! He's meeting with the new Polar contractor, Lockheed Martin. Hopefully, he'll be able to work out a deal with them to continue to work in the Antarctica program. If not, he'll be full-time pizza man!*

*WE CANNOT WAIT FOR YOU GUYS TO GET HERE!!!!!!!!!!!!!*

*I'm so happy for your and Melody's happiness, Davey.*

*Seems like dreams do come true!!!*

*Love you!*

*Kath*

Al wasn't in Washington, D.C., in March, of course; he was in Alaska visiting Trudi Gerhart.

After Trudi's startling information that Kathie hadn't lived with Al for three months, Leif Haugen went back inside the house and confronted Baker. "How long has Kathie been living in Colorado?"

"Since March this year—when I got back from my assignment at the South Pole."

Baker had backed himself into a corner with his many different stories about the last time he saw his wife. Nothing matched.

"Where is she residing now?"

"I don't know . . . I don't even have her address."

"Where would you suggest we look for her?"

"I have no idea."

Baker's stories had become more and more entangled, but each one had to be checked out. Maybe he *had* driven Kathie to the Sea-Tac Airport and let her off there. Maybe he'd suffered a small stroke that damaged his memory and perception of time, but that theory strained credulity. Until investigators actually found Kathie—dead or alive—they couldn't be sure.

Over the past two decades, a number of women have vanished from the sprawling airport, located between Seattle and Tacoma. Some were eventually located, and sometimes reported to the Port of Seattle Police that they had been abducted and raped, as they walked to the airline employees' parking lot, or to the soaring parking garage provided to the public.

Tragically, other women had been murdered, while others were simply "walk-aways." Maybe Kathie Baker was like the ones who had seemingly disappeared through the morass of tunnels and gates as roaring planes took off and landed. Once Al had dropped Kathie off at the departures gate, she would have been out of his sight within moments.

Detective Laura Price and Deputy Leif Haugen met with Al Baker at the Island County Sheriff's South Precinct at 3:00 P.M. on Friday, June 8. Now, Al *did* seem worried; beads of sweat stood out on his forehead and his usually ruddy cheeks were pale. Five days had passed since he—or anyone else, apparently—had heard from Kathie.

No one yet had even hinted that Kathie wasn't happy in her marriage. Everyone who knew them said she doted on Al, called him her "hubby," and smiled widely as she told friends about some lunch or dinner they were going to share. She still sounded like a bride when she spoke about Al. Most of the year, they worked side by side at Harbor Pizzeria, striving to build their clientele. When Al left to spend his three to four months down on the ice, Kathie handled things at the pizza shop.

Indeed, they had celebrated the one-year anniversary at Harbor Pizzeria on June 2 the night before Kathie vanished. Lots of people took pictures to commemorate the happy evening. That film was evidence that the Island County sheriff's investigators certainly hoped to find.

Kathie left the party before Al did, but it was because she was tired—not because they had an argument or anything like that.

Al continued to answer the investigators' questions. He made no effort to convince them that his wife had left him in March. That seemed to be a story he told only to Trudi.

"Kathie usually calls me every few days when she's away," Baker said glibly. "But it can be longer. She's not real good at keeping in touch with her family and friends, but she is *always* available to Raytheon."

Detective Price asked about what time on June 3 Al

had taken his missing wife to catch her plane to Denver. They would have had to take a ferry from South Whidbey Island to Mukilteo on the mainland, and then drive south on I-5 about thirty miles to Sea-Tac Airport.

"We got on the ten or ten thirty A.M. ferry at Clinton, and headed east to the mainland on June third," Baker answered. "When I got to Mukilteo, I missed the I-5 on-ramp so I had to approach the airport from I-405. I dropped Kathie off at the Southwest Airlines departures level around one thirty."

The entrance to I-5 was well marked far in advance of the actual turn. How odd that Baker had missed that.

"How is your marriage?" Price asked suddenly.

"Things are going good," Baker said.

"Was your wife worried about anything?"

Baker shrugged. "Kind of stressed—but she's always stressed about work."

Leif Haugen excused himself as he left the interview room. Now that he had the name of the airline that Kathie Baker had allegedly taken on June 3, he could ask about her record with Southwest.

Port of Seattle's Officer Josh Maiuri followed up within the hour. Southwest Airlines said that Kathie Baker *was* a frequent flyer with them, almost always between Denver and Seattle. She had, however, not flown with them out of Sea-Tac since April 10, 2012! Kathie hadn't flown to Colorado for over seven weeks. She certainly was not on their roster for June 3.

Now it was June 8. Where had Kathie Baker been the last five days?

Detective Mark Plumberg had hit the ground running when he got involved in the probe into Kathie Baker's disappearance. He gathered all the follow-up reports and evidence that had surfaced so far. Plumberg was impressed—and grateful—for all the work that Evan Tingstad, Laura Price, and Leif Haugen had already done. Plumberg and the patrol officers were now trying to sort through any motives Al Baker might have had to kill his wife *if,* indeed, she was dead.

Al said he and Trudi Gerhart were not lovers—and Trudi certainly insisted that they weren't. Even though she had had those two visits from Al at her home in Alaska in the spring just past, and he had assured her that Kathie and he were estranged, and that Kathie was moving back to Colorado. Trudi wasn't ready to commit to a sexual liaison with Al.

Or so she said.

Trudi's mind raced as she tried to absorb the possibility that her good friend, and perhaps her potential lover, was not at all whom she thought he was. She had believed him when Al said Kathie had moved out three months earlier. Now she knew that wasn't true.

At the same time, Trudi herself had become a suspect, although she didn't realize it. She could not have participated in a fatal attack on Kathie; the timing was wrong. She could, however, have assisted Al Baker as he dragged someone who was dead-weight heavy through the house, leaving the large bloodstains. Al was a very small man and Kathie probably weighed about 175 pounds.

Detective Laura Price talked to a convincingly shocked Trudi Gerhart in the house as the male investigators searched the garage with Al Baker. They walked to a door *inside* the garage.

"What's this?" Evan Tingstad asked.

"The laundry room," Baker answered.

"Can we take a look?"

Baker swept his arm widely in an exaggerated gesture, as if he were presenting the room to a possible buyer. He and Tingstad moved into the small laundry room, where they were only inches apart.

Tingstad saw a white bedspread/comforter soaking in the deep sink.

"Did you put this in here?"

"Yes," Baker said. "I had to wash it."

"Why did you have to wash it?"

"It was dirty."

"Dirty with *what*?"

"It was just dirty."

"Where did it come from?"

"The bedroom."

Tingstad lifted the damp comforter and saw what appeared to be a bloodstain about five inches long and a few inches wide. He asked Baker if the stain was blood.

"I don't know," the suspect said, and now volunteered

that he'd misspoken before. Thinking about it, he realized that he hadn't put the comforter in the sink, and he didn't know why it was there.

Tingstad noted that the washing machine in the laundry room was full of clean clothes. He advised Al Baker that he was seizing the comforter as evidence.

"Do you understand that?"

"Yes," Baker said calmly.


It was growing dark, even though the encroaching long hours of Pacific Daylight Time had pushed the Northwest sunset to around 10:00 PM In just twelve days, it would be the longest day of the year.

The detectives all felt an unnerving sense that with the next door Al Baker might open, he would "present" the body of his missing wife. Kathie might be a thousand or more miles away or she might be close enough to touch somewhere on this property that she loved so much.

"Can we look at your truck?" Tingstad asked.

"Sure."

Baker led the patrol lieutenant and Detective Plumberg out of the garage and they headed for his red truck. As they did so, Tingstad glanced to his right and saw a mop bucket with a mop stuck in it; it was filled with dark red water.

They walked to the truck, and Al Baker opened the driver's-side door and stood back. Tingstad peered in, but saw nothing of possible evidentiary value in the cab. Then he opened the hard cover on the truck bed. Fully expecting Kathie's body to be in the truck bed, the searchers braced themselves. But there were only bungee cords, rope sections, two cardboard boxes, a full twelve-pack of Coca-Cola, and an open twelve-pack of Diet Coke.

And no sign at all of Kathie.

"I don't think I want to answer any more questions," Baker said slowly. Then he leaned against his truck for a very long time. The air was electric with tension.

Finally, Baker volunteered that he had a knife in his pocket and asked if it would be okay to take it out.

Evan Tingstad told him he could—"but very slowly."

Baker complied as he drew a folding knife out of his right front pants pocket.

Tingstad slipped it into an evidence envelope and gave it to Detective Plumberg. When Baker said he was cold, Mark Plumberg retrieved the suspect's jacket from the house. Baker was allowed to take one credit card and his driver's license. He had twenty-eight dollars in cash. Plumberg loaned Baker his cell phone so he could call a taxi to take him to his pizza shop where he said there was a back room he could sleep in.

Trudi Gerhart was spending the night of June 8 at the Harbor Inn.

Al Baker wasn't in custody, although it seemed that Kathie Baker must surely be dead. There was just too much blood in her house, but the sheriff's staff had yet to find her body. She could be anywhere—lost forever in the deep waters that surrounded Whidbey Island or in some desolate spot between Mukilteo and the airport.

By 11:00 P.M., the detectives secured the scene. It was pitch-dark; they would have to search for Kathie Baker another day.

As much as they wanted to find her body, the group of investigators let out a sigh of relief. Against all odds, there might still be some hope that Kathie was alive.

On Saturday morning, June 9, the weather was clear with occasional short-lived rain showers. The temperature in Greenbank was in the high fifties. The house, garage, and grounds of the property on Silver Cloud Lane were alive with activity. Not only were there Island County sheriff's investigators, but some members of the Washington State Patrol Crime Scene Response Team were already there, and more were expected. They swarmed over the Bakers' place, looking for physical evidence, but primarily for Kathie. She could be there, hidden someplace on the property. No one but Al recalled seeing Kathie leave on June 3, getting on the ferry, or being dropped off at the airport.

And Al Baker had given so many versions of where Kathie might be and told so many obvious lies that he was hardly a reliable source of information.

Evan Tingstad arrived at Silver Cloud Lane shortly

before 9:00 A.M. and met with Detective Mark Plumberg, who was already there. Plumberg walked state patrol criminalist Mary Wilson from the Washington State Patrol Crime Lab through the scene, pointing out where the sheriff's investigators had searched the night before until darkness forced them to give up. Wilson, the primary investigator from the state patrol, had an assistant and a trainee with her to observe.

Evan Tingstad joined the state patrol team as they were assessing the scene and dividing it into sections for processing. They looked over the bank behind the house and firewood shed, and into the ravine below. Mary Wilson's assistant spotted a suspicious mannequin-sized object wrapped in a silver and blue tarp.

Suddenly, the search for Kathie Hill Baker was over. All this time, she had lain undiscovered only a few steps from the house.

Plumberg immediately called Dr. Robert Bishop, the Island County coroner, and when he arrived Plumberg helped carry the body up out of the ravine without disturbing the tarpaulin tied with bungee cords and short lengths of rope. Plumberg and Dr. Bishop then transported it to a cold room to await autopsy the next day.

Leif Haugen and Evan Tingstad went to Harbor Pizzeria and asked to talk with Al Baker. But his employees said he wasn't there. Then the sheriff's men went to the nearby Harbor Inn and asked if Baker was registered there. He was—and hadn't yet checked out.

"He's in 129,*" the desk clerk told them.

As they approached room 129, Tingstad and Haugen noted that all the curtains were closed and there was a "Do Not Disturb" placard hanging on the door.

They weren't sure what they would find inside. Al Baker had seemed very deflated and morose the night before, when he was read his Miranda rights. There was the possibility that he had committed suicide, or perhaps left by taxi or on foot during the night. He had to comprehend by now that he had nowhere to turn, and perhaps had made a dash for the mainland. Still, it would be almost impossible to hire a taxi on Whidbey Island in the wee hours of the morning without starting rumors. And the ferries didn't run all night.

Deputy Leif Haugen knocked on the door.

The two officers waited. Haugen prepared to knock again when the door opened. Al Baker, wearing only trousers, stood there. He didn't seem surprised to see them.

"We'd like to talk with you about your wife," Haugen said.

"Yes—just let me finish getting dressed. I need to put my shoes on."

When he had a shirt and shoes on, Baker walked outside to Leif Haugen's patrol unit without being asked, and submitted to a search for weapons before he was transported to the South Precinct offices. He wasn't armed;

apparently the knife he'd turned over to Evan Tingstad the night before had been his only weapon.

Lieutenant Tingstad, Leif Haugen, and Baker sat down in one of the conference rooms at the South Precinct.

"Al," Tingstad began, "we're very concerned about Kathie. We want to give you the opportunity to provide a written statement describing what's transpired in the past two weeks."

Baker was given a Miranda rights waiver. He agreed to sign it but wanted to be sure he could later change his mind. Tingstad pointed to the paragraph that said Baker could change his rights form "at any time."

After talking with Baker about his version of events, Tingstad asked if he would like to write his statement, and the suspect nodded. The investigators provided him with statement forms and a pen and moved to the lunchroom; he could see them, and they could see him as he wrote.

Baker, unaware Kathie's body had been found, wrote that they had split up the first week in June, and that she had agreed to leave. (This despite the fact that *she* had provided most of the money for their property.)

"I spent the weekend in my shop, slept there, too. I came up to the house Sunday morning—that would be June 3—and I saw that she had left . . ."

He could not say which day Kathie left—whether it was Friday or Saturday—but he was positive she wasn't there on Sunday. Believing she was gone for good, Baker said he'd headed to the airport to pick up Trudi Gerhart.

Answering a few follow-up questions from Tingstad, Al Baker assured him that he hadn't been in a physical fight with Kathie. But he agreed that some of his previous stories weren't true.

"I was telling two stories to two women," he answered, spreading his hands at the situation he had found himself in. "What would *you* do?"

Baker said he hadn't seen anyone come or go to his house, and had no idea just *how* Kathie had left. The investigators knew her SUV was there in their carport. Her purse, her laptop, and her dogs were still in their house. Her makeup was spread out on a counter as if she planned to use it in the morning.

Furthermore, Baker insisted he knew nothing about the stains in his house, and he told them that the comforter had already been in the deep sink in the laundry room when he'd returned from picking up Trudi Gerhart.

After Al Baker signed his statement, Evan Tingstad continued to discuss with him the multiple versions he'd given of the events on June 3. How *could* he not have noticed the red-brown stains all over his property, known that Kathie was not around, and not be concerned?

*"I didn't see any stains."* He stuck to his litany of lies.

Mark Plumberg had painstakingly checked out the "shop" where Baker said he'd slept. Tingstad stepped out of the conference room and asked Plumberg to recall its condition.

"The futon there was filthy," Plumberg said. "There

were spiderwebs all over and mouse—or rat—droppings. The sink and toilet there had bugs in them. It was clear to me that nobody has stayed there for quite a while."

Al Baker was a fastidious man. Why would he lie about sleeping in the dirty shop? He had bedrooms inside his house. Perhaps he wished to validate that his friendship with Trudi Gerhart was, indeed, only platonic?

Tingstad returned to the conference room and confronted Al with the fact that the investigators did not believe he had slept in his dirty shop.

"You like a clean house—and the shop is filthy."

Al Baker had no answer. He let out a whoosh of air; he had been holding his breath for a long time.

"Why haven't you asked us what we were doing to find your wife?"

"Because *she* left *me*."

Baker had dug his heels in. He insisted he didn't know where Kathie was, and he repeated that over and over.

"What would you do if I asked for an attorney?" he finally asked carefully.

"You can call one," Tingstad said.

"I don't have one—I'm not asking for one. I just want to know what you would do if I *did* ask for an attorney."

"My role doesn't change," Tingstad said. "I still will do everything I can to find Kathie—continue investigating."

As the interview was drawing to a close, Tingstad said, "I know that you know where Kathie is."

"I don't."

Tingstad drew an aerial view of the Silver Cloud property on a yellow legal pad and he slid it over to Baker.

"Show me where to look," he said bluntly.

"I don't know."

The sheriff's lieutenant took the drawing back and made an *X* in the circle where Kathie's body had been found. He pushed it back to Al Baker and began to track the time on his watch.

The room was totally silent, as still as death itself.

Baker said nothing for ninety-seven seconds, and then there was a tinge of anger in his voice. He had never responded with annoyance before, and he never would again.

"What is *this*?" he finally asked.

"You tell me; it's your property. You know," Tingstad said. "I think it's disrespectful to lie to someone who knows you are lying to them—so from now on, instead of lying to me, just tell me you don't want to answer or tell me the truth."

"You lied to me," Baker answered.

"In what way?"

The suspect pointed to the *X* and said, "You know things you're asking me questions about."

"What do I know?"

Baker started to say something, and then retreated before he said too much. Clearly, he was fishing for confirmation that Kathie's body had been found.

The interview ended at 1:40 P.M. that Saturday afternoon. Al Baker was placed under arrest for first-degree murder, and Leif Haugen drove him to the Island County Jail.

He had believed he was so much smarter than the cops, but now the pizza-making scientist was facing an eventuality he apparently had never considered.

After Al Baker was safely locked in the Island County Jail, Detective Mark Plumberg, Lieutenant Evan Tingstad, and Deputy Leif Haugen returned to the now-empty house on Silver Cloud Lane and continued to search for evidence. Al had a number of "man toys"—motorcycles, an MG sports car, and a fishing boat—along with many full boxes and containers stacked there.

On Sunday, June 10, Mark Plumberg observed as Medical Examiner Dr. Sigmund Menchel and Coroner Dr. Robert Bishop performed an autopsy on the body of the woman found in the ravine. It had been a week since Kathie vanished and the weather was warm; any human body would decompose to some extent under such conditions.

The deceased female had physical characteristics reasonably consistent with the descriptions from those who had known Kathie in life, although it would be impossible to identify her absolutely until dental and DNA comparisons could be made.

Even for experienced homicide investigators, it was

appalling to confront what the postmortem exam indicated; the woman before them had a single crushing wound to her head, a circular hole that penetrated through the skull into the brain.

Investigators had found a ball-peen hammer at the Silver Cloud residence, and evidence technician Phil Farr determined that it was the murder weapon. Blood was detected on the flat surface of the hammer, and there were strands of short blond hair caught in the blood. The striking force of the hammer fit precisely into the hole in the victim's skull.

Al Baker had probably attacked Kathie as she slept, bringing the ball-peen hammer crashing down on her head and doing terrible damage to her skull and brain. One would hope that she never wakened to see her killer—the man she trusted so completely, as he struck her.

Perhaps she did not see him. There was, after all, only that single blunt force injury from the weapon, and no defense wounds at all on her hands and arms. Dr. Menchel told Kathie's family that he tended to believe that was the case.

It was a small comfort in their profound time of grief. None of the people who loved her could stand to think of her waking in that last horrific moment.

Her attacker had circled Kathie's neck with some kind of ligature. She had distinctive creases around her neck.

"She'd been dead at least seventy-two hours before they found her yesterday," Dr. Bishop said. "Rigor mortis has come and gone. Her cause of death is blunt force trauma with strangulation by ligature. It's impossible to tell which injury came first."

Because Kathie had been dead for several days, the exact time of her death could not be determined. Tests were negative for any sexual assault.

Two days later, Kathie Baker's dentist confirmed that there was a positive match between the X-rays he had on file for her and those taken during the victim's postmortem exam.

The WSP criminalists continued processing the house and outbuildings. They found blood that would prove to be Kathie's in the master bedroom, throughout the house, in the garage, and just about everywhere they looked. Mixed with the female DNA were occasional samples of male DNA that would later be traced to Al.

The consensus was that after he was sure she was dead, Al Baker had, quite literally, dragged the body of the wife who'd loved him devotedly out of the house on Silver Cloud Lane, wrapped it in a tarp, and tossed it into the ravine. Just in time—because only hours later he escorted the next woman he coveted through his front door.

The calculated cruelty of it all was hard to imagine.

Kathie Baker's two corgi dogs were turned over to Animal Control officer Carol Barnes. Kathie's stepsister, Char, flew up to get the dogs. Her whole family knew how she'd loved them, and it was one of the few things they could do for her. The older dog had fallen ill and was too sick to save, and had to be put to sleep, but as of this writing, the younger dog still lives with Kathie's relatives.

Detective Mark Plumberg attempted to speak with Baker at the jail, but the suspect said he didn't want to answer any more questions. He asked for an attorney.

On June 11, Plumberg contacted authorities at the Washington State Ferries, asking for help locating any extant videos of the red Nissan pickup. He hoped to find images that show the truck and license plate.

Two days later, he received a call from Cadet Andrew Durr of the Washington State Patrol. Durr said they had located videos of traffic on June 3. Drivers who took the ferry from South Whidbey Island to the mainland were quite visible.

"That truck departed the island on the Clinton Ferry at about sixteen hundred hours [four P.M.] on June third," Durr reported.

The driver—who was alone—appeared to be Al Baker. He had paid for two trips. Leaving Whidbey Island, he bought a driver and vehicle ticket, but he added a passenger on his return ticket. Videos of the return trip showed Al and a woman sitting beside him.

That woman was Trudi Gerhart.

*   *   *

If the Bakers' story was a television episode of a show like *Who the (Bleep) Did I Marry?* or *Deadly Vows,* screenwriters could—and probably would—take shortcuts to make it all fit, and it would be over. The credits would start to roll. But this was real life. Island County detective Mark Plumberg's team still had many puzzle slots to fill in.

At the same time, Kathie Hill's family wanted to find out more about the man she had married. Jami Hill stepped into the role of private investigator and tried to find answers.

Meanwhile, the official investigation was ongoing.

Working with stacks of telephone records, emails, and Southwest Airlines and Alaska Airlines rosters, and examining Al Baker's own braggadocio about the many degrees he held, Plumberg began to unravel the life of a man with a penchant for deceit. It would take the Island County detective months to follow the paper trails.

It was a challenge for Plumberg to put together a timeline of the Bakers' actions in the spring of 2012. Some of the puzzle pieces came together in the form of credit card receipts. Kathie and Al had several credit cards, with slightly different end numbers that showed which charges were made by Kathie and which by Al. Al was authorized to access all of Kathie's bank accounts and credit cards.

It was Al who had purchased round-trip tickets to Anchorage, Alaska, at least three times, and Kathie who made the quarterly Colorado Southwest Airlines reservations and also purchased female clothing and makeup. Mark Plumberg found no round-trip plane tickets to Washington, D.C. The story Al had told his wife about flying to D.C. was bogus. An unsuspecting Kathie had been hard at work in Colorado in late March of 2012, while Al was in Alaska. He had been romancing Trudi Gerhart, trying to entice her into an affair.

Quite possibly, Baker had felt there was no need for him to go to D.C. or to be hired for another season in Anarctica. With Kathie gone, he would have their house and business as well as any insurance on her life, rumored to be a considerable amount.

Plumberg talked with Trudi Gerhart in Seward, Alaska. He learned that she and Al had looked at a restaurant for sale. Al had been interested in buying run-down businesses and improving them.

"He told me that he wanted to be 'The King of Whidbey Island' as far as owning businesses," Trudi said and recalled, "He had his eye on a pie shop, and some other small businesses he wanted to buy and remodel."

Out of the hundreds of phone numbers Mark Plumberg had checked with the Bakers' phones via a search warrant for Verizon, he'd noticed several calls from Al Baker's phone to someone called "PAUL WORK" and "PAUL CELL." Plumberg found the same numbers on Kathie's phone, with the name "Paul Sullivan" listed.

Plumberg left messages for Paul Sullivan, asking him to call. Finally, Sullivan called him back.

"I got your voice mail. Figured it was only a matter of time before I was contacted—"

"Why is that?" Plumberg asked.

"I'm Al Baker's boss—have been for years, and I have frequent contact with him."

Sullivan and Al Baker had worked on the budgets for Raytheon the first week of June. This explained the flurry of phone calls from Baker on June 1, June 5, and June 7.

Since Kathie, Al, and Trudi Gerhart had frequently been Poleys down on the ice together, Plumberg asked if Sullivan had ever noticed a romantic connection between Al and Trudi. Sullivan wasn't sure but pointed out that it would be hard to keep something like that a secret since they all lived so close together at the South Pole.

"Come to think of it now," Sullivan mused, "Al and Trudi *did* seem to be together a lot this last year."

As he pored over possible sources, Detective Plumberg discovered that Al Baker's trail led only a short way back; he had reinvented himself continually until his life prior to marrying Kathie Hill was as hard to untangle as a rope soaked in salt water and allowed to dry. He focused, always, on his future, not his past. He usually maintained a façade of success, although he neglected financial matters that a truly competent businessman would never allow to slide.

Far from Al's being a success, in the time before

Kathie's murder, the Bakers were having trouble with their IRS quarterly reports and tax payments. Their payroll deductions for their employees were also overduc. Al just hadn't paid any taxes owed on his employees. He had blithely ignored the IRS, an agency it isn't wise to ignore.

Now the IRS had given them a final deadline to pay what they owed before liens were placed on their property. Kathie tried her best to get things that Al had brushed aside into some kind of order. In an email to her husband in late fall 2011, she'd tried to explain to him how much they owed.

> Hi Sweetie,
>
> Tammy, our tax girl completed her work on quarters 1,2,3 for IRS (Federal and FICA.)
>
> Basically, here's the scoop. To get caught up with the IRS, we need to come up with $19,563.27 at a minimum, as this doesn't include late charges and penalties.

One had the feeling that Kathie was trying to cushion the unsettling news to keep Al from worrying. She might have been afraid that he would blame her for the tax mistakes. She may have only attempted to smooth out his life for him—just as she had always done. She kept assuring him that they would somehow find a way to come up with the money:

*So we're making progress to get ourselves legal.*

*Now, I just need to figure out where we'll get our money and such.*

*That's all that's fit to tell for the moment.*

*I love you, Baby.*

There is little doubt that she did. But, sadly, it appeared that Kathie had become an inconvenience for Al.

Things weren't going smoothly at the pizzeria, either. Al's shabby approach to finances had finally caught up with him.

The amorous pizza man was in deep debt.

Jami Hill was the executor of Kathie's estate. She was determined that Al would not get one red cent of Kathie's assets—not because the Hill family was eager to inherit, but because a heartless killer should not profit from his crime. By Washington State law, killers cannot, in fact, profit from their crimes. But Al Baker would have to be *convicted* of Kathie's murder before he could be prohibited from making a claim against his wife's estate.

Jami found that Kathie's record-keeping was impeccable, with everything stored in a neat file cabinet. But Al had taken out huge loans—one for $28,000 and another for $35,000—from their joint bank accounts, and Jami couldn't find what they were for.

In late June 2012, Jami was sorting out things in the

house at Silver Cloud Lane. There were stacks of documents to go through. One of those was a twenty-five-page document that outlined Al Baker's personal financial analysis as of June 28, 2006.

Jami looked through the pages, and she was shocked to see that Kathie's and Al's insurance coverage was far from balanced. In case Al should die, Kathie would have gotten $50,000. But Kathie's insurance payout, with Al as her beneficiary, would be $275,000!

Jami took the financial analysis to Mark Plumberg. He studied it and instantly saw the disproportion. The detective suspected that Kathie *was* the irreplaceable officer in the Bakers' businesses and made much more than Al did. Still, the insurance coverage between the two of them was vastly different: over a quarter million dollars on her life and a relative pittance of $50,000 on his. According to actuaries, this hadn't changed in the six years since the insurance went into effect.

Kathie had barely managed to hold on to her beautiful home in Aurora, Colorado, by renting it out. And she had really wanted to keep it; it meant she still had a pied-à-terre close to her family. Still, she was willing to sell it to raise money to help Al in his projects and with his debts, and it was listed with a Realtor. Whatever he needed, she tried to supply, believing always that they were a team who had each other's backs.

Beyond his scientific work at the South Pole, Al felt that his pizzeria promised to make money—given enough time and an infusion of funds. Al considered himself an accomplished contractor, and he taught himself to play the piano—and well. In late December 2011, one of his business cards read:

**R. ALLEN BAKER**
*Raytheon Polar Services*
*Science Support Coordinator, South Pole Station*

He had other business cards—to use in whatever fit his current projects.

A check of any rap sheets showing Baker's criminal background drew forth the information that he had been charged with lewd and lascivious sexual abuse of a child in California. The victim was his own stepdaughter!

He was convicted of that crime and served five years in prison.

If Kathie had known that when she met him down on the ice, she would never have married him. But she didn't know. There were so many things about Al Baker that she didn't know.

Now locked in jail and awaiting his trial on murder charges, Al Baker realized he had waited too long to get off Whidbey Island. He had apparently been prepared to leave; investigators had located his backpack with $10,000 in cash inside it. He had broached the subject with Trudi, urging her to flee with him to New Zealand.

He'd been there once on a vacation, liked it, and figured it was a country where they could get swallowed up, far from anyone in America who might be tracking them.

Trudi was horrified to learn what had happened to Kathie Baker. When she was informed that Kathie's body had been found, she broke into tears and seemed to be genuinely grieving. The last person Trudi wanted to go *anyplace* with was Al Baker.

Initially, the Island County investigators had wondered if Trudi might have been part of Al's plan to kill his wife, or at least had guilty knowledge of the crime. But further probing made that dubious. The consensus was that she had been duped—just like so many other women in Baker's life. Whether their relationship was platonic or sexual was another question.

Lieutenant Evan Tingstad got an interesting piece of evidence from the Harbor Inn, where Al Baker stayed the night before his arrest. It was a man's coat—apparently Al's—left behind when he had so hastily checked out. In the pocket, Tingstad found a receipt from the Elkhorn Trading Company on the Island, dated only the day before—on Friday—for the amount of $279.36.

Tingstad visited the Elkhorn Trading Company and found that someone had sold a complete set of Golden Glow Patrician Depression Glass, vintage 1933, on June 8. He looked in the box holding the newspaper-wrapped antique glassware, and he recognized it as one of the boxes in Al Baker's red truck's bed the day before: evidently, Baker had attempted to glean as much money as he could before the arrest he knew was imminent. He was getting rid of Kathie's treasures—or trying to.

(Golden Glow pink, blue, and green glass was given away to moviegoers during the Depression. It was cheap then but it has become an expensive antique some eighty years later.)

Kathie's husband had discarded her as if she were a piece of trash. And he had wasted no time in cashing in on the things that were dear to her.


Even though he was safely locked in the Island County Jail awaiting trial, Trudi Gerhart had a restraining order against Al Baker. He was not to phone, write, email, or contact her in any way. In late September 2012, she called and left a message at the Island County Sheriff's Office.

"Alan's violated his court order."

Mark Plumberg called her back. She told him that she usually picked up her mail about twice a week. She had just received two letters from Al Baker. One had instructions about mailing a $10,000 check to his attorney, and the other held the check itself.

"I don't know what to do," Trudi said.

Plumberg arranged for Detective Doreen Valdez of the Seward, Alaska, police department to pick up the two letters from Trudi. And Plumberg made reservations to fly to Alaska himself.

When he read the contents of the two letters Al had sent to Trudi, Plumberg saw he still believed he could control others—especially women—with his charisma. One held just the $10,000 check, the attorney's address, and a short note: "I apologize for being a pest [please] send that check to my attorneys."

The other was more personal: "You're the only person I trust with this. There are people who believe I did this horrible heinous thing. Most know otherwise. What a nightmare . . . Smile."

"He always signs his letters like that," Trudi said. "And he puts 'Smile' on the envelopes instead of his return address."

That may have been a habit Al Baker learned in prison. Most convicts use "Smile" and draw smiley faces on their correspondence.

Now that she had no more allegiance to Al Baker, it was time to interview Trudi Gerhart in depth.

Mark Plumberg flew to Seward, Alaska, on October 9, 2012, to speak with Trudi and to take DNA samples. She had been pretty much excluded as a suspect, but her DNA still needed to be tested. The investigators were thorough and left nothing to chance.

DNA testing must be very precise, and is perhaps the most important element in a chain of evidence. Plumberg opened new sterile swabs, and then swabbed the insides of both of Trudi's cheeks. The four swabs were then inserted into plastic tips specifically designed to protect the cotton end of each swab, and then they were placed in separate boxes, which were sealed with evidence tape with the case number and subject's name. Plumberg kept the exemplars with him until he returned to Whidbey Island and gave them directly to evidence technician Phil Farr.

Mark Plumberg showed Trudi pictures that had been developed from film in a camera found at the Silver Cloud Lane property. It had been in the bed of Kathie's SUV.

There were six photos taken on the "pickle fork" of a ship—*The Eau-de-Vie*—("Water of Life" in French) in Alaska. They showed a male and a female framed in the doorway that led from the pickle fork into the main passenger area of the ferry. They appeared to be a romantic couple. Trudi identified the couple as herself and Al Baker.

She was not sure of the date the pictures were taken.

Next, Plumberg reminded her that she had once mentioned something to him that she thought was important.

"Oh," she recalled. "It was something Al said after he was first contacted by the police," Trudi said. "He went into the precinct to see Detective Price. I didn't go in with him, but went browsing in an antiques shop. He came back about forty-five minutes later and told me the police wanted to talk to me, too.

"Alan mentioned Raytheon's involvement in searching

for Kathie, and he said, 'I don't know why they didn't call me first.'"

"Did you and Mr. Baker have any kind of sexual relationship while you were in Antarctica?" Plumberg asked.

"Nope," Trudi said emphatically. "We did not. We watched movies and ate breakfast together."

"That [sex] never happened?"

*"Never . . ."*

Mark Plumberg asked about the numerous cards she had received from Baker once they returned home from the South Pole. "Did you ever send cards and letters to him?"

"I asked him for his address, so I could send him cards and letters, but he never gave it to me."

"When did you last talk to Kathie?"

"It was years ago—had to be at least five years, and that was through email. I hadn't spoken with her directly since she was down on the ice."

In response to Plumberg's questions, Trudi said that Baker had flown to Alaska to see her twice, and she'd come down to Greenbank only once. She couldn't recall when he mentioned during a phone call that he and Kathie were having marital trouble. Only that he said things were "heavy."

"Where did you sleep when you came to his home?"

"I slept in the guest room upstairs."

"And Mr. Baker?"

"I presume he was sleeping in his bedroom [the master

bedroom]. He gave me a tour of his house," she said. "I was in his bedroom only once. That was his space and I didn't go in there for anything. It was really neat and tidy for a guy—most guys aren't that tidy."

"When did you notice the stain on the living room carpet?"

"When I first went in. I didn't say anything about it, but I tried to clean it one morning when Alan was at work. It was really ugly; it looked like what happens when a dog scoots its butt across the floor."

"Did it smell?"

"Hey, I'm a deckhand. My nose is shut down to odors I have to clean."

"What did he tell you about the stain?"

"I didn't ask him, and he didn't tell me anything about it, except he blamed it on Kathie's dogs. I finally asked him if he had tried to clean it up. He told me that he'd tried but couldn't get anywhere with it. I said I'd try some of my old boat tricks. In my job as a deckhand, I've cleaned a lot of stains on board. I just used hot water on the carpet stain, and it looked great when it was wet—but it came back when it dried."

Unwittingly, Trudi had only made the stains more permanent. Any housewife knows that bloodstains should be washed with *cold* water.

Trudi said she was puzzled to find Kathie's dogs there. She could kind of understand that exes would help each other out, but Al didn't really like dogs, and it was strange that he would look after the two corgis. On the way from the airport, he'd told her that Kathie was living in Aurora, Colorado.

Trudi said she wanted to refinance her Alaska home, and Al helped her out with that. "I needed verification of employment during the winter months—with more salary than I got down on the ice. He filled out an application that said I worked for him as his 'consultant' who got paid monthly. He was trying to help me with a job, because I needed one and didn't have one."

Trudi told him that she and Baker "left the ice" on February 14, 2012, and parted ways in Los Angeles. Al Baker had long been surrounded by people—his employees at the pizza shop and all his coworkers at Raytheon—and yet no one knew who he really was.

"He touched so many lives," Trudi said. "We'll never know how many. I don't even feel good in my house anymore. I *really* don't want to go in the guest room here. It makes my skin crawl."

What were Al Baker's plans for Trudi? She shuddered to think that she could have ended up the way Kathie had once he had no more use for her.

Baker wouldn't talk to the investigators any longer, but he had had no choice in submitting to the court-ordered DNA tests. Kathie's blood was all over their house, with minimal traces of blood from Al. Testing for bodily fluids and hair in the place where the subjects lived is problematic; residents would normally have left some trace evidence. They found no semen on the scene. A stranger's semen, of course, would have raised the possibility that Kathie had been attacked by someone other than Al.

During Kathie's autopsy, a single long white hair was found on her buttocks. It wasn't hers, but neither Al Baker nor Trudi Gerhart could be excluded. Hairs aren't easy to test; the shaft reveals little of value, but if the root tag is attached, DNA can be determined.

Most likely, the long white strand of hair had been Al Baker's.

Plumberg had more questions for Trudi, and he asked her if Al had given her the impression he was wealthy.

"We'd been talking about his business once," she replied. "and I asked if it was doing well. He opened his wallet and showed me that $10,000 check, saying, '*This* is how well it's doing.' I didn't ask him anything about it—I just figured it was a withdrawal from his pizza business."

Al Baker seemed to have plenty of money, and to Trudi, it had looked like he had adjusted quite well to the breakup of his marriage. She had accepted it all at face value, and told Plumberg that when Al had visited her in Alaska, they had looked at a boat that Al had considered buying.

"Because of his age, Alan wanted to be spontaneous and do fun things—I got the impression that Kathie was much more conservative, but he wanted to go 'this other way.' When he came up to Alaska the second time, we looked at the boat and he said he was ready to sell his pizza business, buy the boat, and set off into the sunset."

Seeing his house and acres of property only added validation to Al Baker's air of wealth. Trudi wasn't doing nearly as well financially as she had believed Al was.

He took her on a tour of his land the second day she was there, and urged her to walk around the acreage. One has to wonder why. Did he want *her* to discover Kathie's body? Would it be some kind of macabre thrill for him? Fortunately for Trudi, she didn't go.

"What did you do while he was working at the pizza shop?" Plumberg asked.

"I crocheted hats for a little business I have here in Seward," Trudi said. "On Tuesday—June 5—we went to a lavender farm and bought some plants for in front of his deck. I spent the next morning planting them."

A man had come by to unload some materials for remodeling Baker's deck, but it had been raining all week, and the carpenters hadn't been working on that project.

Asked if Al had tried to hide her during her visit, Trudi shook her head. They walked around the small island towns, and Baker introduced her to friends and to his employees at the pizzeria. He told them her name and said she was visiting from Alaska.

"He asked me what I'd told the fellow who dropped off the deck materials. I told him, 'I said I was your gardener.'"

"Al asked why I hadn't told the carpenter that I was his girlfriend.

"'Because I'm not,' I said. 'I'm your gardener right now.'"

181

Some of the people who had property Al was interested in had assumed that Trudi was Al's wife, and she hadn't corrected them. And Al never said she was his girlfriend, his wife, or a visitor.

Mark Plumberg would make one more trip to Seward, Alaska—on March 4, 2013. Al Baker's trial loomed, and Detective Plumberg and prosecutor Eric Ohme wanted to be sure there were no loose ends to their intense probe into Kathie Baker's murder and Al's background.

Plumberg showed Trudi a few more photographs that she hadn't yet seen, including the pizzeria anniversary pictures from the night of June 2. Al and Kathie were clearly visible sitting at a table toward the back of the restaurant. They were also in some group photographs.

"Were there any other vehicles at Al's house?" Plumberg asked her.

Trudi nodded. "There was a car in the garage—Al implied that that was his, too. We went to the drive-in once in it. I found out later that it was Kathie's."

The Island County detective took out some emails between Baker and herself that he had recovered. He read them aloud to Trudi. One was a map of how she would get to Whidbey Island from Sea-Tac Airport on a shuttle bus in case she wanted to "drop by." Dated on January 5, 2012, (when she and Al were still in Antarctica), it ended, "We'll be there to pick you up."

That sounded like a smoke screen. If a possible affair between them ever came up, he had this email showing that she would be coming to see both him *and* Kathie. But there were other emails saying he wanted to know much more about her.

Mark Plumberg asked her again about what might have gone on between herself and Al Baker. She shook her head. "He was at my workstation a lot, and we would watch movies in each other's rooms, so we could watch what we wanted instead of what was on in the lodge—and we danced on New Year's Eve."

"Was Antarctica kind of like 'What happens in Vegas stays in Vegas'?" Plumberg pressed on.

"Usually," Trudi answered. "But you never know. No! I don't . . . No. We weren't doing anything!"

Trudi and Al were in their sixties, but she was so adamant in her denial of any sexual activity between them that she might well have been a teenage virgin.

"Is there anything I've missed asking you that you want to tell me?" Plumberg asked.

"I can't think of anything."

The interview was over.


On October 2, 2013, Robert Alan Baker went on trial for first-degree murder. Coupeville, Washington, is a wonderful place to be in autumn. The trees are red and golden as they shelter unique, restored houses, many of them a hundred years old or more. Tourists have gone home, and full-time residents settle into the harvest season, high school football games, and the holidays. All too soon, mighty storms off Puget Sound will lash against their windows with heavy winds and pounding rain.

On this day, the temperature was in the mid-50s, and there was only a trace of rain.

There are no windows in Judge Alan Hancock's courtroom, so there is a cocoon-like feeling once the doors are closed. There were ninety people in the jury pool. Detective Mark Plumberg sat at the prosecution table beside senior assistant prosecuting attorney Eric Ohme. Ohme's assistant, Jenna Knutsen, sat there, too. Knutsen's job was to keep the trial running smoothly—but this trial would be challenging for her. It was full of starts and stops, interruptions, sickness, and unexpected events, all of which meant that Jenna had to arrange for witnesses to switch their normal sequential order.

One of the potential jurors fell ill. Luckily for her, there were two doctors, a physician's assistant, and an EMT in the courtroom. She wanted to stay, but the professionals insisted she should be hospitalized. Paramedics whisked her away to the hospital.

After that crisis, it was too late to go on with jury selection and/or the start of the trial that day, so Jenna Knutsen rearranged the schedules of out-of-town witnesses, somehow managing to get things organized for the next day.

"Jenna did a fantastic job," Mark Plumberg remarked. "Most of the people there had no idea of what was happening behind the scenes of the trial."

Initially, Craig Platt had been Al Baker's attorney, but he had been replaced by Tom Pacher, one of two public defenders in the Island County court system.

Eric Ohme and Pacher had winnowed out thirty prospective jurors by noon of the first day. After lunch, Pacher and Ohme asked questions of the jury pool. How many individuals looked forward to serving on a jury? How many dreaded it? Who had been on a jury before? Did they believe the district attorney has no duty to provide evidence?

"If the defendant doesn't testify," Tom Pacher asked, "would that influence your decision-making process?"

Four responded that it wouldn't be a problem—three had a problem with that prospect.

Ohme asked, "If you should find out there were no eyewitnesses—only circumstantial evidence—could you arrive at a consensus regarding guilt or innocence?"

Everyone agreed that an eyewitness wasn't necessary.

As expected, the answers were as varied as the potential jurors.

The would-be jury was excused to allow Judge Hancock, prosecutor Eric Ohme, and defense attorney Tom Pacher to identify those who would be excused for cause, and to take up preemptory challenges.

When they filed back in, the judge pointed out five women and seven men who'd been selected, with two alternates, both men.

Judge Hancock read instructions to the jury, and court recessed at 4:30.

Robert Alan Baker's trial for first-degree murder was expected to last ten days. Kathie's family had gathered from three states to observe what they sincerely hoped was justice for their much-loved sibling, cousin, niece, and aunt.

The defendant was brought into Judge Hancock's courtroom in handcuffs. He scarcely resembled the Al Baker the investigators first encountered—the man with long hair and a longer beard. Now they were both neatly trimmed, and he wore a white shirt, a tie, and a well-pressed sport jacket and slacks. He took his seat beside Tom Pacher at the defense table and seemed quite calm and contained. He would only rarely speak to his attorney.

One could see why Kathie's family had called him a troll behind his back. He *did* resemble an evil gnome; he was very short and had thick eyebrows that half hid his eyes.

One newspaper reporter described him as "an angry Santa Claus."

Senior deputy prosecutor Eric Ohme made his opening statement the next day. Ohme was in a wheelchair, but he handled it so deftly that no one in the courtroom noticed it after the first few minutes.

"The defendant had a motive for getting rid of his wife," Ohme said. "He had a secret obsession with a woman who was *not* his wife."

Ohme explained to jurors that Baker had met this woman in Antarctica and fixated on her. "This culminated on the night of June 2, 2012—or the following morning—when Robert Baker struck his wife in the head with a hammer and strangled her in their bed."

Eric Ohme didn't have to exaggerate the facts of that murderous night. He merely listed them. He spoke of the sheer violence that had taken place, and of the defendant's efforts to hide Kathie's body.

"Robert Baker dragged Kathie Baker out of the house, through the garage. He wrapped her body in a blue and silver tarp with ropes and bungee cords, and dumped her in a ravine behind the house."

Ohme explained that Al had met Kathie the same way he had met Trudi—while working for Raytheon. Baker's courtship of his newest target—Trudi Gerhart—was a rerun of his seduction of the wife he'd killed.

"Trudi Gerhart felt their relationship was platonic," Eric Ohme said, "but he wanted more; he visited her twice, sent her romantic cards, and invited her to his home in Greenbank, falsely claiming he and Kathie had broken up.

"Robert Alan Baker killed his wife and hid her body before Trudi Gerhart arrived."

Ohme then read off a list of witnesses who would be testifying, and described how each was involved in the Baker case.

Defense attorney Tom Pacher reserved the right to postpone his opening remarks until the prosecution rested. It was an usual strategy, and one that baffled court watchers.

The second week of Al Baker's trial was to begin on Monday, October 7. It did not. Tom Pacher called in sick. Another public defender, Matthew Montoya, sat at the defense table. The jurors were dismissed and told to come back the next day.

The two public defenders resembled one another; both were large men with florid faces whose shirttails were forever coming untucked from their trousers. I sensed that neither was particularly happy with his job and each would be glad when his contract with the county was over.

Eric Ohme had scheduled two witnesses from Colorado. They said they could stay over one more night—but after that, they had commitments to fulfill.

If Pacher should be unavailable the next day, Judge Hancock asked Montoya if he could fill in. Montoya agreed that he would.

But on Tuesday Tom Pacher was back in court. Judge Hancock reprimanded him severely because he had not followed protocol in notifying the court (Hancock) or opposing counsel (Ohme). The judge also lectured Pacher on how important it is to show up once a trial has begun, citing the inconvenience for the jury, witnesses, and others who depended on him to be there.

Jenna Knutsen, Ohme's assistant, had managed to reschedule the order of witnesses and the trial proceeded.

Andrew Archer of Inglewood, California, was the first witness. He was a primary contractor at the Antarctica station for twenty-one years, and he'd known both Kathie and

Al Baker for a long time—since 2001 for Al and even longer for Kathie. Archer said he and his wife had visited the couple in their Greenbank home from May 22 to May 28 leaving less than a week before Kathie's disappearance.

When Eric Ohme asked Archer about the visit and the condition of the house on Silver Cloud Road, the witness said he couldn't see any problems between Kathie and Al.

"The house? It was a very tidy house."

"Did you see stains on the carpet?"

"No—none at all."

Deputy Leif Haugen took the witness stand next to testify about how he first became aware of Kathie Baker.

"Lieutenant Tingstad and I were responding to a 'check on the welfare of' request from Kathie's employers."

They had briefly glimpsed a woman walk by an upstairs window there. Al Baker explained that she was just a platonic friend who had come to visit both him and Kathie.

"We tried to call Kathie on the phone numbers he gave us that first day," Haugen testified, "but the calls either went immediately to her voice mail or rang and rang."

Deputy Haugen said that both Lieutenant Tingstad and himself sensed something was very wrong. Out of sight of the Baker house, they pulled over to compare notes and their initial impressions. They agreed that there was far more to this call than a standard welfare check.

Haugen described the intense investigation that he, Lieutenant Evan Tingstad, and Detective Laura Price had carried out for the next two days, and the many versions of how and when Kathie had left, according to Al Baker.

Mary Wilson from the Washington State Patrol Crime Lab took the witness stand. She told the jury about the grim discovery in the ravine behind the house on Silver Cloud Lane.

Prosecutor Ohme asked what her team had found in their further investigation, and she described every room in the house in detail and the evidence in each one. Of course they had inspected the dried mahogany-colored stains on the carpet.

"We took different kinds of samples," she said. "Saturation, dilute, swipes—many of the stains were 'dilute' because an attempt was made to clean them."

Two carpet runners on the side of the bed in the master bedroom, the mattress pad, mattress, decorative pillow, and even the nightstand next to Kathie Baker's side of the bed had dilute bloodstains. Wilson testified that she followed a trail of stains out of the bedroom, across the living room and kitchen floor, and down a short flight of stairs into the garage.

"We found the bloody comforter soaking in the sink in the laundry room," Mary continued. "And a carpet cleaner filled with water and human blood."

As she testified, Mary Wilson identified sixty-five photo exhibits her crime scene team had taken as they scoured the house for anything that might be of evidentiary value. All were admitted.

Detective Laura Price testified about her contacts with Trudi Gerhart and the defendant and her initial work on the first-degree murder case. In addition to going over Baker's financial records in his computer with him, Price had interviewed Trudi after the detectives realized the woman believed that Kathie had moved out months before.

Price said that Al Baker had showed the sheriff's investigators, including herself, around his house willingly. Laura Price testified that she, too, saw the large splotches of some kind of "brownish-red" stains on the carpet in several rooms, and down the stairs.

"I asked Mr. Baker what caused them, and he told me that Kathie's dogs poop on the carpet."

Laura Price met with Trudi in the motel where she was staying. Trudi couldn't go back to the house on Silver Cloud Lane—nor did she want to. Trudi left the crime scene hours before Baker did; the detectives were still searching and had questions for Al.

Price told the jurors that she gathered up Trudi's belongings and brought them to her.

The next day, June 9, Laura Price visited Trudi Gerhart again at the Harbor Inn—to deliver more of her things, including some unsent greeting cards that were in Al's truck. There were two romantic cards addressed to Trudi.

Price also had appalling news to tell Trudi; Kathie's body had just been found in the ravine behind the Silver Cloud house.

"And how did Ms. Gerhart respond to this?" Eric Ohme asked.

"She cried and appeared to be shocked. She seemed to be overwhelmed with grief."

Tom Pacher's questions on cross-examination made little sense. He was apparently trying to paint Laura Price as an incompetent and a sloppy investigator. He did not succeed. Perhaps he was trying to lay the groundwork for a defense stance that a stranger snuck into the Bakers' house and killed Kathie.

"Did you contact any of the neighbors?"

"No," Detective Price answered.

"Did you know if the Bakers locked their doors?"

"No."

"Do you know Kathie's occupation?"

"No."

"Was Trudi's testimony recorded?"

"Yes."

"Did the Baker pickup have locks on the cover of the bed?"

"I don't know."

"How many doors are there on the back of the Bakers' house?"

"Two."

Price said there were some dog doors, but doubted they were large enough for a killer or killers to crawl through.

Despite Pacher's obvious intent to show Laura Price hadn't done all the things television detectives do, she came across as a thoroughly competent and well-trained investigator.

The premise that some unknown stalker had crawled through a doggy door, made his way up to the master bedroom, where Kathie slept with Al, struck her with a hammer, strangled her, and then dragged her through the house, wrapped her in a tarp, and hidden her body in the ravine would have been almost laughable—if her death weren't so tragic.

Al's lies, of course, had suggested many scenarios, so many that it must have been difficult for the jurors to keep track of them.

The next two to testify were Ray Dunham, Kathie's immediate supervisor, and Bill Sloan, the Raytheon employee who first contacted the sheriff's office. Each of them had tried to get in touch with Kathie during the first few days in June 2012. Dunham remarked that if the defendant said that his wife was at Raytheon headquarters, Al Baker was either lying or mistaken.

"She would provide two weeks' notice for any travel she planned to Colorado," Dunham said firmly. "We usually had daily contact by email or phone."

"When was your last contact with her?" Ohme asked.

"Friday, June 1—by instant message from her," Dunham said. "I tried to get in touch with her the Monday through Thursday that followed. I called the pizza place and they said she was in Colorado—which I knew wasn't true."

Bill Sloan testified that he called the Island County Sheriff's Office the next day, asking for a welfare check on Kathie.

Curiously, Tom Pacher had no questions for either Dunham or Sloan.

The seventh witness was David Hill, Kathie's brother, who was currently living on Whidbey Island. He had previously lived in Colorado for thirty-two years.

Hill said he and Kathie had a very close relationship. He testified that he and his bride, Melody, had visited with the Bakers in April 2012, just a little over a month before Kathie was murdered.

"How was their marriage at that time?" Ohme asked.

"Fine. We all had a wonderful time."

"How did Kathie feel about her two dogs?"

"They were like her children. Al wasn't fond of dogs; they were obviously a source of aggravation for him."

Many of Kathie's family and friends had remarked earlier to the detectives that that was true. She would never give up her dogs because of Al's dislike for them—but she tried to get them safely in their kennels before he got home.

Later, when Eric Ohme asked Detective Mark Plumberg about the dogs, he testified that it was obvious Baker didn't care what happened to them. Plumberg, a dog lover, and Leif Haugen had reluctantly placed the two corgis with Animal Control.

Not only would Kathie never have left her pets behind,

she took exquisite care of them. The week before she disappeared, she had made an appointment with her vet for a checkup for the older corgi. She, of course, did not show up for the appointment.

The eighth witness was Island County Deputy Darren Crown. He testified that he and Leif Haugen had handled the crime scene log, listing who went in and who left and the exact times they did. Crown said that he and Haugen had searched the garage and Kathie's blue SUV. It was they who had located a camera with the undeveloped film. When it was processed, there were the photos of the Harbor Pizzeria anniversary party on June 2, and also of Al Baker and Trudi Gerhart on the ferry in Alaska.

Detective Mark Plumberg was the ninth witness. Before the jurors filed in, Plumberg reviewed and identified thirty-six exhibits. Ohme asked the lead detective about the discovery of Kathie's body and its removal from the ravine.

Plumberg was excused for the moment, but Eric Ohme had the right to call him to the witness stand again.

Prosecutor Ohme had designed a masterful plan for the State's case. Each witness built on the one before. More than twenty-five witnesses for the prosecution created an airtight case against the defendant:

- Number ten, Sausha Branson, who worked at Harbor Pizzeria, described the anniversary party the night before Kathie was killed. She saw both

Bakers at the party, but she never saw Kathie again. Sausha *did* see Al at 9:00 the next morning. "He seemed messier in appearance and really tired. He left at 10 A.M., leaving a note saying that Kathie was going on a trip, and he was picking up a 'Poley' friend."

- Number eleven, Ashley Christie, manager of the pizza shop. Al Baker called her the morning of June 3. He said he was dropping Kathie off at the airport and picking up a family friend.

- Number twelve, Jeff Christensen, one of the carpenters working on the house on Silver Cloud Lane. Ohme asked if he owned a ball-peen hammer, and he said, "No."

- Number thirteen, Randall Hughes, the finish carpenter who, with Christensen, remodeled the Bakers' kitchen and was working on a new deck when Kathie went missing. Both carpenters testified that the Bakers were "very nice people—good, friendly, and articulate."

- Number fourteen, Dr. Robert Bishop, coroner for Island County for eighteen years, responded to Mark Plumberg's call of a found body. (Eric Ohme introduced fifteen photos of the ravine and Kathie's tarp-wrapped body.) Dr. Bishop testified to the arduous procedure of bringing the victim's body up out of the ravine. Bishop explained the autopsy and said it was impossible to tell if she had been struck with the hammer first—or strangled.

- Number fifteen, Lieutenant Evan Tingstad testified about his long days in gathering evidence on Al Baker, from the first welfare check to the interview where the defendant wrote out his own statement, *and* Al Baker's angry reaction to the sketch of the body location that Tingstad drew.

- Number sixteen, Dr. Sigmund Menchel, forensic pathologist for thirty years, testified about unwrapping the victim's body from its silver and blue tarp, layer by layer, and the postmortem examination. Prosecutor Ohme introduced twelve photo exhibits of Kathie's nude body—over Tom Pacher's objections. Answering defense attorney Pacher's questions, Dr. Menchel testified it was impossible to say whether the hammer or the garrote came first, or how long the victim had been dead. Tests for recent sexual activity were negative.

- Number seventeen, Dr. Jean Dieden, the veterinarian who treated Kathie's dogs, said, "She made an appointment for June 5 but she didn't show up. That was *very* unlike her. She always kept her appointments—or called to cancel."

- Number eighteen, Joel Norris, owner of an ice cream parlor in Coupeville, testified that Al and Kathie Baker came into his shop once in a while. He and Al were both from Colorado and talked about that state's sports teams. "The first week of June, Al came by with another woman . . . They were holding hands. Later that week, they came back and Al told me that he and 'Trudi' were going to meet with owners of a restaurant that was up for sale."

- Number nineteen, Detective Phil Farr, Island County Sheriff's Office evidence technician. He was at the crime scene to collect and take control of physical evidence found by the sheriff's officers and the Washington State Patrol Crime Lab. Farr explained each item of evidence to the jury.

- Number twenty, Detective Ed Wallace, Island County Sheriff's Office, a specialist in investigating electronic devices: computers, cell phones et al. At Mark Plumberg's request, he retrieved vital information from two cell phones located at the house on Silver Cloud Lane.

- Number twenty-one, Mary Wilson, lead forensic scientist from the Washington State Patrol Crime Lab, told jurors about locating Kathie's body in the ravine behind her house. She also testified about finding the blood trail in the house, identified a number of photos that she had taken, and explained that the stains on the carpet were "dilute," meaning someone had tried to clean them up. The comforter stains were much diluted, as was the bloody water in the carpet-cleaning machine. A member of her team, Wilson said, had also located a ball-peen hammer stained with dried blood that had blond hairs stuck in it.

- Number twenty-two, Katherine Taylor, whose specialty is forensic anthropology relating to bones and bone structure, testified at Plumberg's request for her assistance in testing a section of cranium (skull): "There are several ways trauma appears in a corpse. In this case, it was blunt force."

- Number twenty-three, Kathy Geil, Washington State Patrol Crime Lab tool mark specialist, testified about a ball-peen hammer and two pieces of skull that the sheriff's office sent her. She had analyzed the hammer for blood type and checked the skull pieces for the damage done by that hammer.

- Number twenty-four, Helmut Steele, Washington State Department of Transportation security officer (previously spent thirty years with the State Patrol), had responded to Detective Plumberg's questions about identifying Al Baker's truck—and driver—as it boarded an eastbound ferry on June 3, 2012, and a possible return trip with the driver and a passenger. Steele provided two DVDs containing the images that Plumberg sought. Al Baker was clearly visible as he left Whidbey Island; several hours later, he could be seen in his truck, this time with a female passenger.

(Detective Plumberg returned to the witness stand for the third time—to review and identify thirty-six exhibits. They were admitted, and he was dismissed subject to recall.)

- Number twenty-five, Deputy Dan Burns testified that he had responded to the crime scene to guard its perimeters overnight.
- Number twenty-six was Trudi Gerhart, sixty-one, of Seward, Alaska.

"Call Trudi Gerhart!"

This was the "other woman" in Al Baker's life. Those watching in the gallery and the jurors sat up straighter. She didn't look like a femme fatale—save for the fact that she had a purple rinse on her graying hair. Eric Ohme asked her if she knew Kathie Baker, and she replied, "She was a friend, and I had a social relationship with her during our tours to Antarctica. I haven't seen her for several years."

But she had seen Al Baker many times, particularly after Kathie stopped working in Antarctica.

Asked to identify Al, she looked at the defense table and pointed him out. Thereafter, she avoided meeting his eyes. Trudi testified that she began her trips to Antarctica in 1995 during the "summer months." At the South Pole, that would be from October/November to January/February. At that time of year, there were about 265 people there in the three stations.

When Eric Ohme asked Trudi if she had had a romantic

relationship with the defendant, she said, "Not in my mind. Sometimes we held hands and we had occasional kisses on the cheek. Back in the U.S. after our last assignment, Mr. Baker would call me or email me. I got cards every day."

The first emails he sent were casual—but they became more personal as time went by. He told her about the "heavy stuff" that was happening in his home, all caused by Kathie, but he didn't want to go into detail.

"On March 1, 2012," Trudi testified, "he told me that he and Kathie were divorced."

That couldn't have occurred unless Baker had filed for divorce in December; it takes three months to finalize a divorce in Washington State. And, in December, Al Baker had been in Antarctica.

Later that month, Al Baker had visited Trudi in Alaska, staying in her guest room. He visited her again weeks later.

"There was no physical relationship," she testified. "But he told me he was in love with me."

Trudi Gerhart accepted Al Baker's invitation to come and visit him in his house in Greenbank, Washington, and he sent her plane tickets. On June 3, he met her at Sea-Tac Airport, and they drove to Mukilteo, where they had dinner in a restaurant before boarding the ferry to Whidbey Island.

"It was dark when we got to Greenbank," Trudi testified. "He gave me a tour of the house and we had a glass of wine before I went to bed in the guest room on the second level. He left early the next morning to do prep work at his pizza place."

Trudi had wakened later and gone downstairs. It was then that she noticed the large stain on the living room carpet.

"I tried to clean it up with boiling water and a rag—but when it dried, the stains were still there."

Trudi Gerhart testified that she had begun to think something was wrong. Kathie's car was still in the garage—they had even gone to a drive-in movie in it.

And it was odd that Kathie's beloved dogs were there without her. When the police showed up, the horrible truth began to dawn on her.

Prosecutor Ohme gave her a large manila envelope that contained five or six dozen greeting cards that the defendant had sent her. Trudi read a number of them aloud, but she wouldn't look at Al Baker.

"What did you think about them?" Ohme asked.

"At first I thought those cards were flattering, but then I began to think they were a little over-the-top. But I'm kind of old-fashioned and I thought if this all worked out, I would put them together and make a collage."

Defense attorney Tom Pacher asked her if she had been restricted from any part of Al Baker's property.

"No."

Mariah Low, a forensic scientist with the Washington State Patrol Crime Lab, was the final State's witness. She explained what DNA was, how she collected it and tested it. Ohme showed her several exhibits—including the ball-peen hammer with hair caught in it, fingernail clippings, and DNA swabs. She identified Al Baker's DNA on some of the critical evidence.

When Mariah Low was excused, Judge Alan Hancock asked Tom Pacher if he was ready to give his long-delayed opening statement. The defense attorney waived it.

It was Friday, October 11, 2013, and both the jury and the gallery wondered if this meant the trial was over.

It did not.

"Call Robert Baker!"

There had been rumors that Baker would take the stand, and the courtroom viewers certainly hoped he would. Still, the shocked spectators gasped as Pacher called what would be his one and only witness: Robert Alan Baker. It is rarely a good idea to put a murder defendant on the stand, although many of them insist, confident that they can convince a jury of their innocence. But once they testify on their own behalf, they leave themselves vulnerable to the State's cross-examination.

Pacher asked Al Baker about Antarctica and his work there.

"I work as a physicist—planning and support for experiments. I specialize in cryogenics."

"And Trudi's?"

"She was a communications officer."

Baker described a typical testing process used for sampling. He came across as very confident and quite brilliant, tossing around technical terms about cryogenics that went over most of the courtroom spectators' heads.

Baker explained that it was a twenty-five-hour trip to get to the South Pole. He would fly to Denver, change planes to one headed for Los Angeles, and then fly on to New Zealand.

"When did you meet your late wife?" Pacher asked.

"In Denver. We had worked three seasons down on the ice until we got married in Colorado in 2007."

"What were your salaries at that point?"

"I made around $90,000 a year, and Kathie made $120,000. We would each make two or three trips to Colorado a year—that's where Raytheon's headquarters are. And Kathie has—had family there."

Baker said that he took an interest in Trudi Gerhart when Kathie stopped going to the South Pole.

"You sent a large number of cards to Trudi?"

"I probably sent her well over a hundred."

"When did you leave Antarctica last year—2012?"

"February."

Pacher asked about his client's time with Trudi down on the ice, and he said he would visit her in the communications center, and they watched movies together.

"Did you intend to strike up a relationship with her?"

"That's hard to say, but I was excited about it."

"Where was Kathie?"

"I thought she was in Denver."

"After your initial contact with the Island County Sheriff's Office, were you concerned?"

"I didn't attempt to contact Kathie, because Trudi was with me."

Al Baker testified that when he and Trudi Gerhart drove up to his house on Sunday night, June 3, he saw that Kathie's car was in the garage. That was odd because it had been gone earlier in the day and he had assumed she'd flown to Denver.

"I thought we were going to have a problem, but she wasn't in the house."

The defendant admitted he had lied to detectives when they came looking for Kathie days later after Raytheon sounded the alarm. He felt caught between two women.

"I didn't want the police to tell Kathie that Trudi was there," he told the jury. "And I didn't want the police to tell Trudi that Kathie still lived there."

If Baker's testimony was meant to show jurors that he was just a "good old boy," it had failed miserably.

The defendant insisted that he knew nothing about Kathie's murder.

*"Did you kill your wife?"* Pacher asked suddenly.

Al Baker's overt reaction was almost indignant.

"NO!" he said. "I swear on everything I hold sacred— my mother's grave. I did not kill Kathie. I did not kill my wife!"

Prosecutor Eric Ohme said he would wait to cross-examine Baker until after the lunch break.

It is often said that he who represents himself has a fool for a lawyer. Al Baker had a lawyer, but he chose to take the witness stand over defense attorney Tom Pacher's objections, and in doing so, he indeed made a fool of himself. Now he faced Eric Ohme for cross-examination.

Ohme systematically reviewed the lies Baker had told along with the reasons they had tripped him up:

"When you picked up Trudi at the airport, Kathie's car was missing from the garage, and upon your return the car *was* there—but not Kathie," Ohme began.

"When you talked to Lieutenant Tingstad at your home, with Trudi present, you told him Kathie was taken to the airport; why wouldn't you tell him how she got there?

"You repeatedly told officers that Kathie went to the airport by herself. On June 3, you placed a call at eleven A.M. to your pizza place advising them you were taking Kathie to the airport."

Prosecutor Ohme went over the plethora of lies Al Baker had told the sheriff's officers, Trudi Gerhart, his pizzeria employees, townspeople on Whidbey Island, even Kathie's brother.

Baker testified that he could not explain how blood got on the carpet runners, decorative pillows, and nightstand in the master bedroom. Nor did he have any knowledge about the dilute bloodstains on the comforter found in the laundry room. It was the same way with the stains in the living room and garage.

"Did you love Kathie—or not?"

"I loved her. There was no thought about splitting up, and I was against divorce."

For a man allegedly divorced numerous times, this last statement was ridiculous.

Ohme went over the absurd discussions Al had with Trudi and businessmen on the island. He had said he wanted to buy another restaurant and soon own several refurbished businesses. He also was thinking of buying a forty-six-foot boat.

"You knew full well you weren't in a position to purchase any of them," Ohme asked, "didn't you?"

Baker's decision to take the witness stand and show the jurors he was an innocent man turned out to be a bad one. He had failed miserably. Most of Baker's answers were vague: "I didn't think about it," and "I don't recall." It still seemed that he didn't realize how many inconsistencies he'd been caught in.

It was time for final arguments, but the shadows outside were growing longer, and the final arguments would have to wait until the next session in Judge Alan Hancock's courtroom.

The Hill family asked Hancock if there was some way they could have Kathie's name changed postmortem—back to Hill. They had representatives in court every day, and they could no longer bear to hear her referred to as Kathie Baker. Judge Hancock agreed, saying he felt the same way himself. Henceforth, she would be called Kathie Hill.

\*　　\*　　\*

Prosecutor Eric Ohme reminded jurors that the defendant did one thing right: he had managed to keep two women from knowing about each other.

But Al Baker had made so many mistakes.

"In order to keep his web of deceit from crashing down, he made a choice on how he could fulfill his fantasy," Ohme began.

The prosecutor described in excruciating detail how Kathie Hill had died and how Al Baker had concealed her body. He reviewed the elements of the case, and all those that were questionable. Then he answered them with irrefutable proof that had been supportive of the State's case during the prior two weeks.

Ohme summarized Al Baker's myriad lies, and asked the jury to remember how the defendant had told constantly changing stories.

"Based on the evidence, you must find the defendant guilty of murder in the first degree."

Tom Pacher never did make any opening statement. And he had said, "No questions," to most of the State's witnesses. One can understand why: he was representing a despicable client who clearly rankled the jury. Now, finally, Tom Pacher rose to make his final arguments.

He began with a statement Matthew Montoya had used in another murder trial on Whidbey Island.

"Don't confuse me with the facts—I've already made

up my mind." The jurors' brows wrinkled as they attempted to understand Pacher's obscure remark.

Then Pacher presented what seemed to be anything *but* facts—loopholes the defense attorney had winnowed out of Al Baker's testimony and circumstantial evidence.

He asked the jurors to consider the logistics. Baker was a small man, and Kathie, Pacher said, weighed 240 pounds (in reality, she weighed about 75 pounds less than that). How could Baker manage what was ironically a dead weight?

The hammer was a "shop tool." And, of course Al's DNA would be found on it, Pacher submitted. He had probably used it to fix or build something around his house.

The item used as a ligature had never been located. The real killer had probably taken it with him when he left.

Tom Pacher insisted that the Bakers' dog door was very large, and strangers in the night could have easily crawled through it and murdered Kathie as her husband slept.

And why hadn't the investigators talked to neighbors close to the house on Silver Cloud Lane?

Then Pacher brought up the fact that both Detective Laura Price and Lieutenant Tingstad were over six feet tall. His poor little client—only five feet six—must have been intimidated and frightened as they loomed over him.

Pacher insisted that Al Baker had *tried* to help the detectives.

Ohme didn't say anything, of course, but one could tell

209

how he felt by the expression on his face. And his face said, "Really?"

"This case is crawling with reasonable doubt," Pacher said. "There is simply not enough evidence in this case to convict him of anything."

When Tom Pacher sat down, court watchers looked bemused. The defense attorney hadn't truly addressed the murder of Kathie Hill. Instead, he had plucked theories out of thin air to convince jurors that his client must be innocent.

Once more, it was Eric Ohme's turn to speak on rebuttal. And Ohme's response was scathing.

The mysterious burglar/dog door theory? The victim had no defensive wounds on her body.

Why was Kathie's expensive diamond ring found in Al's nightstand?

Al Baker had had plenty of time to dispose of his wife's body and clean up. He did what he could, Ohme suggested, but he had still left plenty of physical evidence behind.

Baker's testimony was full of lies. Tom Pacher's theory that the defendant had helped the police was preposterous.

Finally, closing statements were over.

After listening to Judge Hancock's instructions, the jurors were excused at 11 A.M. At 3:20, they signaled that they had reached a verdict—after only four hours and twenty minutes.

was *deeply* in love with Al Baker. I believe he planned this for a long time."

David's wife, Melody, said Baker had done other "disgusting" things in the past.

Char Johnson, Kathie's stepsister, who had flown to Whidbey Island to rescue her two dogs, was next: "She was like a true sister to me."

Amy Gralinger, Kathie's best friend, drew tears from the jury and court watchers as she described what "an incredible, beautiful person" Kathie was. "I knew there was an issue between them over Kathie's dogs. I offered to take them, but she loved them so . . . There is no punishment severe enough for taking Kathie's life."

So many people had loved Kathie Hill, and one by one they took the witness stand to praise her—her kindness, her willingness to help those who were sick or grieving, her brilliance, and her misplaced love for a man who was a monster. Al Baker himself sat silently as he heard the description "monster" over and over.

Maybe he had begun to believe that his lies were true. More likely, he was deaf to what Kathie's family and friends were saying. He didn't care. Indeed, he hadn't seen his own mother for more than two decades—and, then, only at Kathie's urging. On the witness stand, he'd sworn on his mother's grave that he was innocent. One has to wonder how much his mother's grave really meant to him.

Jami Hill testified that the entire Hill family was shocked to hear about her aunt's husband's criminal past.

She had worked for sixteen months since Kathie died to uncover Al's expenditures of Kathie's money; her aunt had kept perfect records, but Baker's records were a mess or missing entirely. Jami discovered that it was Al who had caused the IRS trouble; he'd simply failed to pay his employees' withholding taxes.

Kathie's cousin, Lori Snider, spoke of the deep roots the Hill family had in Colorado, and of how difficult it was for Kathie to leave there and follow Al Baker so far away from "home."

"I would like to visit Whidbey Island—just to walk in her footsteps for a moment. I'm not sure if I can ever get full closure without experiencing a bit of her time there. Hopefully, Kathie will rest in peace now, and her family and friends can start to exhale. Feels like we've been holding our breath for a *very* long time."

The task of following Al Baker's trail was almost overwhelming. But Jami was determined. "You cannot step over a mountain," she told me, "but if you step over pebble by pebble, you'll look back and the mountain will be behind you."

Even to this day Jami is stepping over "pebbles" as she tries to avenge her aunt Kathie.

Jami says that no one really knew who Al Baker was. Jami and her attorney, Charles Arndt, are trying to find out why Raytheon had hired Al to work in Antarctica since his record revealed he had been convicted of serious offenses.

Judge Alan Hancock took a twenty-minute break to gather his thoughts. When he returned, he appeared shaken and touched by the heinous aspects of Kathie Hill's murder. He read Al Baker his rights of appeal. And then he spent several minutes deploring the crime. He had listened well to the witnesses and to the victim's family. It sounded as if the judge was as appalled by the crime as they were.

He sentenced the sixty-three-year-old killer to fifty-two years in prison, ensuring he will never walk free again. "All of us had a relationship with a person we thought existed," Jami told Jessie Stensland, an editor for the *South Whidbey Record,* "but nobody knew the real *him.*"

While researching this book, the suspicious death of Raytheon astrophysicist Rodney Marks was brought to my attention. In May 2000, he died in the South Pole of methanol poisoning. Though not yet officially ruled a homicide, Marks's death is widely referred to as the South Pole's first murder. Did Al Baker know Rodney Marks? Was Baker in Antarctica when Marks died? I do not know, but I hope investigators will look into this.

Only Robert Alan Baker knows the depth of horror of his dark secrets. Maybe one day, he will reveal all. But it is more likely that he will take his secrets to the grave.

Rest in peace, Kathie Ann Hill.

# A ROAD TRIP
# TO MURDER

*Some crime victims know when they are being stalked; others have no idea of danger. Why should they? As far as they know, their lifestyle is safe and far off the pathways traveled by thieves, burglars, rapists, and killers. If anyone told them they were dead-center in the gun sights of killers without conscience, they would shake their heads in denial.*

*And they would be wrong.*

*I don't know which is worse, to meet deadly strangers or to find out too late that someone you have trusted cares nothing for you and is quite willing to dispose of you—forever. The victims in this third case met someone who fit into both categories; the murderers killed indiscriminately.*

*They were full of hate, and heaven help anyone who got in the way of their "project."*

**"DeeDee" Pedersen was** born Leslie Mae Sudds on September 13, 1942, in Everett, Washington, to Clara Belle and Melford Willard Sudds; she was their second daughter. She escaped the nickname "Bubbles" because her older sister, Mildred Elsie, already had it. Their younger brother, Willard, was called "Butch."

Leslie is a popular female name today, but in the 1940s, it was more commonly a boy's name, and Leslie Mae didn't like it. Her name would change often along with the vicissitudes of her life.

Clara Belle and Melford eventually divorced each other and married other people. Though Leslie was thrilled when her stepmother, Karol Sudds, gave birth to a baby girl, Helen, she was not allowed to help care for her. Leslie thought her new sister was the prettiest baby she had ever seen, and she longed to hold her. She was thirteen and dependable, but her overprotective stepmother did not trust her with the baby.

It hurt Leslie's feelings, and she sometimes felt like an outsider in her own home.

It was worse at Clara Belle's house. Leslie's new stepfather, Vernon, would sneak into the room where she slept with Butch and touch her inappropriately. She soon learned that if she changed places with her little brother in the bed, it would discourage her stepfather from molesting her.

This kind of abuse was far more common seventy years ago than anyone knew—or acknowledged. Many families had dark secrets, but few talked about them.

DeeDee Sudds broke the cycle of abuse; she vowed that she would never allow cruelty toward any children she might have one day.

DeeDee graduated from Everett High School in 1960; she was seventeen. She was petite at five feet, two inches, but full-breasted. DeeDee was pretty, with soft brown bangs curling around her face. Nearsighted, she always wore glasses.

She attended Catholic church with her longtime best friend, Jean, but she was confirmed in the Lutheran church. She and Jean remained close friends.

DeeDee was engaged in high school, but that fizzled, as most teenage romances do.

When Jean married a young man named Edward Nemitz, she introduced DeeDee to his brother, Richard.

After her first date with Richard, DeeDee announced to her mother that she had just met the man she was going to marry.

And she did—six weeks later, on April 7, 1961.

The future lay ahead, promising all good things. DeeDee and Richard had their first daughter, Lori Jane, on April 8, 1963, and their second, Susan Beth, on February 5, 1966.

While Lori Jane thrived, Susan was frail and spent a lot of time at what was then called Children's Orthopedic Hospital. Despite the worry over Susan's health, the Nemitz family was happy, and they prospered.

In the summer, they loved to go camping at Crescent Bar in eastern Washington. Lori and Susan learned to swim there, and their father mastered waterskiing. The girls climbed apricot trees and ate the sweet fruit, its juice dripping down their chins.

They had a dog, a schipperke named Tippy Toes, and wonderful neighbors who treated the Nemitz girls like grandchildren.

But the happy times didn't last. After nine years, DeeDee and Richard told their daughters that they were getting a divorce. Confused and shocked, Lori Jane used the news during her class's show-and-tell in the third grade. Her teacher that year and her adviser, who was the vice principal, helped her deal with what, to Lori Jane, seemed unthinkable.

Neither Lori nor Susan approved of their mother's

choices when she began to date again, often coining scatological nicknames for the new men in her life.

"Mom told me later that she always viewed her first boyfriend as her punishment for divorcing Dad," Lori said. "We called him Rick the Prick."

DeeDee dated one man who drove a car painted lime green with glittery flakes in it that the girls found "the coolest."

Another boyfriend was a mountain climber who had once scaled Mount McKinley in Alaska and Mount Kilimanjaro, the tallest mountain in Africa.

But despite the passage of time, DeeDee found no likely prospects for marriage.

And then she met Leroy Marvin Danner, a Vietnam vet. He was solid, a good man who had served his country, and DeeDee was very attracted to him.

Her girls liked him, and they called him Dad, although their biological father was still a big part of their lives, and they often visited Richard Nemitz.

DeeDee and Leroy were married on August 18, 1976.

Leroy had his faults, but he and DeeDee really loved each other, so their marriage flourished. They rolled over the rough patches, and their union grew happier.

They had been together for a few years when Leroy went to Idaho to visit his mother. When he came back, he told a shocked DeeDee that he had a daughter.

"Why didn't you tell me?" she asked.

She knew Leroy had two sons—Leroy Jr.* and Ron*—but he had never mentioned a daughter.

"It was as much a surprise to me as it is to you," Leroy answered. "I didn't know. Not until my mother told me. It seems as though Mom knew, and my daughter, Gracie,* knew—everyone knew but me."

From then on, DeeDee, Lori Jane, and Susan welcomed Gracie into the family. DeeDee had a kind heart, and she considered Gracie her daughter, too.

Leroy Jr. and Ron spent a lot of time with their new sisters—until the boys became caught up in the drug world and gradually drifted away.

Her years with Leroy were quite likely the happiest period of DeeDee's life, but she didn't truly trust it to last; she had had too many dreams dashed to bits.

Lori Jane was fourteen and Susan eleven when they decided they wanted to live with their biological father. That decision was devastating to DeeDee.

"It hurt Mom immensely, which I take full responsibility for," Lori recalled. "Leroy was furious with us. I didn't talk to Mom for six months and only spoke to her again because my dad's attorney called and told me to."

Gradually, Lori Jane and Susan mended the rift in their tattered relationship with their mother. They had acted like bratty teenagers because their mother didn't always let them get their way.

"I knew after talking to Mom that I had made a mistake moving to my dad's," Lori Jane admits. It hurt the girls to hear the pain of rejection in their mother's voice. "After seeing what that did to her, I swore I'd never do that to anyone else."

Susan eventually moved back to live with DeeDee and Leroy, but the wound to their mother's heart took a long time to heal.

DeeDee and Leroy had a happy marriage. When the girls grew older, they traveled a lot. With her second husband, DeeDee found a kind of love she hadn't known before, and she was grateful for it.

But just as she had always feared, the joy would not last. Leroy was having surgery for a hernia when the surgeon discovered an invasive cancer. Ten months later, on March 5, 1995, Leroy died at home with DeeDee by his side. She was overwhelmed with grief. They had been together for more than eighteen years, and she had hoped their marriage would last forever. With the love of her life gone, she never expected to marry again.

She had no choice but to go on. There were bills to pay, and she had never shirked hard work. After twenty years as a legal secretary, DeeDee worked for five years for Snohomish County's Public Utilities Department, and then, before she retired, she worked as a legal transcriptionist and a validator of medical credentials.

DeeDee continued to live in Mount Vernon in the nice mobile home that she and Leroy had bought together, and she devoted herself to her family. She was fun and creative, and her grandchildren adored her.

One of DeeDee's most popular ideas was the Grandkids' Picnic.

"My mom and all the grandmas in our family dressed up in funny old clothes, and the kids just laughed and laughed," Susan recalls. "Then we had a picnic that was really good."

DeeDee was still attractive as she aged, and once, just for fun, she and her sister, Aunt Bubbles, and their mother went to a photo studio and had glamour shots taken.

Though she always took care with her appearance, it was not because DeeDee was trying to attract a man. She was content with her life just as it was. She talked with her daughters daily and had a close relationship with them. Their disagreements from the past were long forgotten.

DeeDee was comfortable in her cozy mobile home. She enjoyed spending time with her grandchildren, and she adored her little dog. The miniature Australian shepherd was loyal and well behaved. Though she missed Leroy terribly, DeeDee counted her blessings. Her life was pretty good.

And then DeeDee met David Jones "Red" Pedersen. It was Valentine's Day, 1997, when a friend of DeeDee's set her up on a blind date with the ex-marine whom everyone called Red for his once-fiery-red hair. His hair was white by the time DeeDee met him, but the nickname had stuck. He was quite handsome and thirteen years younger than DeeDee.

Red was closer in age to her daughters, only eight years older than Lori Jane. DeeDee was both surprised and flattered when Red Pedersen flirted with her.

He was determined to be with DeeDee, and despite her hesitancy about their age difference, they were soon spending time together. Though he was younger, Red was the one with health issues. The pain from arthritis in his shoulders and knees often made it impossible for him to work the long shifts as a truck driver. When his joints ached like fury, Red needed someone to help him.

DeeDee was a nurturer, and looking after a man came naturally to her. The more time they spent together, the less she worried about their age difference. Maybe age didn't matter, she decided, reasoning that past the age of fifty, no one noticed.

Still, she took care to appear as youthful as possible. Large-breasted women tend to droop as they age, and DeeDee was no exception; she had undergone breast-reduction surgery while still married to Leroy. She took time each morning to make sure her hair and makeup were perfect.

Red and DeeDee got along well, and it wasn't long before she fell in love with him. They married on Valentine's Day, 2004, exactly seven years after they had met.

DeeDee had been content to live by herself, but she was really a man's woman, and she loved making Red happy, cooking his favorite meals, and in most of their photos, her hand was in his, or she was touching him fondly. Now that he was in pain most of the time, she did her best to make him comfortable.

Red also liked to pamper DeeDee. When she was still working, he often made dinner and drew baths for her.

Lori Jane and Susan were not as taken with Red as their mother was. They were suspicious of his motivations. Before he married DeeDee, Red had no house and no job. "He used a cardboard box for a coffee table," Susan recalls. Now Red shared the nice home that DeeDee had made, and she supported them.

From the beginning, the girls didn't like the way Red treated their mother.

"He called her an 'old bag,'" Susan says. "And other mean things."

Lori nods and confesses, "We thought he was terrible and that he wore our mom down, but she said that was just his way—he was joking. And she laughed along with him."

"Leroy was a wonderful father," Susan says wistfully. "Red wasn't our dad."

"We were pleasant to him because our mom loved him, and she seemed happy with him," Susan emphasizes, "but we never felt he was part of our family."

While Gracie and Susan were especially wary of Red, Lori Jane was a bit more accepting of him.

DeeDee's daughters never came to completely trust Red Pedersen. They knew very little about his family, and what they did learn didn't exactly reassure them. His first wife, Linda Eilene Pedersen, had suffered from multiple personalities and had been hospitalized several times. Red had married and divorced her twice.

Linda had called him Pa, and he had called her Ma. They had two children, Joseph and Gloria.*

Suspicious of Red, Susan looked into his background. She snooped around but did not learn much—only that he was one of four brothers. One brother had died in an accident as a young man, and another was named Steve. She found no information at all about the third brother.

Red had been open about the fact that he had a son, David Joseph Pedersen, "Joey," who was serving time in an Oregon prison. For what crime, Lori didn't know. And neither did her mother.

DeeDee was vague when her daughters questioned her about the convict stepson she had yet to meet.

"I don't think Mom knew that much about what he was in for," says Lori Jane.


In 2007, Joey Pedersen wrote a letter to his father, inviting him to visit him in prison. "He was incarcerated in Colorado at the time," Lori says.

Red and DeeDee didn't have much disposable income, but they scraped together what they could to pay for a trip to see Joey. But when they got there, he refused to see them.

"They were really disappointed," Lori says. She thinks she knows the reason for his change of heart. She suspects that a relative of Joey's got wind of the fact that he was planning a reunion with his father and stirred up disturbing memories from his childhood, reminding him that Red had not always been kind to him.

Red had made it no secret that he had been abusive to his children, but he never went into specifics.

"Abuse can mean different things to different people," Lori says, explaining that her mom assumed that Red felt guilty for being short with his kids, yelling at them and spanking them. When Red insinuated that he had not been the best father in the world, DeeDee could never have imagined just how bad it had been for his children.

Short-tempered and commanding, Red was a marine sergeant and sometimes treated his children like little soldiers. But that was not the worst part. At least one of his children was sexually abused by him.

David Joseph Pedersen, Joey, was born in Stayton, Oregon, on June 18, 1980, fifteen months after his sister. With an emotionally fragile mother and a demanding and abusive father, the Pedersen siblings had a far-from-ideal childhood.

When life became too much for Linda Pedersen, she sometimes retreated to the bedroom and locked herself in for days. Red took his frustrations out on the children, raging at them as they cowered in fear.

Years later, Joey's sister would tell a reporter that Red did not drop his drill sergeant façade at home. He had no self-control at all, and he exploded at the sight of a messy house.

Red set impossible standards, forbidding his young son to cry. Sergeant Pedersen grew frustrated by the fact that the limitations of his seventh-grade education prevented him from helping his kids with their homework. When he could not understand the assignments, he vented his wrath on his children.

While Gloria tried to behave, Joey had a rebellious streak and would sometimes deliberately defy Red.

Joey was about five years old when his family moved to Camp Pendleton, California, in San Diego County. Red was stationed at the camp, the major West Coast base for the U.S. Marine Corps.

The family lived there for about four years, and despite their dysfunctional home life, there were also some good times for the kids. They got along well with each other, and they swam in the ocean, caught crawdads, and rode their bikes.

Sometimes Joey and Gloria were bounced around, dumped on relatives and neighbors. In 1993, when Red and Linda divorced, neither parent sought custody of the kids, and they became wards of the state. They stayed for a while with an aunt in Stayton, Oregon.

The aunt's house was warm and inviting. She decorated the home for the holidays, and she baked Christmas cookies—something that was apparently so alien to Joey that he would one day describe the scenario to *Portland Monthly* reporter Alison Barnwell, saying, "Those were the best years of my life."

At age thirteen, Joey moved in with his mom in Salem, Oregon, but she kicked him out when he quit school at sixteen.

In June 1996, Joey was arrested for third-degree robbery. He was put on probation until October of that year. Soon robbery became a habit for the troubled teen. He robbed at gunpoint two coffee stands, a McDonald's, and a Plaid Pantry.

In March 1997, Joey was incarcerated at MacLaren Youth Correctional Facility in Woodburn, Oregon. Despite the fact that he was only sixteen, motions were made to move him to an adult prison. On his seventeenth birthday, he was moved to the Oregon State Correctional Institution in Salem.

The incarceration of an underage teen in an adult prison was unusual and could have been the tipping point for an impressionable youth who had an already skewed outlook on the world. He had been behind bars with hardened adult prisoners for about a year when he assaulted someone. He would collect nearly six dozen violations of prison rules during his incarcerations.

While imprisoned, he began to embrace white-supremacist ideology. One of his relatives would later tell a reporter that Joey had not always been a racist and, in fact, had had a black girlfriend when he was fifteen. Many of Joey's opinions were formed while he was in prison, and it was there that he got his tattoos. He grew more violent and angry as the years passed and was written up for harassment of those of other religions and races and also for sexual harassment.

In February 2000, Joey sent a death threat to a U.S. district judge in Idaho. The judge had presided over the trial of Randy Weaver, the former U.S. Army combat engineer and white supremacist at the center of the deadly confrontation with the FBI at Ruby Ridge, Idaho, in 1992. Weaver's wife and son were killed in the mountaintop showdown, and Weaver was apparently a hero to Joey.

More than one hundred prison gangs have been identified by the Oregon Department of Justice, and Joey allegedly belonged to one known as Aryan Soldiers, a radical gang infused with intense hate for those who are different from them. Joey bonded with a member of the gang when he discovered they could speak to each other through a vent in the wall that separated their cells.

He had lengthy conversations with the inmate, who had been incarcerated for shooting his foster mother at age fourteen. The kid had been in and out of foster homes since he was eighteen months old and had lived with his victim and her family for about ten months. After he had moved out, he went back to the house to burglarize it, and he ended up killing the forty-eight-year-old woman.

Joey Pedersen was surrounded by violent people, and his life behind bars was bleak. His prison rap sheet was lengthy. In one of his more shocking crimes, Joey assaulted a prison guard, striking him in the face repeatedly with a hot clothes iron. Joey was in a rage, and he admitted he would have killed the guard if another convict had not stopped him. Bigger and heavier than Joey, the other inmate slammed him from behind and pinned him to the wall.

Joey had a difficult time getting along with others, but he could not cause much trouble in solitary confinement, and he spent so much time in forced solitude that he earned time off for good behavior. On May 24, 2011, Joey Pedersen was released from the Oregon state prison.

A fellow convict, paroled shortly before Joey, was involved in cage fighting, a particularly violent sport of mixed martial arts, with no holds barred. It sounded exciting to Joey. It was something he'd always wanted to try. Joey's ex-con friend coached him, and Joey competed in three bouts and lost all three. He shrugged it off, saying, "You're supposed to train for six months before a bout, and I only trained for two weeks."

DeeDee and her daughters were unaware of Joey's activities and did not realize he was planning a visit. They couldn't have known that Red's son was filled with rage.

As September drew to a close that year, the vine maples' leaves were edged with the brilliant orange that would soon turn them into solid flames.

Susan and Lori Jane were both struck with a premonition that something bad was about to happen. The title of the classic Ray Bradbury novel came to mind: *Something Wicked This Way Comes*.

The sisters found themselves quoting the words of the ominous title to each other in the following days as they felt the cold shadow of foreboding. Neither could pinpoint just what it was that worried them, but they were compelled to make frequent welfare checks on members of their family, especially on their mother.

Susan and Lori Jane took turns checking on her, calling her every day.

September had always been a bad time for their family, and it seemed most of the deaths of those close to them happened in that month. Maybe that was why they were so jumpy. The sisters remembered one particularly bad September when they had lost a cousin in a horrific way. As far as they were concerned, it was murder, but no one was ever held accountable for the death of Timothy Hartley York.

Tim was only twenty when the tragedy happened. It was September 26, 1984, and Tim was standing near a bonfire when another youth foolishly threw a can of gasoline onto the fire. Tim sustained serious injuries in the resulting explosion, and he died soon afterward.

Lori and Susan hoped that their fear was caused by

nothing more than bad memories of past tragedies. Still, they felt something was not quite right in their mother's world. They knew that she and Red were struggling with financial difficulties. But it seemed that something more might be bothering her.

DeeDee's sister sensed it, too. Bubbles and DeeDee met for lunch in early September 2011. Aunt Bubbles would later tell her nieces that something was obviously troubling DeeDee. But whatever it was, DeeDee kept it to herself.

Then one day, out of the blue, Joey Pedersen showed up on his father's doorstep. He brought his girlfriend along, and DeeDee welcomed them warmly.

Joey had his father's fiery red hair, cropped close to his skull. He looked like the stereotypical ex-con, tough and covered with tattoos. Holly Ann Grigsby, twenty-four, stood about five foot four and was slightly underweight and plain.

She barely responded to DeeDee's attempts to make friendly conversation. While she knew that Joey's past was less than pristine, it is unlikely that DeeDee was aware that Holly had been in and out of Oregon prisons for the past five years and that her rap sheet included five felony convictions.

If DeeDee was startled by Joey's tattoos or put off by Holly's glum demeanor, she didn't mention it to anyone.

She was a good sport, and she went along with Red when he took Holly and Joey to a shooting range near Arlington, Washington, on Friday, September 23.

She may have put on a cheerful face, but shooting guns was not DeeDee's idea of a good time. The employees at Norpoint Shooting Center noticed that DeeDee did not seem excited to be there.

After briefly firing a gun at the target—a silhouette of an upper torso—DeeDee put down her weapon and went to sit outside, where she flipped through magazines as she waited for the others to finish.

The foursome was at the range for just half an hour, and employees were glad to see them go. Their presence made them uncomfortable.

Joey frightened them. His tattoos spoke volumes about his mind-set. Covering his neck and creeping up onto his face, the ink marked him as an angry racist: *SWP*. It stood for Supreme White Power.

Holly, too, made people uneasy. She was too quiet, a gloomy kind of quiet, as if something dark smoldered inside her. Holly participated in the shooting but barely spoke a word to those with her or to the employees at the range.

Employees at the gun range were unaware that the young couple had both been convicted of felonies and that they were not allowed to handle guns. Joey and Holly had signed the standard liability waiver with the names Josh Spencer and Melissa Wright.

The guns belonged to Red, and he and DeeDee signed their real names to the waivers. They had nothing to hide, certainly no criminal records. And there was no reason for them to think that the two young people shooting beside them were plotting something evil.

As usual, DeeDee was a gracious hostess. She cooked and cleaned and did her best to make their guests comfortable in her mobile home, which was a little crowded with Joey and Holly sharing the space with them.

DeeDee was more than four decades older than Holly, and she was as vivacious as the younger woman was introverted. On the surface, it appeared the two had nothing in common. But though they did not know it, DeeDee and her sullen female houseguest did have something in common.

Holly Grigsby had been molested as a child, just as DeeDee had been violated. Both Holly and DeeDee had been around age seven when their mothers married men who preyed upon their children.

Holly had been just a year old, her sister three, when her parents split. Her mother would marry twice more over the next few years.

According to Holly's relatives, she was a happy, helpful child, but she began to rebel around the age of thirteen when she got involved with drugs. The next years were chaotic, and Holly lived with her father, Fred, for a time while she tried to get off of heroin and meth.

Fred wanted to help the troubled teen, but Holly was out of control. She made some feeble attempts, but she lost the battle with her addictions. Her father was upset when he discovered she'd been doing drugs in his bathroom.

One night, she came home yelling racial slurs. Fred had had enough. The police were called, and Holly was told she was not allowed to return to her father's home.

Fred would later tell a reporter that it broke his heart to send his daughter away. "It was terrible," he said. "It's a hard thing to tell your child."

Miraculously, Holly seemed to pull herself together. She attended Parkrose High School in Portland, Oregon, and graduated in 2005. She was the first one in her family to earn a high school diploma, and her family was proud of her.

An uncle helped her rent an apartment, and Holly got a secondhand truck. She worked two jobs, and she seemed determined to make something of herself.

But a few months after graduation, Holly was in trouble again. She was arrested for trying to steal a trailer. She stood in the Multnomah County Courthouse in October 2005 as Judge Kathleen Dailey sentenced her to eighteen months' probation and offered prophetic words of warning. "I worry for you, Miss Grigsby," Judge Dailey said. "If you don't get a handle on this, your life will just go down the toilet."

The judge's words apparently had little impact on Holly. In January 2006, shortly before her nineteenth birthday, she once again faced charges in Multnomah County Court, this time for two Class C felonies: identity theft and unauthorized use of an automobile.

Holly told Judge Michael McShane that her boyfriend

(who was also her stepbrother) was violent and that he beat her if she refused to steal for him to get money for drugs.

Judge McShane sentenced Holly to thirteen months in prison and told her, "The one thing I don't want you to do is go back with crappy men."

The judge may have zeroed in on Holly's most salient problem. According to her family and friends, her fatal flaw was her taste in men. She found "bad boys" attractive, and she was easily influenced by them.

Holly would collect a total of five felonies over the next several years. The friends she met in prison further entrenched her already twisted perspective on the world.

She had a swastika tattoo on her right ankle, and during one prison sentence, she bonded with Sandee,* the only other female there with the same offensive image branded on her flesh. The two Caucasian girls with their Nazi tattoos stuck together, set apart from the rest of the prison population as they flaunted their unpopular philosophies.

Sandee had been thoroughly programmed to believe her race was superior, and she took Holly under her wing, reciting the same lines that she had been fed about white power. Holly wholeheartedly embraced the hate.

When she was released from prison in 2007, Holly soon hooked up with Mick Buttram,* nineteen years her senior. Both were in treatment for drug addiction. They quickly moved in together, and before long, they were both addicted to heroin.

Holly and Mick were married in November 2008, but their life was anything but stable. Holly ended up back in prison, serving twenty-six months for ID theft, forgery, and theft. She was also pregnant. Her baby boy was born while she was incarcerated, and the state of Oregon swiftly took custody of him.

Released from prison in 2010, Holly went directly into a drug-treatment program. By spring 2011, she had kicked her heroin habit and was thrilled to have her little boy back. Holly and Mick moved into a southeast Portland apartment, and she devoted herself to their toddler. She read stories to her son, who was by then two and a half. She wrote poems in her spare time and helped support her small son by working in a pretzel shop in a Portland area mall. Her boss recalled that she was doing a good job there.

And then she met Joey Pedersen. He was the "baddest" of all the bad boys she had ever known. For her, this was the perfect man.

The two met through a mutual friend, and Holly was intrigued by the redheaded man who shared her controversial beliefs. He was passionately anti-Semitic and not hesitant to voice his hatred for people of color. Holly found his prejudice a sign of masculinity and confidence.

She told her husband, Mick, that she thought he would like Joey Pedersen. Holly introduced them, and Mick attended some of Joey's cage-fighting matches.

Before long, the young mother fell under Joey

Pedersen's spell. Holly and her husband broke up over Labor Day weekend in 2011. Labor Day fell on Monday, September 5. It was unseasonably warm in Portland, with temperatures creeping to nearly ninety degrees.

Summer would be over in less than three weeks, the days inevitably turning gray and drizzly, but Holly did not look back. Joey had become her whole world, and she would follow him anyplace. Mick Buttram would one day tell an *Oregonian* reporter that his estranged wife had "painted a happy picture" of what her life with Joey would be like.

Some close to Holly believed that she was attracted to Joey partially because of the fact that he was clean and sober. Ironically, Joey neither drank nor took drugs.

Still, they refused to believe she would abandon her son and were sure she would come back for him. They found her heedless and foolish, but they expected she would find life with Joey nowhere near as idyllic as she expected.

No one could have guessed that before the month was over, Joey Pedersen and Holly Grigsby would dominate national news headlines.


On Saturday morning, September 24, 2011, Lori Jane got a phone call from her mother. "Come on over," DeeDee said happily. "I want you to meet Red's son. Joey and his girlfriend, Holly, are here."

Lori Jane drove the short distance to DeeDee's trailer, where she met her mother's houseguests. She was instantly taken aback by Joey's tattoos. His arms were sleeved with ink from his wrists to his shoulders. She tried to suppress her shock as she took in the large tattoo of the letters *SWP* across the front of his neck, a wheel-like design on one cheek, and a tattoo of Adolf Hitler on his abdomen.

Lori was fairly sure that all of her new stepbrother's tattoos were linked to white supremacy. She didn't think her mother was savvy enough to recognize what they represented, and Lori didn't comment on them. But to herself, she thought that Joey Pedersen looked every inch the ex-convict he was.

Despite his appearance, Joey was polite and friendly. He got up off the couch the moment Lori stepped into the room, and he greeted her with a smile.

Holly Grigsby sat in a corner, obviously listening carefully to Lori Jane and Joey's conversation but not participating. She wore a sullen expression. Maybe she was bored, perhaps angry at Joey for dragging her along to see his family. It was impossible to tell.

Lori Jane was surprised when she heard that DeeDee had accompanied Red and their visitors to a gun range the day before. Her mother hated guns. Why on earth would she agree to go to the gun range?

But then, Lori Jane thought she knew the answer to that. Her mother wanted to please Red. She would do whatever was necessary to keep her marriage intact.

Lori Jane and her sister, Susan, continued to dig into the backgrounds of their mother's houseguests, and what they found didn't alleviate their concerns. They learned that Joey was a member of a truly violent gang and that Holly was still married to another man and had a young son. They were shocked to find that Joey was most certainly a devout white supremacist with a criminal history leading back to his teenage years.

What a mess of snakes their mother had become entangled in! Could they extricate her from it?

On Sunday, September 25, Red went to a friend's house to watch the Seahawks football game on TV. He brought Joey and Holly with him, but DeeDee decided to stay home. She said she was not feeling well.

On Monday, the 26th, Susan had a phone call from her mother, and they talked for a long time. DeeDee asked about the grandchildren and great-grandchildren, and Susan filled her in on all the latest news. DeeDee was in the middle of asking how Lori was doing when her tone suddenly changed. Hurriedly, DeeDee said, "Gotta go." The phone went dead.

Susan stared at the phone in her hand, perplexed. Should she call her mother back or wait for her to call? She decided to wait.

But there were no more calls.

Later, Susan phoned Lori to see if she had spoken with their mother since her abrupt good-bye. But Lori hadn't heard from her, either. The sisters took turns calling Red and DeeDee, and they grew more anxious as a day passed and then another without a word from either one of them.

They considered asking the Everett police to make a "check on the welfare of" the elderly couple but decided not to embarrass them. Red would be angry, and their mother would be humiliated.

Lori and Susan drove by the mobile home but saw nothing suspicious, other than that the lights were out. DeeDee's daughters called her several times a day, and when there was no answer, they figured that the older couple were probably shopping or visiting friends and had not yet figured out how to set up the new answering machine.

It was still September, their family's unlucky month, and neither Lori nor Susan could find many more simple reasons for why their mother hadn't gotten in touch with them.

On the morning of September 28, the sisters talked to each other, and when they learned that neither had heard a word from their mother, Lori decided she had better go by the mobile home to make sure everything was okay.

At the same time, she dreaded it. DeeDee had never been gone so long without letting her or Susan know where she was. Lori was afraid of what she might find.

But then she rationalized again that with Joey and Holly visiting, they probably were all going on day trips that extended far into the evening. It was no wonder Lori couldn't catch them at home.

Lori's neighbor called her on that strange and horrible day in September and asked if Lori could take her and her dog to the vet's, and she said she would. She felt relieved at the delay. What was it that she was afraid to find? She wouldn't allow her mind to go there.

After Lori dropped off her friend, she drove toward her mother's place. She turned slowly onto the lane where her mother's mobile home was located on 84th Street.

"I saw that their car wasn't there, and my heart sank," Lori Jane recalled. "I tried the back door, and it opened easily. It wasn't locked. I called out her name, and she didn't answer. I noticed that the bedroom door was closed. I opened it just a little, and I could see Mom sleeping under a comforter. But there were no sheets on the bed, and I could smell the blood. I could see her elbow, and I called her name, but she didn't answer—and then I knew she wasn't asleep."

Even in her shock, Lori Jane knew her mother's bedroom was now a crime scene and that she should not touch anything.

Numb, she picked up the phone and called 911. It seemed only five minutes or so passed before Everett police squad cars pulled into her mother's driveway, followed by an unmarked car from a detective unit.

Frostie, DeeDee's dog, had run into the master bedroom when Lori opened the door, and he refused to leave his mistress's side. The police helped corral the small dog.

In a daze, Lori barely heard the officer's questions.

"She was single . . . married?" a male voice kept repeating.

"She's married," Lori finally managed to answer. "To Red Pedersen."

"Think he did this?"

"Red? No! Red would have died protecting my mother. He's an ex-marine."

And suddenly, Lori realized that was true. Red would have given his life to save her mother. He might call her demeaning names and tease her, but he loved her.

But where was he? The patrolmen searched every inch of the mobile home. Red was not there. Both he and his car—a 2010 Jeep—were gone.

Lori explained the recent household setup to Detective Sergeant Gary Woodburn. DeeDee and Red usually lived alone, but Red's only son and his girlfriend had come up for a visit. "I think they're still here—or they've just left."

Joey didn't have a car; the couple had come from Oregon by bus. While they were in Everett, Joey had driven Red and DeeDee's car.

The last time Lori Jane had talked to her mother, DeeDee had said that Red was planning to drive Joey and Holly to the bus station in Everett the next day or the day after.

Lori told Detective Sergeant Woodburn that Joey had recently been released from the Oregon state prison on parole. Woodburn perked up at that.

The police had three good suspects in Leslie Mae Sudds Nemitz Danner Pedersen's murder.

And all of them were missing.

The Snohomish County medical examiner's office was informed by Everett Police Detective Sergeant Woodburn at approximately 6 P.M. on September 28 that there appeared to have been a murder in the mobile-home park.

Woodburn had arrived to find an elderly Caucasian woman lying on her left side in the back bedroom. She wore a blue denim blouse and capri pants. Her feet were bare, and there was duct tape hanging from her ankles. She had several purpling bruises in her neck region—but strangulation was not the cause of her death.

There were at least two large, gaping incised wounds on her neck. The forensic examiner later would determine that the mechanism of death was the right jugular vein's being severed. The victim then bled to death. The knife wounds were what had killed her. There were no sheets on the bed, only a bare mattress. That was soaked with a dark magenta liquid: drying blood.

Woodburn put out a wants-and-warrants for Red's vehicle, a 2010 black Jeep Patriot with Washington plates, license number ABZ7996. The front license plate was a U.S. Marine Corps plate. If spotted by law officers, the driver and any passengers were to be held until the Washington State detectives arrived.

On September 29, 2011, police in Corvallis, Oregon, recovered a backpack from a garbage can in a park. Inside the backpack, the officers found four credit cards—three belonged to Red, one to DeeDee. There was also bloody man's clothing and a Ka-Bar fighting knife.

The Kershaw Ka-Bar knife matched the kind of weapon that had been used to slice DeeDee's throat. Investigators knew that Red had a knife like that, but it would be a stretch to say it was the same one that Red owned.

Whatever had transpired in the Pedersen trailer in Washington was still not clear. DeeDee Pedersen was the only known victim, while Red was a missing person. Was Red a hapless victim, or was he involved in the murder of his wife?

Both Holly and Joey had long records, but Red appeared to be a law-abiding citizen. By all accounts, he loved DeeDee and treated her well. But detectives could not rule anything out—not until they found Red, dead or alive.

Investigators had few facts, and they were certain of only one thing: the suspects had to be stopped before they hurt someone else.


On Saturday morning, October 1, 2011, Susan Stewart hugged her nineteen-year-old son, Cody, and they said to each other what they always said: "I love you."

Cody Faye Myers was excited about going to the annual jazz festival held in Newport, a coastal town in

Lincoln County, Oregon, and a popular tourist destination dubbed the "Dungeness Crab Capital of the World."

The "Jazz at Newport" festival was celebrating its eighth year, and its organizers, the Oregon Coast Council for the Arts, proudly showcased world-class jazz. The festival attracted the most talented musicians from all over the state and beyond, and Cody was looking forward to the performances.

Cody drove away from his Lafayette, Oregon, home in his white 1999 Plymouth Breeze, headed southwest toward the Pacific Ocean. Lafayette, near the larger and better-known city of McMinnville, was about an eighty-mile drive from Newport, and Cody could expect to arrive at the festival within two hours.

Cody loved music. The teenager was making plans for his future—a future he was sure would include music. He hoped to be a concert jazz guitarist, and he practiced every chance he got.

Susan encouraged her firstborn son. In fact, she bought him his first guitar when he turned fourteen. He hadn't asked for it and seemed a little perplexed by the gift, but he smiled at his mother and thanked her. The guitar was set aside until a musically inclined uncle visited, bringing his own guitar along. He showed Cody a few chords, and the teen was hooked.

Everyone was impressed by how fast Cody took to the guitar. After a few months, he was playing as if he had been strumming for years.

Susan wasn't surprised to see how quickly Cody mastered the instrument. The kid had always been exceptional, and his mother sensed that from the start. "I fell in love with him from the moment I was pregnant with him," she said.

Born on April 24, 1992, Cody Myers was a happy baby. His mother noticed his intelligence early on. At age two, he took a pile of Legos and created a structure that rivaled those built by children far older.

He had the potential to become an engineer or an architect or just about anything else he wanted to be. In addition to hoping for a career in music, Cody was drawn to another vocation. He seriously considered becoming a minister.

He was a devout Christian who was active in his church, and he loved people. He was also considering the possibility of becoming a missionary so that he could both help people and travel the world.

But Cody was only nineteen, his future not cast in concrete. He had every reason to believe that there would be plenty of time to decide.

Though Cody was close to his mother, he was no mama's boy. He was a tall, strong young man and quite independent. His mother worried, as most mothers do, and she was horrified to learn that he had once slept on a bench in Portland when a night out grew too late for him to find a decent place to stay.

He was also known to spend the night in a sleeping bag

on the Clackamas Community College campus. It was an hour's drive from his home to the school, and Cody slept on the grounds on nights he had lingered too long practicing his music and did not want to risk being late to class the next day.

At six foot three and 220 pounds, Cody felt he could take care of himself. Few predators would choose to tangle with anyone Cody's size. He thought his mother worried too much, but he humored her, and he checked in with her regularly when he was away.

Cody was expected to return from the festival on Saturday night, and his mother brushed aside her worries as it grew late and he had not returned. He was a considerate kid, and it was not like him to forget to check in with her if he was going to be delayed. He didn't answer his cell phone, but Susan knew that could mean he was out of range, or perhaps the phone battery was dead.

Susan went to sleep, confident that she would wake the next morning to find her son home. When she heard his alarm blaring at 10:30 A.M., she figured he was ignoring it, sleeping in after a late night out.

She went to wake him and found his bed empty. She pushed down her panic, forcing herself to consider all the logical reasons Cody had not returned. His car could have broken down, or maybe he had run into friends and lost track of time. Still, as the agonizing hours slid by and there was no word from him, Susan was sick with worry.

Her biggest concern was that Cody had been in a bad

car accident. Frantic, she phoned all of the hospitals between the Lafayette and Newport areas. Cody hadn't been admitted to any of them.

Susan even called the jails, though she knew it was highly unlikely that he could have been arrested. Still, it would have been a relief to find he had been. Anything was better than what she feared.

When Susan heard a knock at her front door, she opened it and immediately slammed it in the face of a startled deputy. The sight of the man in blue had turned her blood cold. "I thought he was there to tell me that Cody had been in an accident," she said.

Susan did not want to hear the bad news she was sure the deputy was there to tell her, but she worked up the courage to open the door again. The officer, however, was not there for the reason Susan thought. He was looking for Cody. He told her Cody was suspected of serious criminal activity. Not only had his car been spotted moving erratically down the freeway, but its license number had also been caught by the surveillance camera of a Salem convenience store—the apparent getaway vehicle for someone who had tried to use a stolen credit card. The police suspected Cody.

"I stood on the porch and argued with him for half an hour," Susan says.

She tried to tell the officer that Cody was missing and that if there was any illegal activity, then he was the victim, not the perpetrator.

The deputy offered her reasons for why her son might have turned to a petty crime. He suggested that Cody might have met a girl at the jazz festival who influenced him to walk on the wild side with her.

But Susan shook her head, adamant that Cody could not be involved. No, she told the officer. That was simply not possible. She knew her son. He would never have gone willingly with the sort of people who would commit crimes.

What came next was the kind of nightmare that no mother should have to live through. The media had jumped on the story of runaway homicide suspects Joey Pedersen and Holly Grigsby, and their faces flashed across TV screens as Susan Stewart watched in shock.

Was the fate of her son in the hands of dangerous fugitives who had murdered an elderly woman?

While security cameras had captured the pair with Cody's car, the teenager himself was nowhere to be seen. It did not look good for him. The mother, sister, and three brothers who loved Cody so dearly were not alone in their affection for him. He had many friends and relatives who prayed for his safe return. He was a good guy, and people liked him. Maybe he had managed to charm the cold-hearted pair. Maybe he was simply a hostage.

But the story of the beloved musician who was kind to everyone ended tragically. On October 5, 2011, he was found in a wooded area near Corvallis, fatally shot in the chest and head, most likely killed the day he went missing.

Susan Stewart has yet to hear the truth about her son's encounter with Holly Grigsby and Joey Pedersen. The story shifted, and the "facts" changed, depending on the whims of the convicts—the only two people left alive who truly know what happened.

Some of it makes sense to Susan. Holly approached Cody and asked him for a ride. The boy did not hesitate to help her and her tattooed boyfriend.

Everyone said that was just like Cody. He'd help anyone who needed it. Of course he agreed to give them a ride. Susan does not dispute that part of the story.

But she still questions the killers' claims that Cody fought them for his car after he had been taken by gunpoint to a secluded area. Cody would have been just fine, his killers insisted, if he had just let them drive away in peace. According to them, their unarmed captive dove through the driver's-side window to try to prevent them from leaving.

They almost made it sound like self-defense. But Cody was levelheaded; there was no way he would have done such a foolhardy thing.

On another occasion, Susan noted, the killers had confessed that they had planned to murder all their victims, leaving no witnesses along their wicked trail.

And yet another reason given for the bloodshed was so heartless that every decent human being who heard it was stunned. White supremacists Joey Pedersen and Holly Grigsby proudly declared that they were on a mission of hate, with a goal of obliterating those whose genetic makeup or religious faith did not meet their perceived standards of superiority.

Cody was murdered because "Myers sounds like a Jewish name," the killers explained.

The name Myers, in fact, is not a Jewish name but originates from the ancient Anglo-Saxons of England. But that is beside the point. The murder was senseless no matter the roots or race of the victim.

In still another contradiction, Holly Grigsby told a reporter for the Marysville, California, *Appeal-Democrat* that the media had gotten it wrong. They hadn't known his name until after they had killed him and looked in his wallet. They could only hope, she said, there was a reason he deserved to be killed.

When Cody was murdered, his loss caused immeasurable emotional pain. Sadly, the fugitives were not finished, and they soon encountered another kind soul with a heart as big as Cody's.

Reginald Alan Clark, fifty-three, had lived in Eureka, California, since he moved from Chicago in the 1980s. Born into a big family with twelve brothers and sisters, he learned early on how to get along with people, and he made new friends everywhere he went. Forever smiling and cracking jokes, he instantly put people at ease.

According to his friends, he was a gentleman, who was always willing to help someone in need. "Kids loved him," Tim Guyette told Patrick Fealey, a reporter for *The*

*North Coast Journal* weekly. "He was gentle and respectful around women. He never cussed in front of a woman."

It was not just his friends who loved him; Reginald was also adored by his fiancée and her children. He had helped to raise her kids, and they considered him a father figure.

His many nieces and nephews looked up to him, and one niece remembers that when she was six years old, Uncle Reggie had spent days looking for the very Barbie doll she wanted, after he saw her crying because her mother would not buy it for her.

Reginald had had some rough spots in his life. He wore a pacemaker because of a heart defect, and he had been homeless for a while. One winter, he slept in a friend's truck, but he still managed to keep himself clean, and he always looked well groomed.

Despite his own troubles, he was generous to others. Once, when he heard that a friend was broke, he handed him forty bucks and told him to keep it.

A hard worker, Reginald had held a variety of jobs, including a stint washing pots and pans at St. Vincent De Paul. He was trying to better himself, and in the fall of 2011, he was making plans to go to truck-driving school.

Reginald was optimistic about his future, but his dreams were dashed when he crossed paths with Joey Pedersen and Holly Grigsby.

At about 10:30 P.M. on October 4, Holly approached Reginald outside a Winco Foods, a grocery store in

Eureka, and asked if he would give her and Joey a ride. True to his character, Reginald did not hesitate. It was his last kind act.

Joey and Holly climbed into Reginald's truck—a 1989 Ford. Reginald had had the truck just two weeks, after saving up for a year and a half for the one-thousand-dollar down payment.

Joey shot Reginald in the back of his head, and then he left his body in the truck he had been so proud of.

On Wednesday afternoon on October 5, California Highway Patrol Officer Terry Uhrich, forty-two, was on a routine patrol in the Yuba County foothills when he heard the dispatchers announce a 187—police slang for murder.

"I didn't pay that much attention," says Uhrich, explaining that the message was for I-5 patrol units about a hundred miles away. They shared the same radio frequency, so officers often overheard announcements for faraway units.

The "be on the lookout" (BOLO) specified a white car with Oregon plates and two occupants—a male and a female.

A short while later, as Uhrich drove along a quiet road, he noticed a white Plymouth Breeze pulled over, with a young female standing beside it. Three of the doors were open, and the officer noticed that the car was cluttered with junk.

Uhrich pulled up next to the car and asked, "Is everything okay?"

"I'm just stretching," the woman replied.

It was not unusual to find people living in their cars in this area, and he figured she was just another person down on her luck.

Uhrich drove away, but it suddenly dawned on him that the Plymouth had orange plates. He knew that Oregon license plates were orange, and he remembered the BOLO he had overheard. He had not seen a male—only the lone female standing outside the car. As he turned his car around, Uhrich called dispatch and asked for a repeat of the license number.

The white Plymouth was on the move, and he followed a safe distance behind, as the license number was confirmed. He felt a rush of adrenaline as he realized that this was the murder suspects' car.

For nearly three miles, Uhrich tailed the vehicle. They were headed in the direction of the backup patrol car, so he waited before he finally activated his rotating lights and pulled over the suspect car.

Waiting for backup, he stayed seated for the longest three and a half minutes of his life. "It felt like three and a half hours," he confides.

The patrol car was parked a few feet away from the suspects' car. The male, who had apparently ducked down when Uhrich had first approached the Plymouth, now called out, "What's this about?"

"Stay in your car," Uhrich answered. The officer's hand was on his gun, prepared to shoot if necessary. "I was ready," he remembers. "If it was going to go down, I was ready."

Uhrich did not know the suspects were white supremacists Joey Pedersen and Holly Grigsby. And he did not know that Holly had a .22 between her legs and that she turned to Joey and said, "Let's shoot him."

Joey took one look at the hairless Uhrich and said, "No, he is one of us."

"I'm bald and I blame my grandfather for that," Uhrich now jokes.

To Pedersen, the officer looked like a skinhead—a racist who had shaved his head to make a statement.

Uhrich's grandfather had passed on what had seemed like some undesirable genes, but in this instance it was a blessing. It prevented a shoot-out that could have left Uhrich wounded, dead, or with blood on his hands. The last thing he wanted to do was to shoot someone.

"I did not take my eyes off of them," Uhrich explains. He was aware of their every movement, and when the two began kissing, he wondered if they were preparing to go down in a blaze of gunfire.

When Uhrich's backup arrived, Joey and Holly were arrested without incident. The suspects were separated, and Holly rode in the back of Uhrich's patrol car. He had been instructed not to "Mirandarize" or speak to the suspects.

Uhrich flicked on the radio, and Holly immediately

began to sing along with Zac Brown's country-western tune, "Not a Worry in the World," a song about sitting on the beach, carefree and drinking beer. It was a tragic irony, considering that the place where Holly was headed was nothing like the beach.

Holly Grigsby was later videotaped as she gave a shocking five-hour interview. The investigators in three states had always considered Holly as a ride-along, not a partner in crime.

Though rare, females participating in bloody crime sprees are not unheard of. Bonnie Parker—of the infamous Bonnie and Clyde—certainly was an active participant in the pair's bloody wanderings across America. In more recent times, there have been cases where the female half of a couple joined in the actual violence.

Holly Grigsby spoke in a flat voice as she explained, "We came up from Oregon to kill Joey's father and to steal from him."

Joey had told her that his father was wealthy and stressed that there was no reason they had to be poor and go without. They needed to fund their "project." They didn't even have a car, when his father had everything.

Once they arrived in Everett, Joey had modified his plans. He had to pick the right time and place to kill his father and, of course, his stepmother, DeeDee, too. They couldn't leave a witness behind.

Joey decided to strike when Red drove them to the bus station in Everett for their trip back to Oregon.

"The old man will be in the driver's seat," Joey told Holly. "And you will be beside him in the front passenger seat. I'll be behind him, and I will shoot him in the back of the head, see? Once he's dead, you will take control of the car."

Holly began to ask how she could manage to get over Red's body, seize the steering wheel, and straighten out the car. "What if we have an accident?"

"You will figure it out. Just do it."

The Oregon detectives listened as Holly calmly told them that she and Joey had stolen numerous items from the mobile home, everything of possible value, including Red's 2010 black Jeep Patriot.

She didn't say whether the thefts occurred before Red's murder or afterward, when they had returned to their victims' mobile home.

The detectives felt sure that Joey had murdered DeeDee, but when they brought this up, Holly interrupted them.

"No," she said. "I'm the one who duct-taped her—around her mouth, wrists, and ankles."

That seemed almost impossible, but her next revelation was even more startling: "I killed her—with two different knives."

Holly confessed to the detectives that she and Joey were also responsible for a murder in Oregon. They had killed the "kid," she told them.

"Why?" they asked her.

"Because Myers sounded like a Jewish name," she replied matter-of-factly. "When we were arrested, we were on our way to Sacramento to kill more Jews."

The killers were like a pair of mad dogs on the loose, frothing with hatred for anyone they perceived as different, their rage exacerbated with each kill.

Holly told the Oregon State Police where they could find Red Pedersen's body. The victim and his vehicle had been dumped in a wooded area about sixteen miles east of Sweet Home, Oregon. The investigators followed Holly's directions and found the Jeep near a logging road in the Yellowbottom Campground area north of Green Peter Lake.

The Jeep had been pushed off a gravel road and down a precipitous embankment. Once they managed to climb down the steep incline and look inside, the mystery of Red Pedersen's whereabouts was solved. His body was inside, with a single bullet wound in the back of his head just behind his right ear. A sign pinned to Red's shirt read, "Child Molester."

Red's remains had been found about a hundred miles away from the Newport jazz festival. Early news reports had indicated that Cody Myers had met his killers in the coastal town. Investigators made a public request, asking to see any photos or videos taken at the jazz festival during the weekend of October 1, in hopes that images of the victim or his killers might have been recorded.

But from a geographical standpoint, it made more

# A ROAD TRIP TO MURDER

DeeDee with her first husband, Richard Nemitz, at their wedding in 1961. (*Nemitz family*)

DeeDee with her daughters Lori (left) and Susan, in the late 1960s. (*Nemitz family*)

DeeDee in the 1980s. Life was not always easy for her, but she was optimistic about the future. (*Nemitz family*)

Though she was a down-to-earth lady, when she hit middle age, DeeDee had some glamour shots taken just for fun. (*Nemitz family*)

Red Pedersen was good to DeeDee, and she had no idea her husband had a shadowy past that would come back to haunt them. (*Nemitz family*)

Red Pedersen mellowed with age, but when he was younger, he terrified his children. He never dreamed his son would one day seek revenge. (*Nemitz family*)

Joey Pedersen was filled with hate, and he took his anger out on innocent people. (*Author's collection*)

People said that Joey was a nice little boy, but when he entered adult prison as a teen, he learned to hate. (*Author's collection*)

Holly Grigsby, pictured in a mug shot, liked bad boys so much that she followed one to the gates of hell. (*Author's collection*)

Judges got tired of seeing Holly Grigsby appear before them, in trouble again, because of a man. In this mug shot, she appears to be a bit tired of the process herself. (*Author's collection*)

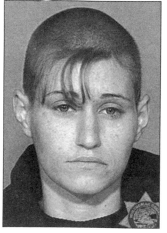

Sporting a female skinhead cut in this mug shot, Holly was proud of her racism and she would kill to prove it. (*Author's collection*)

Cody Myers never hesitated to help someone in need. Sadly, a good deed turned tragic when he met evil on the road. (*Susan Stewart*)

Cody with his brothers. They were very close, and they miss him desperately. (*Susan Stewart*)

Holly Grigsby's scrapbook gave the impression she was happy with her husband and baby. But when she was mesmerized by darkness, she threw it all away. (*Komo News*)

Reginald Alan Clark cared about people and went out of his way to help them. When the strangers asked him for a ride, he did not hesitate to help. (*Author's collection*)

After Reginald Clark was murdered, some wondered if Holly Grigsby could be the next woman to face the death penalty in California. Louise Peete, pictured in this mug shot, was among those who were sentenced to die in the Golden State. (*Author's collection*)

Barbara Graham died in the gas chamber, leaving behind a young son, Tommy. There was a chance that Holly Grigsby could face the same fate, leaving her son behind in a tragic repeat of history. (*Author's collection*)

California Highway Patrol Officer Terry Uhrich was credited with nabbing two of the Northwest's most dangerous killers. (*Uhrich family*)

sense that the young man had met the dangerous couple in Corvallis. When Cody left his home in Lafayette on Saturday morning, he probably traveled south on Highway 99W. It was the logical route for his journey. Halfway there, he would have arrived in Corvallis and then taken U.S. Route 20 to Newport. As the midway point, Corvallis was the most likely spot to stop for gas or a snack.

It was also the same city where the backpack with the bloody clothing, knife, and stolen credit cards had been found in the park trash on September 29.

It was easy to see how Pedersen and Grigsby could have ended up in Corvallis. If they'd hitched a ride headed out of the Green Peter Lake area after dumping Red, it was a straightforward fifty-mile trip to Corvallis.

Corvallis is a college town, home to Oregon State University. The killers may have hung out in the city for a couple of days, and if Joey wore the turtleneck shirt that covered his tattoos, they could have easily blended in with the hundreds of students who roamed the streets there. A couple of bedraggled young people with backpacks would not have stood out.

On October 8, Joey Pedersen initiated contact with the police in Yuba City, California. Three days in a jail cell had evidently made him much more eager to talk about what had transpired in the twelve days since September 26.

Maybe he was jealous that Holly was getting all the

publicity when he was the one who had planned all the crimes. Perhaps he regretted what he had done—which seemed hardly likely, particularly when he wanted to tell Yuba City detectives about a fourth murder victim.

Joey said it had occurred in Humboldt County in Eureka, California. This victim hadn't had anything that Joey wanted. Joey killed him because he hated him—though he did not even *know* him. The victim was African-American. That, of course, made him a prime target for violent racists Holly and Joey.

The Yuba City police called detectives in Humboldt County and asked if they had any recent murders with an MO similar to Joey's crimes.

They did. Reginald Alan Clark had been recently discovered, shot to death beneath a pile of clothes inside his blue 1989 Ford F-150 pickup.

On October 9, Joey Pedersen summoned a reporter from a local paper and held an abbreviated press conference.

He wanted to be sure that everyone knew that Holly Grigsby had nothing to do with his crimes and that he was solely responsible.

It was not the first time he had shown concern about Holly's predicament. At the time of Joey's arrest, authorities had found a note he'd written to Holly, promising her that he would make sure that she was eliminated from suspicion.

It was yet another of his grand plans that would not pan

out as he hoped. His goal of vindicating Holly would be difficult to achieve, now that she had confessed to killing DeeDee Pedersen and participating in other murders.

Joey was showing an odd kind of gallantry, or so it seemed. He had murdered his own father and two strangers, and yet he was trying to save Holly, who had admitted to the vicious stabbing of an elderly and vulnerable woman who had shown her nothing but kindness and hospitality.

Perhaps Holly possessed all the traits a man like Joey was looking for.

Joey's white-supremacy "enterprise" called for enriching its members and associates through murder, robbery, and the use of unauthorized devices and promoting and advancing a white-supremacy movement to "purify" and "preserve" the white race and "reclaim our country and culture" through acts of murder on the basis of race, color, and perceived "degenerate" acts, including sexual abuse, vagrancy, drug abuse, and other "riffraff."

Members were also instructed to target Jewish leaders and others of the Jewish faith. All through their "by-laws," the word *murder* was the first suggestion. It was an ugly, hate-filled document but one that people like Joey and Holly adhered to.

Given Joey's preferences, who knew how many bodies were yet to be discovered out there in the forest that was now ablaze with orange vine maples, red sumac, red kinnikinnick, and yellow poplars? The weather would soon grow cold, there would be snow in the higher elevations, and finding hidden bodies would be next to impossible.

The investigators felt a sense of urgency.

Back in Everett, a "celebration of life" was held for DeeDee. Many mourners attended, although few of her friends had known her as the Leslie named in the obituaries. Most people knew her as DeeDee.

"I don't think she fought Holly very hard," her daughter Susan says sadly. "Once she realized that Red wasn't coming home—ever—she didn't want to be alone again. She grieved for my dad—Leroy Danner—for a long time, and she really loved Red. She wouldn't have wanted to go on alone."

Lori Jane nods in agreement. The sisters believe it would have been very difficult for their mother to carry on with life after Red was murdered. She had lost one husband to divorce, the second to cancer, and the third to murder by his only son. If she hadn't been home that morning when Red drove Joey and Holly to the bus station, DeeDee would have survived but suffered the horror of waiting for days to learn what had happened to him, only to find out the worst of her imagining was true. The rest of her life would have been full of nightmares.

If they hadn't been stopped by Officer Terry Uhrich, at the rate Joey and Holly were cutting killing swaths through the three western states, they might have taken their places in infamy alongside Perry Smith and Richard Hickock, Bonnie Parker and Clyde Barrow, Charles Starkweather and Caril Ann Fugate, plus numerous other cross-country murderers.

The 2011 holidays approached, and the killing couple remained locked up. They had both been charged with two counts of aggravated first-degree murder. The Snohomish County prosecutor, Mark Roe, and his deputy, Craig Matheson—who would handle the prosecution in the murders of DeeDee and Red Pedersen—requested that Joey Pedersen be evaluated by a panel of forensic psychiatrists. Was he fit to stand trial? The question "Is the subject a danger to himself or others?" was deliberately excluded from this evaluation. He had already demonstrated that he was.

On January 25, 2012, three psychiatrists met David Joseph "Joey" Pedersen in a secure ward (F2) at Washington's Western State Hospital. His social worker and one of his attorneys warned him that the fruits of this intense interview would be nonconfidential, and he accepted that easily.

An attorney was at Joey's side in the room, and Joey seemed pleased when he was told that he could refuse to answer any question and also consult privately with the lawyer when he wished.

He was pleasant and agreeable—not what one might expect from a "mad-dog killer." When he gave his version of his life, the three psychiatrists noted that this was only

Joey's perspective. They knew better than to take his word as gospel.

Asked about his childhood, Joey said he had spent half of his life in prison, beginning with his first arrest when he was sixteen. "I was kept inside the joint, more or less, for the next fourteen and a half years."

He told them about his sister, Gloria, who was fifteen months older than he was. He felt he had a reasonably "intact" family when he was growing up. His father was in the Marines, and his mother did not work. "That was before women felt the need to work outside the home," Joey explained.

Asked if he or his sister was ever abused by their father, Joey said that Red had acted "in a less than ideal manner." And then he softened the vague comment even more by adding that everyone had his or her definition of abuse. Later in the interview, Joey referred to his father as a "child molester" but then refused to give any details about that.

He said that his parents were at "opposite ends of the spectrum," with his father being extremely strict and his mother very permissive.

"My parents separated when I was nine, and my sister and I went to live with my aunt, who had lots of foster children, too," Joey said. "Those were the best four years of my life."

When describing his move to his mother's home at age thirteen, Joey explained, "My mother suffered from depression all her life and also multiple personality disorder." Joey said that she had been hospitalized for inpatient psychiatric care numerous times in both Oregon and California.

"I believe she did make suicide attempts," he commented. Remembering his time with his mom in his mid-teens, he said, "She let me play hooky because she didn't want me to leave her."

Joey said the schools he went to were always too easy for him (a fact supported by his court-ordered IQ tests). He was bored in class, but he had never had the opportunity to participate in any gifted-student programs because his family was always moving to different school districts.

It was clear that Joey Pedersen considered himself superior to most other students. "In the classroom, they teach to the lowest common denominator," he said. "So I'm waiting for them to get it through some idiot's thick skull. I finally dropped out of school."

With school behind him, he worked at fast-food joints and also was employed laying carpet and doing other manual labor, all the while seething over the unfairness of it. He was superior, but no one seemed to understand that.

The attitude of superiority would escalate. (This may well have been the root cause that led him to join a white supremacists group.)

Asked about the specifics of his robbery crimes, Joey was careful about how he answered: "I pled guilty to robbing a few espresso stands, a Circle K, and a McDonald's . . . I was treated as an adult—even though it was my first arrest." His original sentence was for six years, but his prison infractions kept adding time to his sentence.

In 2012, Joey was in danger of facing "The Big Bitch." In convicts' jargon, three felonies meant life in prison. Three strikes and you're out.

It seemed a moot point; he was already facing four first-degree aggravated-murder charges. He was sentenced to six years in an adult prison when he was sixteen, but he actually more than doubled that, serving fourteen and a half years for infractions inside, including those for the assaults and his threatening letter to an Idaho judge.

For a man who bragged about how smart he was, Joey Pedersen had done some really dumb things. And paid for them. His parole in May 2011 was the first time he'd seen the world on the other side of prison bars since he was sixteen. Now he was thirty-one. He'd met Holly Grigsby soon after he was a free man. And he still pled her cause. "She shouldn't be sitting under two counts of aggravated murder," he said. "She should be at home with her kid."

Joey had never married, never had children, never served in the military; he had been incarcerated during the years when most young men laid down the foundation of their lives. Asked about any use of drugs or alcohol, he said that he'd seen his father's alcoholism, and he had vowed that he would never use drugs or alcohol.

"I tried beer once and marijuana once, but I've never used meth, cocaine, heroin, or any of that stuff."

Joey explained his multiple tattoos, including the *SWP* (Supreme White Power) across the front of his neck, a swastika on his chest, and the image of Adolf Hitler on his belly. The psychiatric team was looking for any indication that he might have mental-health issues and if there were more members of his family—other than his mother— who might be psychotic.

He denied a widespread family propensity for mental problems. Indeed, he seemed calm and cooperative in this interview, entirely appropriate in his responses, even making jokes that suited the situation. His worldview had begun to form when he was seventeen to eighteen. Joey was eager to deny that his philosophy was a concept formed because he'd joined white supremacists in prison as a means of survival. He refused to be seen as a "simplistic stereotype."

If he had to label what his beliefs were, Pedersen said that the right answer would be "white racialism."

"I see everything as a battle—and race is paramount. I see our culture as Europeans being threatened."

Joey Pedersen's philosophies were disturbing, but his intelligence was apparent to the staff in Ward F2 and also to the forensic psychiatric panel. His overall IQ was 107, in the high normal range. His vocabulary was impressive for a man who had been in prison since he was a teenager. He spoke with a fluidity and grasp of the English language that many college graduates don't have.

He obviously enjoyed being at center stage and fencing with his audience.

One of the psychiatrists felt that while Joey was not insane—medically or legally—he was suffering from at least two personality disorders: anxiety disorder and anti-social disorder. Joey denied any major psychiatric symptoms. He was, according to the panel, "well organized and reality based."

Joey Pedersen attended every ward group offered, and he was popular with the staff, flirting with female guards as he sought more food or treats. He was polite and could be wickedly humorous; it became difficult to picture Joey as a roving killer when he presented as such an affable, bright, cooperative prisoner.

But he was the epitome of a sociopath. Like a chameleon, he could assimilate the personality that would do him the greatest good at any particular time. And this would allow him to maintain his need to appear perfectly sane and in control.

Joey requested a visit from his mother, who still lived in Oregon. "I'm going to death row," he said calmly. "I'm indifferent to being executed. Seeing Mom is for her to have a last hug. I saw her and hugged her in August 2011 after I got out of prison."

His request was denied.

Joey Pedersen's racism was twisted. He said he had no regrets whatsoever about the people he had killed. He was disappointed only that he hadn't made it to Sacramento, where he'd intended to kill more Jews.

"I have no intention of using an excuse that I was an abused child to beg for leniency," Joey said firmly. "I know what I did, and I have no regrets. I did what had to be done, and there's no changing the facts. I killed those people, and they needed to be killed."

According to Joey, his father truly deserved it because he was a "child molester," and his stepmother, DeeDee, did nothing to mitigate Red Pedersen's behavior.

That made little sense. By the time Red married DeeDee, Joey was grown and serving time in prison. She hadn't even met Joey until he showed up with his plan to murder them.

Furthermore, he had denied being abused in his childhood, other than to say that Red's behavior was "less than ideal."

He commented that the "criminal class" generally didn't take responsibility for their actions, but he wasn't like that. "I'm not going to try to weasel out of it. I act on my convictions, and I'm not going to shame myself by begging for leniency."

Joey did acknowledge that he had suffered from anxiety since he was sixteen, but fifty milligrams a day of Zoloft helped calm that, and he now had periods of heightened anxiety only once every few months.

Asked if he minded that his two attorneys were Jewish and that the psychiatric panel members were Hispanic, African-American, Asian, and Portuguese, Joey shrugged. It didn't matter to him, as long as they did a good job for him and were fair.

Many of the staffers in his ward were members of the races he claimed to hate, and he got along well with them.

Initially, staff notes said he had tended to stay away from African-American inmates and security officers, but that ended after a week, and he currently joked with them and seemed very comfortable.

Exactly who was David Joseph Pedersen? It's likely that even he didn't know the answer to that. Apparently raised by an angry father and a psychotic mother, he spent the entire second half of his life in prison. He was gripped by anxiety but brushed that aside. He was clearly full of rage, misdirected as it was.

The suspects were behind bars, but there was a lot of work ahead for prosecutors, who would fight to be sure that they would never be released to kill again.

The four homicides were committed in three different states, and numerous other laws had been broken as the suspects traveled hundreds of miles down the West Coast in their deadly quest. If each crime was to be prosecuted in a separate jurisdiction, it could take many years before a resolution was reached.

The wheels of justice were already grinding in Washington State, with Snohomish County prosecutor Mark Roe at the helm, when the feds stepped in during the summer of 2012 to consolidate the bulk of the remaining crime charges against Grigsby and Pedersen.

In March 2012, Joey Pedersen had pled guilty to two counts of aggravated murder in his father and DeeDee's case in Snohomish County. He was sentenced to life in prison without parole.

He still faced charges for the Oregon and California cases. Holly had not yet been prosecuted in Snohomish County, and charges there against her were dropped to make way for the three-state consolidated prosecution.

Roe applauded the move by the U.S. Department of Justice and said he had pushed from the start for the case to be prosecuted at a federal level. Trials scattered across three states would not only waste taxpayer funds but would also be devastating for the families of the victims, Roe noted. He told reporters, "A three-state prosecution up and down the West Coast could take a decade or more. I can't imagine a series of more agonizing road trips for everyone involved."

Indeed, for the families of the victims, drawn-out trials requiring thousands of miles of travel and months out of their lives could be more than they could bear.

DeeDee Pedersen's daughters, Lori Jane and Susan, and Cody Myers's mother, Susan, were among the loved ones of the victims who vowed to be present in the courtroom as

Grigsby and Pedersen were brought to justice. If necessary, they would have gone any distance and spent any amount of time to honor DeeDee and Cody with their presence in the courtroom. But it was a relief for them to know that it could all be over in one fell swoop.

The U.S. Department of Justice officially took over the prosecutions of Grigsby and Pedersen in Portland on Friday, August 17, 2012, with the unsealing of a twenty-four-page, fifteen-count indictment.

U.S. attorney Amanda Marshall also released a statement: "The indictment in this case alleges horrendous crimes were committed as part of defendants' white supremacist campaign to kidnap and murder targets on the basis of race, color, religion and perceived 'degenerate' conduct. We hope this indictment brings the victims' families one step closer to justice."

The indictment fell under the Racketeer Influenced and Corrupt Organizations Act (RICO).

Charges included conspiracy, robbery, kidnapping, carjacking, identity theft, credit-card fraud, and, of course, murder.

There was another plus to consolidating the cases. Roe acknowledged that while the federal prosecutors would be allowed to include evidence from all four of the murders under its theory of the case, he likely would not have been allowed to tell the jury about the murders of Cody Myers and Reginald Clark, because they had occurred after the murders in Everett, Washington.

Before the federal prosecutors stepped in, however, many hours on the Pedersen and Grigsby case had been logged in courtrooms in Oregon, Washington, and, briefly, California.

Susan Stewart notes that when she first saw Holly Grigsby in the courtroom in 2011, the young woman did not seem to take the situation seriously. "She was giggling with her attorney," Susan recalls. But with each court appearance, Holly grew more somber. It was as if the hazy world created by drugs was wearing off, and she was beginning to be aware of the awfulness of her actions.

Eventually, Holly began to lift her chin and look directly at Susan. Holly's eyes were filled with sadness. She appeared remorseful, and Susan took some small comfort in that. Both were mothers of sons, and Susan believes that Holly finally began to imagine herself in Susan's shoes, how she would feel if her child were murdered.

If Holly Grigsby was indeed swept up in a foggy nightmare that overwhelmed her rationality, then her emergence from that bad dream would have been a shock.

No one can really know what went on inside Holly's head, but her relatives insisted she was not an evil person. Holly's mother, Janet Miles,* told *Oregonian* reporters, "She is a good person. I know no one will believe it now."

Her daughter's cruelty was impossible for Janet to comprehend, and she wept as she said, "I'm terribly sorry, from the bottom of my heart and soul . . . I am so so sorry for all the families."

The suspect's estranged husband, Mick Buttram, echoed Janet's comments, telling KPTV reporter Laura Rillos that Grigsby was a "really sweet, loving girl," overwhelmed by the pressure to be a good mother.

Mick acknowledged that on the surface, Joey Pedersen had appeared to be a "nice guy," and he said that he could understand how his wife might have been charmed by him. He thought Pedersen had "got into Holly's brain and convinced her he was her savior."

In the November 2011 KPTV interview, Mick shared scrapbooks created by Holly. The pages are filled with artistically placed photos of her, Mick, and their son. She had decorated the pages with stickers of hearts and stars and smiley faces.

Next to some of the photos were carefully printed words and phrases. At first glance, it appeared sweet, with phrases such as "obsessed with motherhood" and "family love." But smack in the middle of one page is the chilling phrase "Save the white race."

Still in shock over learning his estranged wife was a killer, Mick denounced her actions but said that she had given him a beautiful son and that he would always love her.

Holly Grigsby's husband brought her small son to one of the court hearings, and Mick said that their child was overjoyed to see his mother. But the toddler had started to wail as legal proceedings began, forcing them to leave.

Though he made it clear that he did not agree with the

path taken by his estranged wife, Mick Buttram remained in her corner—even when a shocking news report suggested that he, too, had been on her hit list.

Portland's KATU-TV reporter Meghan Kalkstein interviewed Mick and asked about his reaction to the jailhouse interview that his wife had given to the California newspaper the *Appeal-Democrat*. The paper quoted Grigsby: "It was my plan to go back and kidnap my son and take care of Mick, but I didn't get to do that."

Mick scoffed at that and explained that his estranged wife had had the opportunity to "take care of him" but made no move to do so. He was certain that she never had any intention of harming him.

Mick revealed that Holly showed up after the Everett murders but hadn't stayed long. He had no idea that she was in the middle of a killing spree, and he asked her if she was going to stay and visit with their son. But Holly had rushed off with no explanation.

Had Holly really been plotting to murder Mick when she stopped by his apartment? According to him, she had never planned such a thing and had probably made up the story because her feelings were hurt by something he had said to her in a phone conversation as she sat in jail. He had told her that he had no respect for what she had done.

At one point during the interview with Kalkstein, Mick addressed his wife. "We've been through hell, Holly," he pleaded. "Just let it go." He asked that his face not be filmed during the interview, although he did allow the photos of himself in Holly's scrapbooks to be shown.

Kalkstein continued to cover the case for KATU, and she also interviewed Joey Pedersen, who sent letters to the TV station on yellow legal paper. In small handwriting, he wrote, in part, "We are sitting in cages with no means of purchasing envelopes and calling cards to contact our family and friends, or basic hygiene items such as soap and deodorant."

In his communication with KATU, Pedersen made it known that though he would not do a recorded telephone interview, he was willing to do an in-person interview—possibly a joint interview with Holly—if jailers would allow it. He added that he would like them each to be compensated one hundred dollars so that they could purchase necessities from the prison commissary.

Kalkstein made it clear that it was against KATU policy to pay for interviews and that they would definitely not compensate Joey.

It was not the last time the public would hear complaints from Pedersen and Grigsby about jail conditions.

In February 2012, while incarcerated in the Snohomish County Jail, Holly Grigsby made the news again because of a dispute over breakfast cereal.

Jailers had forbidden her access to her favorite cereal, Cocoa Puffs. The media jumped on the story, twisting headlines with the obvious play on words, "Cereal Killer," and almost gleefully using the General Mills slogan for the product as expressed by its mascot for the chocolate cereal, Sonny the Cuckoo Bird: "Cuckoo for Cocoa Puffs!"

Authorities said they had blocked Grigsby from using the commissary, where she might purchase the sugary cereal, candy, and other sweet snacks, because of her history of brewing "jailhouse hooch" or "Pruno." The alcoholic concoction requires sugar and is often made by inmates who manage to conceal it in their cells during the days it takes to ferment. Sometimes they place the mix in a plastic bag and hide it in toilet tanks.

A two-hour hearing on the cereal conflict was held in Snohomish County Superior Court. Attorneys for Grigsby and Pedersen had complained about jailhouse conditions and the fact their clients were not allowed access to the jail commissary. Grigsby's attorney, Pete Mazzone, argued that it was against her constitutional rights to deny her access to the commissary.

A judge ruled against the inmates.

In December 2012, Holly Grigsby became the subject of yet another bizarre news story when she became involved with high-profile inmate Andrew Barnett.

Barnett was Holly's type of guy, a bad boy with obvious intelligence but misplaced loyalties. Andy Barnett and Joey Pedersen were both very angry young men. They were the same age, born a few months apart. Instead of using their brains to move their lives forward in a positive way, their schemes just drove them deeper into pits they could not crawl out of.

Andrew Laud Barnett, born in 1980, had had trouble with the law since his teens. He had felony convictions for third-degree robbery, first-degree burglary, and theft of a vehicle. Convictions also included a 2004 assault of a corrections officer.

In January 2008, Barnett was incarcerated at the Oregon State Penitentiary in Salem, serving a seven-year sentence for assault, when he found a way to make more trouble.

The Oregon state penitentiary is the state's only maximum-security prison, yet Barnett, who was twenty-seven at the time, managed to send a letter to the Washington County Sheriff's Office, threatening the lives of the sheriff and three deputies.

Then, in August 2011, while awaiting trial proceedings for the 2008 case, he threw a container holding a mixture of feces and urine into the face of a Multnomah County deputy.

He was awaiting trial in April 2012 for both the 2008 and 2011 cases when he mailed yet another threatening letter, this time to the federal prosecutor who was prosecuting the previous two cases. The envelope held a white powder that the letter indicated was anthrax. The letter read, in part:

> *I want things in life.*
> *1. I want you gone!!!*
> *2. To see Pink Floyd live!!!*
> *3. I want to lean [sic] VOODOO.*

The receptionist at the U.S. Attorney's office routinely opened the mail there, and when she opened the envelope, the fine white powder tucked inside filled the air, and she accidentally inhaled it.

Hazardous-materials personnel were rushed to the courthouse to investigate. Paramedics cared for the terrified woman, who suffered hours of emotional trauma before the powder was identified. It was not anthrax. It was a penicillin-based antibiotic that had been ground into a powder.

It was a relief, of course, but the receptionist reportedly now suffers from post-traumatic stress disorder and is afraid to open mail.

Andrew Barnett was moved to the Columbia County Jail in St. Helens, Oregon. Because he was representing himself in the federal charges for the anthrax hoax, he was given access to the jail library, a room with three aisles of general books and one aisle of law books.

Inside the library, Andrew discovered an air vent that connected to the women's housing unit in the next room. He managed to contact Holly Grigsby by shouting through the vent.

The two began communicating through letters hidden inside books in the library. The scheme included marking books with stars, other symbols, and numeric codes, so that Holly could locate the ones with the clandestine letters inside.

In November 2012, a jailer found a four-page letter

concealed in one of the books. The "love letter" to Holly was allegedly "vulgar" and sexually explicit and also contained rants about an African-American judge.

It was soon discovered that at least two other inmates were using the library books for underground communication, referring to it as their "email system." The elaborate communication setup was apparently designed by Barnett.

Upon learning about the letters, prosecutors asked for a hearing before Senior U.S. District Judge Ancer L. Haggerty, and they argued that because Barnett had abused his library privileges, he no longer deserved to represent himself. The suspect, they said, would find and exploit another loophole if he were allowed free rein.

Barnett told the judge that Holly Grigsby had typed up a recent court motion for him. "I don't consider my constitutional rights a loophole," he said. "Cutting off my law library privileges—that's cutting me off from Holly Grigsby. That's the only way I can communicate with her."

Haggerty ruled that Barnett could continue to represent himself.

The authorities relocated the jail's law library, putting an end to the vent communications. The jail library rules became stricter, so that only law books were accessible via the library. All other books were made available only through the cart that was pushed from cell to cell.

Andrew Barnett was convicted for sending the death

threats and throwing the foul mixture at the deputy. Without the added crimes, he could have walked out of prison a free man in May 2015. The new convictions added five years and three months to his sentence.

He was allowed to write only with a special pencil with a distinctive orange lead. Should anyone else receive an anonymous threatening letter from Barnett, the orange writing would lead straight to him.

The clandestine romance between two of the state's most controversial convicts was delectable fodder for the media, and once again, the story made newspaper headlines and television news.

While a lot of noise was made over smuggled letters and forbidden breakfast cereal, there were far bigger legal concerns for Joey Pedersen and Holly Grigsby.

The question of the death penalty had been looming since the moment the two were arrested and was a troublesome one for both the prosecution and the defense. California, Oregon, and Washington are among the thirty-two states that allow capital punishment, and there was the very real possibility that Pedersen and Grigsby would pay for their violent crimes with their lives.

In California, the condemned inmate can choose between lethal injection and lethal gas at the San Quentin state prison. If a decision is not made in writing within ten days of being served with the warrant for execution, then the death penalty is carried out via lethal injection. California's death row is the largest in the country, with more than seven hundred condemned prisoners currently waiting to face death.

In Washington, inmates are given a choice between hanging and lethal injection. (Washington is one of three states that still executes by hanging. The other two are Delaware and New Hampshire.) If no choice is made, the condemned will die by lethal injection. Since 1904, sixty-six Caucasians, seven African-Americans, two Asians, two Hispanics, and one native Alaskan have been executed in Washington.

Condemned inmates in Oregon are executed via lethal injection, with no other choice offered to them. Since 1904, sixty men have met their deaths by execution at the Oregon State Penitentiary in Salem. They were fifty-six Caucasian, one Native American, and three African-American men.

Joey Pedersen was full of bravado in the spring of 2012 when *Oregonian* reporter Lynne Terry asked him about the possibility of the death penalty.

"How do you not kill a Joey Pedersen?" Pedersen asked, referring to himself in the third person. "I want to get the show on the road. If they're going to kill me, get the rope out already."

Pedersen had admitted many times to committing the four murders. But he had not been consistent. In October 2011, in court in Everett, Washington, both Pedersen and Grigsby entered pleas of not guilty for the murders of Red and DeeDee. Even when Pedersen displayed a cavalier attitude about the prospect of his own death, his attorneys fought for him.

Snohomish County prosecutor Mark Roe had his work cut out for him, and he carefully plotted his strategy. It was decided that Grigsby and Pedersen would be tried separately, with Pedersen facing charges first.

The question of capital punishment weighed on Roe, and he did not take it lightly. He was no stranger to the issues of the death penalty. He had been on the team that prosecuted James Homer Elledge, a janitor at a Lynnwood, Washington, church. Convicted of murder in 1975 and in and out of prison until he murdered Eloise Fitzner, forty-seven, in the church basement in 1998, his conscience haunted him, and he begged to be executed. Elledge got his wish; he was executed in Walla Walla by lethal injection on the morning of August 28, 2001.

When prison guard Jayme Biendl, thirty-four, was slain in the prison chapel in Monroe, Washington, in January 2011, it was Mark Roe who prosecuted killer Byron Scherf and made the decision to seek the death penalty. Scherf, fifty-two, was a convicted rapist, serving life in prison without the possibility of parole, when he ambushed and strangled the female guard he outweighed by one hundred pounds.

It took jurors less than three hours to decide that Scherf should die. It had taken them less than half an hour to convict him.

Would jurors be so quick to condemn Joey Pedersen to

death? Roe didn't think so. While the veteran prosecutor believed that the death penalty was an appropriate punishment for the heartless murders, he knew that the mitigating circumstances in the Snohomish case could tilt the decision in favor of the defense.

Roe was concerned with the allegations of abuse that Joey said he and his sister had suffered at the hands of their father. In a statement released on March 12, 2012, Roe said:

> The police investigation revealed that many years ago when his children were young, the late David Pedersen engaged in child abuse. Significant, credible evidence exists that he engaged in multiple acts of child sexual abuse, victimizing his own children, and others. The defendant has repeatedly confessed to killing his father, and cited some of that abuse as a reason why. Whether that was his true, sole or only motivation is less certain, but what is certain is that any jury considering his fate would first hear hours, days or perhaps weeks of testimony on the subject, some of it from the actual victims of the abuse.
>
> Neither my senior attorneys, I, nor members of the investigation team believe that with what a jury would hear, there is any reasonable chance of them unanimously returning with a verdict of death for this defendant. As such, I will not seek a death

sentence I believe we cannot realistically achieve, despite my feeling that such a sentence would be justified.

Mark Roe had carefully considered the feelings of Red and DeeDee's family and had met with them four times before making his decision. He addressed this in his statement:

I told surviving family and friends my decision at our most recent meeting last Tuesday. They were disappointed, but I believe understand my decision and my reasons for it. Since the public also has the right to know why I decided not to seek the death penalty for this defendant, I am issuing this press release. The family and friends of the victims have already had an opportunity to review it.

In the statement, Roe also stressed that DeeDee Pedersen had absolutely no guilt in Red's past actions:

By all accounts, Leslie Pedersen was an incredibly lovely person who hadn't harmed anyone in her entire life. She was not married to David Pedersen in his younger years, when he was raising the defendant and the defendant's sister, and was therefore in no position to either know about, or prevent the decades-ago activities of her husband, which this

murder investigation brought to light. Leslie Pedersen was not even in David Pedersen's life at the time.

Roe addressed the fact that Red Pedersen had apparently not committed any crimes in recent years:

Nothing can justify this defendant's actions, and
in fairness to the late David Pedersen, it should be
noted that no evidence has come to light of any recent wrongdoing by him.

Joey Pedersen pled guilty to two counts of aggravated
first-degree murder for the deaths of his father and stepmother.

At his sentencing in mid-March 2012, he called Roe
a coward for not pursuing the death penalty against him.

His anger toward the prosecutor, at least one reporter
speculated, might have been because he did not want to be
in the general population at the prison and had hoped for
a more comfortable cell on death row.

Joey's sister did not attend the sentencing, but she
wrote a statement that was read by a victims' advocate. It
said that she thought her brother's actions were vile and
asked the judge to show no leniency. She said she feared
her brother and believed that if he were ever freed, he
would harm others. Gloria stressed that despite the abuse
that she and her brother had suffered at the hands of their
father, it did not justify murder.

Snohomish County Superior Court Judge Linda Krese sentenced Pedersen to life in prison without parole.

He would not face the death penalty for the Washington State murders, but there was still the possibility that he could face the death penalty in Oregon and California courtrooms.

And what of Holly Grigsby? Could she face death for her cold-blooded murders?

Prosecutor Mark Roe mentioned Grigsby in the statement he had released about his decision not to seek death for Pedersen:

As for the co-defendant, I expect to receive a mitigation package from the defense shortly, and my announcement about whether I will seek the death penalty will be made after a separate review and consultation process.

Grigsby still faced a possible death sentence in California, Oregon, and Washington.

While more than thirteen hundred men have been executed in the United States since 1976, the legal execution of females in the nation is rare by comparison, with fifty-three receiving irrevocable death sentences since 1900. As of this writing, sixty-one women wait on death row in the United States, while more than three thousand condemned men await the same sentence.

Still, when a crime is heinous enough, jurors might not spare a female the same punishment they would mete out to a man. Holly Grigsby had confessed to horrific murders, and she was a viable candidate for the death penalty.

While Washington and Oregon have no history of female executions, California has put to death four women in the gas chamber, beginning with Juanita "The Duchess" Spinelli at San Quentin. Spinelli, her boyfriend, and two other men—all gang members—drowned nineteen-year-old Robert Sherrard to prevent him from squealing on them about another murder they had committed.

Spinelli had hoped that Governor Culbert Olson, perhaps filled with the spirit of the season, would grant her a Thanksgiving Day stay of execution. He had granted her a reprieve before. But there was no word from Governor Olson. Juanita Spinelli was executed the day after Thanksgiving, on November 20, 1941. She was fifty-two years old.

Southern belle Louise Peete was the next female to earn a spot on California's infamous roster of female executions. She was convicted of murdering two people, twenty-four years apart. In May 1920, she shot Jacob Denton, a wealthy Los Angeles widower who had lost his wife and child to the influenza epidemic. Louise thought he was ripe for the picking, but he easily resisted her.

When Denton mysteriously disappeared, Louise had a perfectly logical explanation for his absence. She told everyone that he'd had an argument with an angry Spanish woman who had hacked off his arm with a sword and that he was so embarrassed by his missing limb that he had gone into hiding. Oddly, few questioned her story, and Louise had a wonderful time throwing parties at her victim's home, where he was buried in the basement.

Denton was hidden beneath the ton of dirt that Louise had ordered the Denton caretaker to dump there. She explained that the dirt was for the mushroom garden she planned to plant in the basement.

Denton was eventually found when police, acting on a tip from Louise's lawyer, unearthed him. He had no missing limbs, but he did have a bullet in his neck.

Louise Peete served eighteen years in prison for Denton's murder.

In order to qualify for parole, she needed a job, but prospective employers were understandably wary of her violent past. Margaret Rose Logan, a kind middle-aged woman, took pity on her and hired her as a housekeeper for her Pacific Palisades, California, home.

In 1944, after a dispute over a forged check, Louise shot and killed Logan, burying her in the backyard beneath a row of flowerpots. She got away with the murder for several months, forging Logan's signature on the parole reports.

One day, an alert corrections officer compared the new parole reports with the older ones and noticed that Logan's signature had changed dramatically. The parole board immediately suspected that Louise had been forging her employer's signature. They investigated and found that Logan hadn't been seen for a long time. It didn't take long for authorities to find her body. Louise was again convicted of murder, but this time, she did not get parole.

Louise Peete walked into the San Quentin gas chamber with a smile on her face at 10:03 A.M. on April 11, 1947. Though she appeared calm on the surface, her hands were visibly trembling. She was pronounced dead at 10:13 A.M.

Next on the list was Barbara Graham, whose life, crimes, and execution were the inspiration for a 1958 film starring Susan Hayward as the killer, *I Want to Live!* Hayward won an Academy Award for her performance as the glamorous Barbara Graham, who was convicted of strangling a sixty-four-year-old disabled widow, Mabel Monahan, in Burbank, California, during a robbery. Graham was executed on June 3, 1955.

It was seven years before another California murderess's crime was considered heinous enough for her to face the death penalty. At age fifty-four, Elizabeth Ann Duncan hired two men to strangle her pregnant daughter-in-law. Olga Kupczyk Duncan was thirty years old, seven months pregnant, and the unfortunate competitor for the affection of Elizabeth's lover, the older woman's very own son. The incestuous relationship that resulted in the tragic murder made for sensational newspaper headlines. Duncan was executed in San Quentin on August 8, 1962.

Would Holly Grigsby go down in crime history next

to Juanita Spinelli, Louise Peete, Barbara Graham, and Elizabeth Duncan? Was the young mother even aware of the crimes of the four infamous women who had preceded her—the killers who received the state's harshest penalty for spilling blood on California soil? Probably not.

But Holly was most certainly aware that she could face the death penalty. And that was enough to send the Grim Reaper slithering through anyone's nightmares.

There was still the question of whether or not Holly had done the actual killing of DeeDee Pedersen. Joey claimed that it was he and not Holly who murdered the defenseless grandmother. But Holly had already admitted many times that she was the one who stabbed DeeDee.

In fact, in October 2011, Holly had told a reporter that she had killed DeeDee because Joey adhered to white-supremacist protocol. White supremacists, she explained, believe that men should not murder women.

Any reasonable person would have regretted her words once faced with the specter of the death penalty. No longer in a drug-induced fog, Holly had nothing but time on her hands—time to contemplate her depressing future and possible court-mandated death.

In May 2012, Mark Roe announced that he would not seek the death penalty for Holly Grigsby for DeeDee Pedersen's murder.

Grigsby's crimes, Roe said, "almost defy description." Still, prior to the recent murders, Holly had no violent history, a factor that might sway jurors.

Instead of the death penalty, Roe planned to seek life in prison for Holly Grigsby. But just weeks after his decision, federal prosecutors stepped in to take over the case.

Now, both Joey Pedersen's and Holly Grigsby's fates would be decided by U.S. Attorney General Eric Holder.

Before the question of the death penalty was settled in the federal case, Joey Pedersen made what some might consider a suicidal move. He asked to be his own attorney and represent himself against the federal charges. In a January 2014 U.S. District Court hearing in Portland, Oregon, Pedersen stood before Senior U.S. District Judge Ancer Haggerty.

Asked if he understood the seriousness of the charges, Pedersen replied, "I understand them."

The judge asked if Pedersen realized that if he were to be found guilty on counts three, four, five, eleven, or twelve, he could face the death penalty.

"I understand," Pedersen said.

Judge Haggerty pointed out that Joey's attorneys— Renee Manes and Richard Wolf—had worked very hard on the case and were "top notch."

Pedersen was not dissuaded as Haggerty explained to him that he would have limited access to legal materials and court filings and that he would also have little control over witnesses.

Haggerty asked if he had ever represented himself before, and Pedersen replied that he had represented himself in a trial when he was charged with assault in Malheur County. He was referring to the attack on the prison guard with a hot iron. That trial ended with three extra years being added to his existing sentence.

Judge Haggerty granted Pedersen's request, but he offered him this caveat: "I think it is unwise to try to represent yourself. A trained lawyer can represent you better than you can represent yourself."

Less than two months after Pedersen's win to represent himself, he changed his mind, and Manes and Wolf were back on his case.

Meanwhile, those in the Joey Pedersen and Holly Grigsby camps had been sweating it out, waiting for Holder to announce his decision about the death penalty.

In February 2014, Holder announced that he had decided against seeking the death penalty for both Pedersen and Grigsby. The process leading to the decision was confidential, U.S. Justice Department authorities said, and the public would not be privy to the reasons.

Cody Myers's mother, Susan, was not upset by Holder's decision. "Cody would not have wanted them to get the death penalty," she said. And neither did she. "This may sound crazy," she said. "but I can't muster up hatred and anger" toward either Joey or Holly.

Susan blames the justice system more than she blames Pedersen and Grigsby. It was while they were incarcerated that they learned to hate.

While she has no hate in her heart, her grief is excruciating. "There are times when I just want to die, but I have other children, so I can't give up," Susan says.

There are photographs of Cody all over Susan's house, and while she glances at them, she does not allow her eyes to linger. "I never allow myself to look him in the eye, because I will fall apart," she confides.

Susan is admittedly very private and normally keeps her emotions to herself, but she takes some comfort in sharing Cody's story. She wants people to know about the young Christian man with forgiveness in his heart.

Cody cared about people and went out of his way to help them. If he had lived and pursued his plans to become a missionary, he would have touched many lives.

A pastor who knew Cody talks about him in his sermons to children, and that makes Susan "beyond proud. It's one of the things that help me get by," she says. "Kids have come to know Christ because of Cody."

Besides Holly Grigsby, Joey Pedersen had drawn others into his murderous project. As a convicted felon, Joey wasn't allowed to purchase a gun on his own. But he had mesmerized other members of his circle.

He had a Svengali quality about him, and the psychiatric panel could attest to that—although they weren't taken in by his charm. He had been out of prison less than two months when he had begun looking for someone who would buy a gun for him.

Max Lewis,* twenty-eight, and his wife, Cacee,* thirty-two, were only too happy to purchase a Hi-Point Model C-9 9mm Luger pistol for Joey. Cacee lied to a licensed firearms dealer when she said the gun was for her own protection. She knew full well that it was intended for a convicted felon.

The U.S. Department of Justice filed a federal indictment against the Springfield, Oregon, couple in mid-June 2013. Max and Cacee Lewis faced federal counts of conspiracy, straw purchase of a firearm, unlawful disposition of a firearm, and accessory after the fact and misprision of a felony (concealing a felony or failure to report a felony).

Like Joey, Max was a mixed-martial-arts fighter, and he was already incarcerated for unrelated charges at the time of the indictment. Cacee was accused of purchasing the gun in July 2011.

When U.S. attorney Amanda Marshall announced the indictment, she said that the Lewis couple could face a fine of $250,000 and prison sentences of three to fifteen years.

While Pedersen expressed no guilt over the deaths of the four murder victims, he was concerned about Max and Cacee. They were his friends, and now they were in deep trouble for doing him a favor.

He couldn't save Holly Grigsby from her imminent long sentence, but he said he was sorry for all the pain he had caused to those who helped him.

Just as he had tried to get Holly off the hook for her part in the crimes, he tried to help the Lewises. As it turned out, Joey ended up with an unexpected and powerful bargaining chip, and it was practically handed to him on a silver platter by the very people who were trying to punish him.

Prosecutors Jane Shoemaker and Hannah Horsley had sterling reputations and were working long hours to bring justice to the victims of the Pedersen hate crimes. They had always had good experiences working with law enforcement, and they were shocked when they learned that one of the detectives they counted on was accused of mishandling evidence.

The Department of Justice authorities were tight-lipped when questioned by reporters, but court filings revealed that the suspect detective could face criminal charges for withholding documents that should have been turned over to the defense, losing evidence, and listening to confidential recordings between the defendants and their attorneys.

It was a blow to the entire prosecution team. It threatened to damage the reputations of those who had gone by the book and could even result in a dismissal of the federal indictment.

The prosecutors had only recently learned of the omission of evidence by the accused detective. They had never tried to hide anything and were as stunned as everyone else to discover the problems.

An audit had indeed turned up evidence that should have been given to the defense: twenty-seven banker boxes of evidence.

A hearing was held in April 2014, with Judge Haggerty considering the request by Pedersen's attorneys to find that the prosecution had violated the defendant's Sixth Amendment right to counsel and had acted in bad faith.

The hearing lasted for four days, with both defense and prosecution tense and sometimes snapping at each other. Judge Haggerty intervened to ask counsel on both sides to avoid "tit-for-tat" arguments, so that the tedious process could be sped up.

In addition to missing crime-scene photos, interviews with Pedersen's family members could not be found. The "death-penalty interviews" may have made an impact on both defense and prosecution arguments in considering a capital-punishment verdict.

Whether the mishandling of evidence by the accused detective was sloppiness or deliberate deceit was questionable. He had been put on administrative leave, and the rest of the team was left to pick up the pieces.

At least one member of the prosecuting team had acted in bad faith, Judge Haggerty ruled. Though he was not named in court, it was assumed that the judge was referring to the detective. The prosecution team testified that they had never listened to the taped conversations between the defendant and his attorneys, but the fact that the confidential tapes had been given to them displeased Haggerty.

The Justice Department's prosecution team was wary. Now Pedersen had something to bargain with. After the four-day hearing, in an unusual and complicated plea bargain, Pedersen agreed to stop the motions against the prosecution in exchange for leniency for Max and Cacee Lewis.

The federal prosecutors agreed to give Max eighty-nine months (just less than seven and a half years) instead of fifteen years. Cacee was already expected to get probation. The deal would work only if Pedersen and the Lewises all pled guilty, and the overseeing judges agreed to the terms. Holly had no part in this arrangement.

Pedersen, it was noted, would not be benefiting from the deal. The death penalty was already off the table, and he had received a sentence of life in prison without parole for the Washington case.

In April 2014, David "Joey" Pedersen pled guilty to two counts of carjacking resulting in death, one for Cody Myers and the other for Reginald Clark.

In August 2014, Pedersen was sentenced to two life terms for his federal crimes.

Holly made a plea deal with the federal prosecutors, and on March, 11, 2014, she stood before U.S. District Court Judge Ancer Haggerty as he questioned her about her role in the death of DeeDee Pedersen.

"Yes, I aided in the commission," Holly acknowledged.

"Did you in fact stab her to death?" he asked.

"No."

Holly had changed her story, and her response brought gasps from DeeDee's relatives.

"Are you saying your co-defendant did that?" the judge prodded.

Holly said quietly, "I have nothing to say about Joey."

Holly Grigsby pled guilty to racketeering, one of fourteen counts against her. As part of her plea deal, she will not face further charges in Washington, Oregon, or California, and she will be sentenced to life without parole.

Holly threw away everything to follow a man full of hate. How sad. Her little boy will grow up without a mother.

If he lives out a thirty-year-old man's average life span, Joey may go down in criminal history as the prisoner incarcerated the longest. It is a world he knows, and, indeed, possibly a world where he feels safer than when he is outside the walls.


Cody Myers's family will mourn for him for the rest of their lives. Reginald Clark will be forever missed by the many friends and family who loved him.

There won't be any more Grandkids' Picnics for DeeDee Pedersen's grandchildren or family gatherings in DeeDee's mobile home in Everett. When she met Red Pedersen, she marveled at how lucky she was.

She had no idea what evil stalked them both.

# MURDEROUS EPITAPH FOR THE BEAUTIFUL RUNAWAY

**She was born** and raised in a world where private schools, debutante parties, and high society reigned. She was brilliant and lovely in a patrician way, the kind of young woman who would become more beautiful as she grew older. She was slender but full-breasted, with high cheekbones and dark hair that hung a full twenty inches down her back. Her family had been wealthy for generations, and her father held a responsible position with the State Department. She could have had the whole world, but, like so many other young women in the 1970s, Britt Rousseau* chose to follow the beat of a different drummer.

Britt was only eighteen when she left her family and the luxurious trappings of wealth she was used to in late 1976 to begin her wandering odyssey across America. She was legally an adult, and nothing her family could do or say could dissuade her from leaving, setting out on foot with her backpack and only a bicycle for transportation. She had to "find" herself.

Britt's family sent telegraphed money orders whenever they knew where she would be for longer than a day or so. They waited and prayed and worried. It was agonizing for them to wonder just where she was, if she was safe. And the months passed as the wanderer moved farther and farther away from home. Maybe, just maybe, she would miss the world of Washington, D.C., and the rolling countryside of Maryland that she'd left behind. Horse country. Maybe she would return and finish her schooling closer to home as the thrill of the open road and undiscovered territory began to pale. Maybe.

On Christmas Day, 1977, Britt Rousseau was alone, walking down the empty, rain-washed streets of Portland, Oregon. Portland is a friendlier town than most, but no city is very welcoming on Christmas; everyone who has a family is at home, and even the street people are lined up to find shelter and a free holiday dinner.

Britt looked at the closed stores and the deserted streets, and she sighed, wondering where she would go next. She had a little money left, although not much, and everything she owned was in the backpack she shouldered.

Suddenly, a man yelled at her from across the street. She turned, and he waved. She didn't know him, but he looked all right. She waited as he crossed over to join her.

"Where you headed?" he asked.

She shrugged. "Flip a coin—you've got it. I could go south for the sunshine. Anything would be better than this. Or north. I've never been to Washington State. I hear they have some good colleges up there."

The man studied her. She was as tall as he, at five-foot-six, and probably weighed about the same. She was younger by more than a dozen years, and yet she seemed to have a certain insouciance about her, as if she could handle anything that came her way.

"I'm going up north," he offered. "You want to join up with me? It's rough being alone on Christmas, and it's easier anytime to travel in partners. What do you say?"

"No strings?" she countered.

"No strings."

"Okay. Just remember, I go my own way. I don't answer to anyone, and I get nervous if somebody tries to tie me down."

He laughed. "I'm with you. I'm not asking you to marry me. I just want a traveling buddy."

He was a nice guy, she decided, as they cemented their pact over a beer in one of the few taverns open on Christmas. Then they hitchhiked over the bridge crossing the Columbia River and into the state of Washington. Britt called her family, and they agreed to wire fifty dollars to her, which she could pick up in Centralia, Washington, eighty miles farther north. It wasn't the kind of Christmas present they would have liked to give her, but at least they knew she was safe for the moment. She promised to keep in touch.

Britt's traveling companion told her his name was Don

Fabry,* that he was thirty-three, and that his folks lived in Oregon near the state capital of Salem. They decided that they would look for work, but neither of them was apparently very adept at it. They hitched across the Cascade Mountains to Wenatchee, the apple city. Wenatchee was overflowing with jobs for migrant laborers from spring through harvest, but there weren't any in the bleak days after Christmas. It was freezing cold, and the snow was deep, so the pair soon decided to thumb their way back to Seattle, where the chances of a job would be considerably better. Britt thought she might be able to get a grant to go to school if her luck ran well.

She seemed to have an extremely easygoing approach to life, and Fabry warned her that she trusted too many people. "I'm okay . . . but you didn't know that. You have to be careful who you go with."

She laughed and told him that she hadn't had any trouble so far and didn't expect that she would.

Nonetheless, Fabry talked her into opening a checking account in Seattle. "When you're on the streets, even fifty dollars can be enough for somebody to knock you on the head. Put your money in the bank, and then draw it out when you need it," he urged.

She thought he was being overcautious, but she agreed. They didn't have enough money to get a room in the Queen City, and the pair went to the Salvation Army, where someone arranged for them to have a room in the Morrison Hotel, an aging structure kitty-corner from the main headquarters of the Seattle Police Department.

It wasn't much of a room, but it was shelter from the rainy days of the New Year. There was a view of the gray buildings of Seattle's lower Third Avenue. Furniture had been culled from rejects here and there: an iron bed, a 1920s vintage dresser, a worn gray armchair, and some old tables. Cooking was not allowed in the rooms, but everyone did. There was a sink, but the bathroom was down the hall, and heat came only grudgingly from the radiator near the window.

Britt parked her ten-speed bike next to the bed. If she'd left it in the lobby, it would have been stolen.

She talked to Don about possibly moving on to Bellingham, up near the Canadian border, so that she could go to college at Western Washington University, but mostly they just kind of coasted. Although they had established a physical relationship, she still warned Fabry that she didn't belong to him or anyone else and that she didn't want to be questioned if she wanted to spend some time without him.

Perhaps if she had decided to go to Bellingham, a much smaller town than Seattle, she would have been safer. The campus of Western Washington University was definitely more benign than a seedy hotel on skid row in Seattle.

It was approximately 2:15 on the afternoon of Sunday, January 15, when the emergency operator at the

Seattle police dispatch center received the report of a "dead body" at the Morrison Hotel. Patrol officers were dispatched. Calls regarding dead bodies were not especially unusual when they emanated from the crumbling old hotels of skid row. Most of the rooms were occupied by transients or elderly people getting by on pension checks. Many of them died, either from old age or loneliness or because they drank too much cheap Tokay wine. Only two days before, one of them had been found dead on the roof of the Morrison.

But when the officers looked into Room 114, the body they saw before them was not that of an elderly transient; it was a beautiful young woman, nude from the waist down.

They spoke to a husky man about thirty who said that he had been the renter of Room 128 but that he hadn't been living there; he'd moved into a larger room on the fourth floor with his girlfriend. He had discovered the body and called police.

The first responders secured the room and called over to the homicide unit to request a crew of detectives. Detective Sergeant Craig VandePutte and Detective Wayne Dorman didn't have to bother picking up a car; instead, they grabbed their cameras and equipment and walked across Third Avenue. The temperature was a relatively balmy fifty-two degrees on that Sunday afternoon, and although it wasn't raining, there was a layer of threatening clouds overhead.

VandePutte and Dorman made up two-thirds of the

skeleton homicide crew on the weekend and had expected they might have a chance to catch up on the ever-present paperwork of their department, but this was to be no quiet Sunday.

Officer Meyers met them at the door of Room 114.

"No one's been in since I got here," he told the detectives. "She's over there—on the bed."

VandePutte and Dorman stepped into the room, which measured fourteen feet, seven inches by twelve feet, six inches. It was hot and fetid. Someone had covered the room's two windows with blankets so that the place was half lit, and the radiator hissed steadily, keeping the temperature up around eighty degrees. Oddly, both faucets of the sink were turned on and running at full tilt. Dorman attempted to shut them off, but they were stuck open.

The room was furnished with a single twin bed and other assorted furniture.

The girl lay on the bed or, rather, half on and half off. The upper part of her body rested on the end of the bed, while her hips and legs dangled over onto the floor.

She appeared to be fully clothed above the waist in a T-shirt and waffle-knit long underwear. The T-shirt bore the inscription of a well-known fraternity, Sigma Alpha Epsilon, and the victim's bra had been pushed up over her full breasts. The victim still wore socks—mismatched— on her feet. A pair of panties lay near her right leg, and the detectives found a pair of jeans between the bed and a small wooden trunk.

Dorman lifted the sheet that covered the girl's face and saw that she had been very pretty. Her long dark hair cascaded over the bedding. There was just a trace of blood marring her forehead.

The dead girl had pierced ears with earrings in place, and she wore a silver wire necklace around her neck. Her neck was scratched and bruised, as if someone had strangled her manually.

She had not been dead long. The body still felt warm on its nether side, although her exposed lower body was cold.

Green slivers of broken glass littered the bed and were caught in the victim's long hair. The label was still intact on the wine bottle; it was Thunderbird, a relatively cheap wine popular with skid row habitués.

Sergeant VandePutte took pictures of the victim, the bed, and the surrounding area, which was cluttered with blankets and a light green man's shirt and gray sandals.

It looked as if the victim had put up a tremendous fight for her life, but though she appeared young and healthy, she was thin and would have been no match for a man intent on rape. One drop of blood flecked her pale skin just above her pubic hair, and there was a bit more on her right leg. If rape had not been accomplished, it had surely been attempted.

At 3:20 P.M., the King County medical examiner, Dr. Donald Reay, arrived.

"She's been moved," Reay commented. "The lividity

pattern shows that she lay on her right side for some time after she died. Then someone moved her to the position in which you found her. That's why you see the darker red on her side and the lighter pink staining on her back. When the heart no longer pumps, blood drops to the lowest portion of a body."

Discovery of blood marking the pillow that rested at the top of the bed appeared to confirm this.

Taken rectally, the victim's body temperature was ninety-two degrees, which would pinpoint time of death within the previous two or three hours, with some allowance made for the fact that the room was very warm. Dr. Reay took swabs of the victim's vaginal canal and mouth.

When VandePutte and Dorman had finished bagging and labeling all the clothing and other evidence found in the room, the body was released to the medical examiner for postmortem exam, and the room was officially sealed.

There were many tangled stories to unravel. The victim had been tentatively identified as Britt Rousseau, who, had she lived nine more days, would have been twenty years old on January 24. She was rumored to be from Baltimore, Maryland.

While VandePutte and Dorman worked inside the death room, Detective Jerry Trettevik had interviewed the man who said he was Britt's traveling companion. Don Fabry recounted to Trettevik his meeting with Britt on Christmas Day. He said they'd come to Seattle about nine days before, had stayed two nights in the Union Gospel Mission, and then had been placed in the Morrison Hotel by the Salvation Army, in Room 128.

"Then she didn't die in your room?" Trettevik asked.

Fabry shook his head. "No—the last time I saw Britt was about ten this morning. She did a little grass and a little acid when she could afford it, and she borrowed some money from me this morning and said she was going to buy some joints."

"Did you ask her from who?"

"No . . . she was independent. She didn't like to be questioned."

Fabry explained that he and Britt shared Room 128, and they had become acquainted with several other residents at the Morrison. The room in which she had been found belonged to Joe Rogers.*

"But Joe wasn't living there. He'd moved in with his lady, Misty,* up on the fourth floor. So Joe was letting Kurtis Andersen* live in it."

Andersen was described as being a very tall, very strong man of about thirty who was living at the hotel because he was estranged from his wife.

"When did you hear about Britt's being killed?" Detective Trettevik asked Fabry.

"Just before we called the police. Rogers came down to my room and said, 'Come to one-fourteen. Your old lady's dead.'"

Fabry had run down the hall and seen Britt's legs

dangling off the bed. Rogers had insisted right away that Kurtis Andersen was responsible and had run to call the police.

Andersen was the only principal who was not on the scene at the Morrison, and no one knew where he was. He appeared a short time later in the police patrol division offices and told Officer Nick Carnovale that he wanted to talk to someone about a murder. Detectives Bill Baughman and George Marberg, who had been called in to help with the murder investigation, contacted Andersen and brought him to the homicide unit for questioning.

The hulking man was obviously under the influence as he began to recite his version of the events of the afternoon. He told Baughman and Marberg that he was in a room over at the Morrison Hotel around noon, and he wasn't sure of the number but thought it was 114. "Anyhow, I know it's on the first floor."

Andersen said he'd been drinking Thunderbird wine with a white female about twenty-three years old when a man came into the room. "He was black, about thirty-two, and had a mustache and beard, and I think he's called Butch. Anyway, this guy comes bustin' in, and he accuses the woman of stealing some Ritalin from him. He starts slappin' and beatin' and chokin' her, and I get up and try to stop him, and he pulls a switchblade knife on me. So I just took off and left them in there."

The detectives studied the man before them. He was six feet, five inches tall and weighed close to 250 pounds.

It would seem he could have put up a stronger fight to aid the woman being attacked—if his story was true.

Andersen went on to say that he'd wandered around the hotel for about twenty minutes, trying to visit other friends who wouldn't let him in. When he arrived back at 114, he said he'd found the woman lying half off the bed and "all bloody in the face."

"I didn't want to get the guy in trouble—the one who's lettin' me stay there—[Rogers], so I tried to pick her up, and I was gonna put her in the garbage can, but she was too heavy for me. So I left."

At the very least, Andersen lacked a lot in chivalry; at the worst, he looked like a pretty good candidate as the killer himself.

Andersen said that he'd been very annoyed when Butch showed up, because he had been planning to "make it" with the girl and thought he might have been able to if they hadn't been interrupted.

"What did you do after you left the hotel?" Detective Marberg asked.

"I went down to the railroad tracks, thinking I'd hop a freight train out of town . . . but I waited, and nothing came along, so I walked up to Mary's Cafe in Pioneer Square. I got to thinking I should tell somebody about what I saw—so I came over to the police station."

Andersen said he didn't know the woman's name. All he knew about her was that she lived at the Morrison with her "old man." He said that Joe Rogers, his benefactor, had moved out of 114 and into Misty's room on the fourth floor and let him live there free until the rent ran out.

"What'd you do with your bottle of Thunderbird?" Detective Baughman asked.

"I took it with me when I left."

Andersen said he didn't have any permanent address and just stayed wherever he hung his hat. He'd been in the Seattle area since he got out of the service in 1965, he said, and he had a pretty good job as a pipe fitter in a shipyard.

Both detectives noticed that Andersen had blood on his hands, on his pants, and on a matchbook he pulled from his pocket. When they mentioned this to him, he became very agitated and blurted, "I should have just kept going and never reported this!"

"If you'd kept going, we would have come looking for you," Marberg said quietly.

At this, Andersen jumped out of his chair and screamed, "What for?"

"For murder," the detective said in the same quiet tone.

Now Andersen became very antagonistic and surly, and he refused to answer any more questions. He took on the attitude of the outraged innocent who had only come in to do them a favor and was being rewarded for his good citizenship by an accusatory attitude on their part.

Kurtis Andersen was arrested and booked for suspicion of murder.

Before the day was over, however, three men were

jailed on suspicion of murder in the case of Britt Rousseau's death: Don Fabry, her traveling companion and sometime lover; Joe Rogers, in whose room she was found and who had discovered her body; and Kurtis Andersen. None of them had a very good alibi, and all of them had had ample opportunity to kill her.

Andersen was the only suspect who'd borne signs of blood on his person and clothing. Marberg took eight swabs of Andersen's fingers for blood residue, and his clothing was retained for evidence.

Early the next morning, Detectives Mike Tando and Duane Homan were assigned the case for follow-up. On the surface, it looked not too difficult. In actuality, the problem was going to be winnowing out the real killer from the three suspects.

The victim's parents had been located in Bethesda, Maryland, and informed of their daughter's death. They said that they hadn't seen her in about a year but had wired money to her a few weeks before. Her real name was given as Brittania Louisa Rousseau. Her family had no information about whom she traveled with or what her plans might have been. They had prayed that she would come home, and she had talked of going back to college, but her decision hadn't been firm about that.

Homan and Tando began their investigation by checking for prior records on the three suspects. Neither Rogers nor Fabry had any convictions. Andersen had been charged with rape in 1973 but had been acquitted.

They pulled the file on that case and studied it. According to the complainant, a seventeen-year-old girl, she had been approached by Andersen, whose wife was a friend of hers, at a bus stop. The girl had been on her way to work, and Andersen, she said, had urged her to come with him to visit a friend in a nearby building. He'd explained that the friend was disabled and didn't have many visitors. The girl had refused several times but finally agreed to go along with Andersen after he'd promised to see that she got to work on time.

There had been another man in the apartment they went to visit, but he had gone out shortly after they got there, and the girl had reported that Andersen had forced her to have intercourse twice and had threatened to break her neck if she didn't comply. She had been shocked and frightened at this violent side of Andersen's personality and had considered herself lucky to get out of the apartment alive.

The victim had not been a good witness in court, however, and was so upset to be in the same room with the man who had raped her that she could barely speak.

Kurtis Andersen was acquitted of those rape charges.

Now, Andersen's estranged wife was interviewed, and she said that the suspect had beaten her often and that she was afraid of him because he did things during his "blackouts" that he didn't remember or believe he had done. Lucretia Andersen* said he liked to drink. His preference was vodka or bourbon when he had money and Thunderbird or "Mr. Death" (MD-20) when he was broke.

323

Andersen's wife became distraught when she realized that the victim looked amazingly like herself; she said she believed he had killed Britt thinking that he was killing her.

"I was so afraid of him. I tried to get a restraining order, and I put the kids in a foster home because they were terrified of him. I finally had to go to a home for battered women."

Andersen had fingered still a fourth suspect: Butch. They located a subject through the narcotics files named Jacque Francis Renault—or Butch.

Butch was twenty-four and five foot seven and weighed 135 pounds. It was rumored that he did occasionally frequent the Morrison Hotel, but his home address was not known. A "question and detain" notice was put out on Renault.

Investigators Homan and Tando talked to Don Fabry. Fabry evinced considerable anxiety about being in jail, a new experience for him. He recalled how he'd met Britt and their brief partnership. "She trusted people—everybody."

"You say you saw her Sunday morning?" Homan asked.

"That's right. About ten . . . she was going out to buy some joints. Like I told the other officer, she didn't like to be questioned, so I didn't ask her just where she was going."

"What was she wearing when you saw her last?" Tando inquired.

"A sweater, I think, and jeans. They were way too big for her, and she must have been in only stocking feet. She left her black combat boots in our room."

Fabry said that he had stayed in their room. Rogers and Misty had come to visit him and had borrowed a radio from him. "Then they came back, and they were real shaken. Joe said, 'I think your old lady's inside one-fourteen. And I think she's dead.'"

Fabry said that he was afraid to look at first and ran downstairs to call for police. He'd ridden up on the elevator with the policeman and had forced himself to look into the room, and he'd recognized Britt. "Then I walked down the hall and sat on the window ledge with Misty, Joe's girl, and we were both kind of sick and really upset."

Fabry said he wanted to take a polygraph test, because he'd had nothing whatsoever to do with Britt's death.

"When was the last time you were intimate with Britt?" Homan asked.

"Maybe Friday, Saturday night, last night. I'm not really sure."

"Have you had a vasectomy?"

"No, sir . . ." Fabry looked at the detectives curiously. "What's that got to do with anything?"

"We just need to know for analysis of lab reports."

The autopsy on Britt's body had shown that she had died from manual strangulation. The hyoid bone in the back of her throat was fractured, indicating the extreme hand strength required. She had a head cut and a bump on her head. There were scratches on her face and in her anal canal. Because she'd bitten her nails too short, it was impossible to obtain scrapings that might lead back to her killer. DNA testing was fifteen years in the future, but forensic scientists could test for blood type and even racial markers.

Britt's lovely dark hair was full of minute green glass fragments. It seemed likely that she'd been struck with the wine bottle and subdued or knocked unconscious before being strangled.

There was another substance found in her hair: mucoid matter identified as semen. Washington State crime-lab criminalist Chesterine Cwiklik found that there was no sperm in the seminal fluid, indicating that the ejaculate was from a male who had had a vasectomy.

Don Fabry had assured the detectives that he and Britt had engaged only in vaginal intercourse on their last intimacy and that they'd never had anal intercourse. The scratches found in the victim's anal canal indicated that her attacker had attempted to commit an act of sodomy on her.

Investigators Tando and Homan talked next with the third suspect, the owner of the room, Joe Rogers. The room monitor at the Morrison Hotel had told them what Rogers had said immediately after finding the body: "That goddamned Andersen did it, and I'm going to tell the police."

"What made you so sure that Andersen was the killer?" Tando asked. "Don't you know anyone they call Butch?"

Rogers acknowledged that there was a guy known as Butch, but he doubted that Butch had anything to do with Britt Rousseau's death.

"Butch isn't all that swift," Rogers said, "and he never seemed mean or violent. He mostly just hangs around with this young, hippie-looking guy who has a room over at the Reynolds Hotel. I think his name is Lenny or Benny something. I can't see why Butch would kill Britt."

Joe Rogers said that he remembered that Kurtis Andersen had been drinking that Sunday morning, and he said that Kurtis had taken it upon himself to mediate a fight that Rogers and Misty were having. He had seemed very interested in playing the love counselor until Britt had approached his room, and then Rogers had seen Andersen direct her into the room. Suddenly, Andersen had been in a big hurry to get rid of them. Andersen had hurried through his speech: "You both love each other, so why argue and disagree? Go home now. Rap it out and settle it."

"He just wanted us out of there, man. He had something planned with that young chick."

Rogers said he had left his bottle of Thunderbird wine in the room when he and Misty left to go upstairs and make up. He said that later on, they'd been invited to have a pickup lunch with some friends on the fourth floor, but they were supposed to bring their own plates and silverware, so they'd gone back down to 114 to pick up some plates Rogers stored there.

"I knocked on the door, but there wasn't any answer. It was just about noon then," Rogers told the detectives.

Joe Rogers and Misty had gone into Britt and Don's room then, but Britt wasn't there. Don had offered them some beer and peanut butter and crackers, and they'd remained to talk with him for a while. Then they'd gone back upstairs to Misty's room. When they came back down in an hour or so, the room where Rogers had seen Britt last was still locked.

"I got the monitor to open the door. And it was like when the police found her. Misty got real sick, and then we went down and told her old man."

Kurtis Andersen was rapidly emerging as the prime suspect among the three arrested. When it was determined that only Andersen had had a vasectomy and the other two passed polygraph examinations, they were released from jail.

On January 20, Officer Masterson brought in Caswell Rombough,* the second "Butch" in the investigation. Rombough was the Butch who hung out at the Morrison from time to time and who had a gentleman friend named Lenny. As Homan and Tando questioned this Butch, they were aware that his intelligence was either limited to begin with or severely blunted by his fondness for the grape. He answered their questions haltingly and said he did drink a bit.

Rombough had some dark reddish stains on his clothing, and he admitted that he'd dropped by the Morrison Hotel on Sunday the 15. It seemed bizarre that this man could turn out to be a killer—just as Kurtis Andersen had said—and Homan asked Rombough what he remembered of that Sunday five days earlier. He replied that he'd been taken to the detox center at his own request that day and that he'd fallen there, and that's when he'd bled.

"You been wearing these same clothes all week?" Homan asked.

"Yessir, I guess I have."

Rombough said that he survived on checks forwarded to him by a wealthy aunt in California.

Homan asked Butch about Britt Rousseau's murder. "I've never hurt anyone. I don't even know who some lady named Brick Rizzo is."

Butch seemed quite confused about the whole thing. Homan placed a call to the detox center, which cleared the newest suspect. Caswell Rombough had been admitted to the center at 9:49 on the morning of January 15—at least two and a half hours before Britt Rousseau died. He had indeed fallen at the detox center and bled enough to stain his clothing.

Detective Dorman had taken fingernail scrapings from Kurtis Andersen shortly after the huge suspect was booked. Criminalist Cwiklik compared these scrapings with traces of food particles (starch grains, starch clumps, cellular matter) found adhering to the pubic hairs of the victim and removed by combing during the postmortem. The two sources produced some particles that were microscopically alike in class and characteristics.

A body hair removed from the undershorts Andersen was wearing when he was arrested was found to be microscopically similar to body hairs of the victim. In addition, head hairs removed from the undershirt and T-shirt that Britt was wearing when she was killed were found to be microscopically similar in class and characteristic to Andersen's hair.

None of these comparisons could be considered as damning as a fingerprint match. Before DNA, hair matches consisting of the root of a hair could only be considered as a "probable," while a fingerprint match was and continues to be an "absolute." Still, the hair evidence—combined with the circumstantial evidence—enhanced the Seattle detectives' belief that they had the right man.

They had little doubt that Kurtis Andersen had invited Britt Rousseau into his room—probably offered to sell her a few marijuana joints—in the belief that he would have no trouble seducing her. He'd been drinking, and the investigators had been told that drinking tended to produce irrational and violent reactions in the suspect.

Although Britt had been friendly and trusting, she had had no interest in Andersen. And she'd suddenly been faced with a situation she couldn't handle. Undoubtedly, reasoning with him hadn't worked, and the slender girl wouldn't have had a chance against the six-foot-five-inch man who was intent on having sex with her.

A few raps with his fist and a crack over the head with the wine bottle, which had shattered on impact, and Britt would have been virtually helpless. Apparently, she'd continued to fight until the breath was choked out of her, her throat crushed. As a final indignity, Andersen himself had admitted he'd picked up her body, intending to throw it away like so much rubbish in the garbage can.

Kurtis Andersen was charged with second-degree murder. Although Homan and Tando believed that he had planned to kill Britt Rousseau if she didn't submit to him willingly, they had no proof of that. And then they bumped into a helping hand from a most unexpected quarter.

As Andersen was being led off an elevator, the detectives spotted a grizzled and bedraggled character who appeared to be studying the prisoner. Later this man came over to the investigators and said, "I just wanted to be sure they got the right man."

"How would you know that?" they asked him.

"I was there. Right there in the Morrison that morning. This great big guy comes up to me, and he asks me, did I see a naked woman go running by? I've been asked some funny questions before, but—"

"Go on," Detective Tando urged.

"So, like I say, I'm getting ready to say I never saw no naked lady, when here comes this lady—naked from the waist down. She sees him, and she runs faster, and this guy takes off after her. He's yelling 'Brittany' or 'Bitsy' or something like that after her, but she won't slow down."

"And when was this?"

"On the fifteenth . . . right over there in the hotel. About noon. I saw him running after her, and then I hear they found the girl dead—so I just thought I'd check and be sure you got the right man."

"Why didn't you tell somebody before?"

"Like I said, I heard you arrested somebody, so there didn't seem no point in it, but I got to wondering if it was that great big man, so I moseyed over here to take a look."

With an eyewitness to the period just before Britt Rousseau died, an eyewitness who had actually seen the pretty girl running for her life, the charge against Kurtis Andersen was amended to first-degree murder.

Andersen's first trial ended in a mistrial when he indignantly fired his attorney in the presence of the jury. In a second trial, Andersen was found guilty of first-degree murder.

Britt Rousseau came three thousand miles from the good life in Bethesda, Maryland, to end her life in a run-down hotel on a bleak January day. Her belief that she could trust everybody proved false.

# TRACKS OF A
# SERIAL RAPIST

**It was harrowing** enough to be subjected to his frenzied rape assaults, the pretty victims said, but then he added insult to injury by forcing them to listen to nauseating boasts about his prowess in areas that gave them too much information.

Despite the proliferation of books, articles, and television discussions on rapists, there are still many people who believe that most sex offenders who attack women do so because they are losers in the dating game, men too unattractive to obtain sexual satisfaction through socially acceptable means. Only rarely is that true.

In the spring of 2014, there was a horrific killing spree in Santa Barbara, California, by a young man who *thought* he was unattractive and that women rejected him because of that. Full of rage, he shot and killed his two roommates, their friend, and two sorority girls who lived close by.

Elliot Rodger, twenty-two, the son of a successful movie director, was, in reality, quite handsome. But he saw the world darkly.

He left a manifesto behind called "My Twisted World":

*All I ever wanted was to fit in and live a happy life amongst humanity, but I was cast out and rejected, forced to endure an existence of loneliness and insignificance, all because the females of the human species were incapable of seeing the value in me.*

Elliot Rodger wasn't a rapist, but his mind was fixated on sex, and he was crazed with it. Reportedly, no one realized how dangerous that made him until it was too late.

Many rapists are good-looking enough to pick and choose among the feminine population. But they don't get their most all-encompassing thrills with a willing female. They are turned on by the terror they evoke when they grab a woman by force in the dark, making her submit, and the satisfying crunch of their fists against a soft cheek.

These are the men who alarm sex-crimes detectives. The psychic scars left by a "gentle" rapist are bad enough; the injuries helpless women suffer at the hands of a punitive rapist tend to increase with each attack and often result in the death of a victim.

A man who terrorized Seattle women for four months in the late winter and spring of 1975 was a good-looking ex-con who liked to brag that he looked like Peter Fonda. He expected compliments on his sexual prowess and technique and left his pretty victims bruised and battered. There was a definite pattern to his attacks, but unfortunately, several women had to suffer utter terror before that pattern began to emerge.

Ordinarily, Kitty Gianelli* would not have been out so late on a Sunday night, but on February 16, 1975, the young nurse had a visit to make after finishing her swing shift in the emergency room of a hospital in the North End. Her fiancé was in the hospital, about to undergo emergency surgery, and she stayed with him until after 1 A.M., when he was wheeled away to the operating room. Then she left to go home for a few hours before returning to sit with him.

Kitty lived with her family in a quiet residential neighborhood, but the others were away for the weekend. She had left the lights on at home so that it wouldn't seem quite so much like returning to an empty house.

The porch light was on. She felt safe as she drove into her own driveway. But as she locked her car, she heard footsteps. She turned around and suddenly felt a fist crashing into her forehead. The blow made her knees sag.

She screamed. There were neighbors close by. Asleep, probably, but there was the slight hope that someone would hear. Before her scream had even died in the quiet night air, however, strong hands grabbed her coat and pulled it over her head, and a voice ordered her to be quiet or she would be killed.

Kitty screamed again—a muffled scream now, which no one heard. No one had heard the first scream, either.

The neighborhood's windows were all closed; the drumming heavy rainstorm had dulled sound even further.

The man who gripped her was tall and very strong. Pinning her arms to her sides, he walked her northbound away from her yard. The first house they passed was vacant; the second had lights on, but she didn't dare scream again.

Evidently not satisfied with the location, the man walked back past Kitty's own house and into the backyard of the next house.

Suddenly, the man threw her onto the ground, ripped off her slacks and panties, held her coat over her head, and raped her.

The coat blindfold did not work; Kitty Gianelli had seen the man's face in the porch light that shone on that Sunday evening.

When he was finished, he asked her for money.

"It's in my purse," she said, sobbing.

Displeased with the mere two dollars he found there, he began to beat her with his fists. Over a dozen times, his blows thudded against her face.

"That's too bad about the money," he grunted. "I need more than that." He ripped two rings off her finger, one a diamond worth five hundred dollars and the other a rare opal valued at almost two hundred dollars.

As if to justify his brutality, he told her, "Don't think I'm sick or a junkie, but I have a hundred-and-eighty-dollar-a-day habit." He laughed. "I'm sorry that you have to be a victim of this sick society."

And so, indeed, was Kitty Gianelli. "Take what you want, but don't hurt me," she begged.

"I won't hurt you, sweetheart. Don't get up for a couple of minutes, and you'll be okay."

After the man left, she lay still, fearful he would return. But in a few minutes, she heard a car start. She estimated that the attack had lasted almost twenty minutes. Painfully, she made her way back to her car and drove to the emergency room where she had gone off shift earlier in the evening. Almost hysterical, she fell into the arms of a friend, whimpering, "Oh, Mary—I've been raped."

Kitty's clothes were almost all torn off; she was covered with dirt and had a contusion on her forehead and multiple abrasions on her face. A vaginal exam confirmed that the nineteen-year-old girl had been raped.

When she was calmer, she told Seattle police officers that her attacker had been a man in his early twenties, Caucasian, tall and slender, with shoulder-length dark hair cut in a shag, a scraggly goatee, and a pointed chin. She hadn't seen his car but believed he had left in one.

After she had been treated for her injuries, the officers accompanied the young nurse to the yard where she had been attacked and helped her recover her property abandoned there. They found her coat, one shoe, her purse, and the contents of her purse, which had been scattered over the ground.

In a city the size of Seattle—half a million people— there are, unfortunately, a number of rapes reported almost every day. Sex-crimes detectives Joyce Johnson and William Fenkner had learned to evaluate the MOs used in sexual assaults. A rapist rarely stops with one rape, and he tends to follow an almost fetishistic pattern.

Shortly before Kitty Gianelli was attacked, another young woman was raped by a tall, thin man with shoulder-length hair who had followed her after she got off a bus in the North End of the city. He had walked past her and grabbed her around the neck and head and forced her into a garage off an alley. After the attack, he stole two dollars from her and told her to count to fifty before she left the garage.

On March 10, Joanne Bixler* left her apartment in the North End at 12:30 A.M. to walk a few short blocks to a friend's house. At the corner of 39th and Linden Avenue North, a man stepped from the shadows and grabbed her from behind with a hand over her mouth. Although she fought, he was much stronger, and he began to drag her into the bushes. Her screams did not seem to deter him in the least. Her purse fell onto the sidewalk as the man threw her down beneath a bush.

He ripped off her clothes and wrapped her coat around her head before he raped her, all the time hitting her in the face and stomach with his fists.

The man's voice was quiet and soft, an odd contrast to the violence of his fists and the threats of death he was spewing. When he had ejaculated, he turned his thoughts to money and asked Joanne where her purse was. She pointed to the sidewalk where it had fallen in the struggle, and he left her to retrieve it.

As soon as he let go of her, the plucky young woman got up and ran across the street, between the dark houses, until she reached heavily traveled Aurora Avenue. There she found a motel office still open and begged the manager to call the police.

Patrol officers and K-9 units responded at once. But the rapist was gone, gone so completely that the highly trained German shepherds could not track his scent much beyond the spot of the attack. He had probably gotten into a vehicle.

When Joanne talked to detectives Johnson and Fenkner, she revealed a decidedly strange aspect of the rapist's personality: "After he had raped me, he made me lie there, and he kept telling me, 'You're dead. Just act like you're dead.' And then he started throwing dirt on me. Just like he was trying to bury me."

The rapist had taken Joanne's purse with him. On March 18, some of her papers turned up in a coincidental fashion. A Seattle robbery detective received a call from a friend whose Volkswagen had been stolen and recovered in poor mechanical condition. A garage mechanic working on the Beetle discovered some identification belonging to Joanne Bixler under the seats. The car's owner had never heard of anyone by that name and commented on it to the robbery detective, John Boatman.

Boatman had heard the name and knew it was that of

the young woman who had been the victim of a vicious rape-assault-robbery the week before. Evidently, the rapist had stolen the VW for his getaway car and had inadvertently left Joanne Bixler's ID on the floorboards after he'd rifled through her purse.

It was a good—though frustrating—lead. At this point, the VW was of no use for fingerprint evidence; most of its surfaces had been touched by half a dozen people in the garage, and any latent prints were destroyed. And the car thief, presumably the rapist, had removed any of his own property.

The sadistic attacker was out there, and so far, he had been clever at avoiding detection. His victims knew he was young, slender, tall, and strong and that he had a mustache and dark shaggy hair down to his shoulders. Detectives knew he would probably not stop his attacks until he was caught.

For almost two months, things were quiet; none of the rape reports coming in sounded like the man who'd tried to bury his last victim—either actually or symbolically. It was quite possible that he was still active and his victims had been afraid to report him, a not unusual circumstance that benefits nobody but the rapist.

It was near closing time at the huge Northgate Shopping Mall in Seattle on May 13 when the rapist surfaced again. Lynn Rutledge* walked toward her new car, which was parked near the Bon Marche. She had just put her purse in the backseat when someone walked up behind her and muttered something unintelligible. Then he demanded that she give him her purse.

"I've only got a few dollars left," she answered, and tossed her keys out onto the parking lot. Then she kicked him as he pushed her into the car, and he called her "Bitch!" as he retrieved the keys.

"Get in the car!" the man ordered. He hit her in the face twice before she could react. He pushed her in and got beside her, forcing her head down toward the floor. "Keep it down," he growled.

It was close to 9:00 at night and fully dark as the man drove away from the lot, and no one had seen them. He drove to the corner of 95th and Fremont North and ordered her out of the car, pointing toward a thick cluster of bushes.

The man ripped her blouse down the front, tearing the buttons off. Then he stripped the rest of her clothes off, spread them on the ground, and forced her to lie on them. He put his own shirt over her eyes and raped her.

When he had finished, he allowed her to get dressed and made her walk in front of him back to her car. Then he drove back to the shopping mall, telling her that he had friends waiting for him there.

He couldn't find his friends and became upset.

The nightmare began a replay. "Get your head down, bitch," he snarled, and he called her "bitch" again and again. He drove aimlessly around, perhaps looking for his friends—if they really existed. She could see him well now. He looked to be about twenty-five, was tall and slender, and had a medium-length, sloppy, grown-out shag haircut and a small mustache. She studied him covertly, memorizing every detail of his clothes: a white pull-on shirt with short sleeves and a three-quarter zipper, light-colored brushed denim pants, and old cowboy boots.

He talked continually. "Would you believe I have a college degree?" he asked, and she nodded, figuring that flattery might save her life. He told her that he had majored in sociology and then served in Vietnam, where he had become hooked on heroin. "The Army didn't help me, so now I have a hundred-and-fifty-dollar-a-day habit. I was a parole officer before I was drafted."

He bragged that people told him he looked like the actor Peter Fonda, and Lynn quickly agreed with him, adding, "You wouldn't have to kidnap a girl—you could easily find one who wanted to go with you."

Trying to be sympathetic to his drug addiction, she suggested that he might try the methadone program, but he said they couldn't help him even though he wanted to quit.

None of her talking was doing any good, however. The abductor was driving her car right back to the same corner where he had raped her a short while before. She balked at walking into the berry patch again, because she had lost her shoes, but he started calling her "bitch" and pushed her into the bushes. He punched her twice in the face and picked her up and threw her further into the brush.

Even through her fear, she was reminded of a child who

was having a tantrum. He had apologized to her after the first rape, told her he had a wife and child, and said he was sorry he had hit her, had almost pleaded as he asked, "I've been good to you, haven't I? I didn't hurt you, did I?"

She had tried everything to placate him, but all of her amateur psychology had only landed her back in the dark lot.

"Oh, no! You don't want to do this again?" she asked in horror.

His answer was to punch her in the left jaw, and she staggered, and he hit her again. She began to cry, and that angered him, too, so he thumped her on the back. She stopped crying and submitted.

Oddly, she hadn't been afraid he would kill her, but now, as he raped her for the second time and threatened to inflict various perversions on her, she realized he might very well murder her. She moaned in terror—and that seemed to please him. He asked if she was enjoying the sex act, and she finally lied and said yes.

She meant to stay alive if she could.

But nothing seemed to satisfy him. He threatened sodomy, and she cringed. She knew she would scream and that he would wring her neck if she did.

Finally, her attacker was finished with her. Was he going to force her back into the car again? No, he was gathering her clothes and preparing to leave. She begged him to let her have her clothes, and he finally relented, tossing them back at her.

"It's my first rape," he crowed. "Wow! I just raped somebody!"

She cowered in the bushes, wondering if he was so enthused about his conquest that he'd turn back to her, but no, he was leaving.

"I'll leave your car at Northgate," he called back.

Lynn had hidden her diamond ring under the seat. If he found that, he might be furious and come back and hit her again or kill her. As soon as she heard the car drive off, she put on her ruined clothes and ran to a nearby house and begged the owner to call 911.

Patrol officer G. Weyers responded to the call, and on the way, the officer received a "possible" sighting report of the stolen car, but it turned out to be an identical car, not Lynn Rutledge's. The officer drove the injured kidnap victim to a hospital for treatment of her many cuts and bruises. Then the brave young woman volunteered to go with Weyers in a search for her car—and the man who had abducted her.

They looked all around the parking lot at the Northgate Mall, but they couldn't find her car. Lynn, however, spotted it parked along the street near the Wallingford police precinct. It was impounded for processing, and fingerprint expert Jeanne Bynum was able to lift one good partial latent print.

But the shaggy-haired rapist was long gone once again. It was likely that he lived in the neighborhood where the car was found; several of the other attacks had occurred in the same general vicinity. The latent would do no good alone; it would be vital if a suspect was found with prints to compare.

On June 2, Detective Fenkner got an anonymous call saying that the Northgate kidnapper was one Michael Smith, late of the Monroe Reformatory. Fenkner pulled Smith's file and found that the twenty-three-year-old parolee had a rap sheet going back to 1968 but not involving sex offenses. Smith's bookings had resulted from auto theft, grand larceny, burglary, and assault. He had served thirteen months at the penal facility at Shelton and fourteen months at the Monroe Reformatory for parole revocation. He had been released from Monroe two days before Christmas in 1974. In February 1975, he had been arrested as a burglary suspect.

Smith's current location was unknown, but a look at his mug shots revealed that he fit the general description of the man who had been terrorizing women in the North End of Seattle: born April 27, 1952; six feet tall; 165 pounds; brown hair and blue eyes. He occasionally had worked as a carpenter.

While Fenkner and Johnson attempted to track down the elusive ex-con, the rapist was still busy. It was two days later, at 11 P.M. on June 4, when twenty-six-year-old Carol Brand drove up in front of her home in the North End. She parked and got out, idly noting that a man was walking eastbound along the sidewalk.

Carol had just reached her front steps when the man

ANN RULE

called out, asking her the time. As she turned to answer, he grabbed her, covering her eyes with her coat. She screamed several times while he dragged her to the yard of the house next door. Her first thought was that he was trying to force her into a car, and she told him she would do anything he wanted.

The man was evidently confident that she had no choice in the matter anyway, and he continued to drag her behind a fence, where they would be hidden from the street. Once there, he tore off her slacks and panties. He forced his fingers roughly into her vagina, bit her breasts, and raped her.

Not satisfied, the man committed acts of both oral and anal sodomy. During the entire attack, he tried to keep her eyes covered. The coat over her mouth and nose was smothering her, and when she told him she couldn't breathe, he let up the pressure on her face a little.

She heard the sound of other voices—children's voices—asking her attacker what was going on and the man answering, "We're making love."

"Are you all right, lady?" a young voice called.

She was terrified. The man had hit her in the chest before, and she feared he would beat her to death if she called for help now. The kids would be incapable of stopping him and might be hurt themselves. She managed to tell them she was all right, hoping that they would realize that she wasn't and go for help.

She heard their feet running away. The rapist seemed

nervous. No, he sounded ashamed. He asked if she was "okay" and allowed her to put her clothes back on.

Then he fled.

The youngsters had run to their mother and cried, "Mommy, there was a man, and he grabbed a girl, and she screamed, and he dragged her into the bushes and put his hand over her mouth!"

The woman called police, and Wallingford precinct patrolmen arrived almost at once. But just as before, the rapist had disappeared into the night, leaving only blood from his feet, which had been cut by nails on the fence. That wouldn't help; the technology for DNA matching would not be developed for more than a decade. Carol Brand was taken to a hospital, where doctors confirmed she had been sexually assaulted. And she had received deep scratches on her neck, sternum, and back.

Carol gave detectives a now-familiar description: tall, thin, ragged shag haircut, mustache, twenties. Her attacker's MO matched that of the earlier attacks almost exactly. The man stalked lone women late at night, kept their eyes covered, and not only subjected them to sexual indignities but also seemed to enjoy beating them.

What was most alarming was the increasing frequency of the assaults. It was quite possible that the rapist assumed his victims had not seen him, that he felt perfectly free to continue his pattern. He had gotten away clean every time. If he felt safe, he might slip, feel overconfident, and thereby betray himself.

Or he might just kill his next victim. The number of rape victims who have ended up dead through strangulation or beatings is overwhelming. Sometimes the rapist goes further, uses more force than he intended; sometimes the "thrill" of "simple" rape is no longer satisfying enough to the rapist, and he progresses to murder.

It is a very thin line.

On June 10, eighteen-year-old Moira Drew* attended a party at a friend's house in the North End. There were several people she knew there and a few she didn't. One was a tall, good-looking man with a mustache. As she left the party between 1:30 and 2:00 A.M., the man approached her and asked if he could have a ride to Aurora Avenue.

"Sure." She nodded and pointed to her car.

She felt no apprehension. After all, she had met the man at a friend's house.

Once on their way, the man, who had told her his name was Paul Smith, changed his mind about his destination and asked if she would mind taking him to North 91st and Linden Avenue North. It was only a few more blocks out of her way, and she agreed.

"Hey, move closer to me," he said, as she pulled up to his corner.

It seemed like a simple pass. She shook her head and refused.

As quickly as a cobra strikes, the man's hand reached out and seized her by the throat, powerful fingers cutting off her air entirely. A black curtain dropped over her eyes, and she saw pinwheels of light as she fought to breathe. With her last strength, she leaned on the horn.

"If you don't shut up," the man hissed, "I'm going to kill you."

But Moira kept her hand on the horn, its bleating staccato shrieks blasting through the early-morning air. A car pulled up and paused, and the driver looked curiously over at Moira's car.

It was enough to spook "Paul Smith," and he leapt from her car and took off running.

Moira Drew was not a fragile little girl; although perfectly proportioned, she was five feet, eight inches tall and weighed 145 pounds. She had fought her would-be strangler with such ferocity that she had forced the brake pedal of her car to the floor, making the brakes inoperable. She didn't realize that until she pulled into a nearby all-night market and found she had to pull on the hand brake to keep from crashing. There was a police car parked there, with Officer G. J. Fielder inside.

The distraught teenager approached the police unit, and Fiedler could see the angry red marks on her neck—perfect imprints of a strong man's fingers.

This time—finally—the rapist had run out of luck. He had attacked a woman who knew people he knew, and with Detective Fenkner's instructions, Moira called her host at the party and asked who the "tall, good-looking man with the mustache" was.

"Oh, him—that's Mike Smith," the man responded.

Michael Smith. Already a suspect but unaware that sex-crimes detectives were closing in on him, he had continued in his proclivity for brutal attacks on women.

Burglary detective Bill Berg had been investigating Mike Smith, too, and had information that tied in with his fellow detectives' case. Even better, he had a line on where Smith could be found: near an address on Northwest 56th Street. Berg arrested Smith on suspicion of rape in the case of Lynn Rutledge. The suspect would now have to face his accusers in a lineup arranged by sex-crimes sergeant Romero Yumul.

On June 11, the ex-con moved across the lineup stage with several other men who looked a great deal like him. He had always been very careful to cover the eyes of his victims, nearly smothering some of them, but they had seen him, and they had remembered him.

Kitty Gianelli, the young nurse, recognized the man who had beaten her nearly unconscious. Carol Brand, raped, beaten, and tormented, recognized him. Moira Drew recognized him. Lynn Rutledge, kidnapped from Northgate and raped twice, recognized him. The youthful witnesses to Carol Brand's attack recognized him.

Joanne Bixler, whose attacker had thrown dirt on her after the rape and tried to bury her, was not sure, nor were the other young women who had been kept in pitch blackness while the attacks were carried out.

But there was enough. Deputy prosecutors Paul Bernstein and Lee Yates filed charges of rape, robbery, and kidnapping (in the case of Lynn Rutledge) and three further charges of rape and sexual assault (in the cases of rape and sexual assault of the other young women who had picked him out of the lineup).

With the arrest and confinement of Michael Smith— held on a one hundred thousand dollar bail—the attacks on women in the North End stopped. The physical evidence on Carol Brand's rapist was piling up. He had cut his feet on the picket fence as he ran from the sound of approaching police sirens. Partially healed wounds on the soles of Smith's feet looked like nail punctures. And Berg was aware that bloody male clothing, discarded by Smith, had been found. Semen samples from the rape victims matched Smith's blood type.

Smith had no alibis at all for the times the attacks had occurred. The burglary charge for which Berg had arrested Mike Smith in February had many aspects that made it look much more like a rape attempt than a burglary. Pry marks had been visible around the windows of the home where Smith was caught, and inside lived a particularly beautiful young woman—alone. Smith had claimed that he had only been siphoning gas, and his trial on that charge had ended in a hung jury.

Detective Berg wanted Smith, felt he was potentially dangerous. Now he would work countless off-duty hours to help prosecutors Bernstein and Yates build their case. The investigative trio revisited each attack site and took pictures. They interviewed and reinterviewed the victims—all women who not only were intelligent but also had fantastic memories for detail. The case file grew as the prosecuting attorneys and the burglary detectives gave their own free time to compile a loophole-free dossier against the brutal rape suspect.

They learned much about Smith's relationships with women, and an interesting psychological profile emerged. There had been no dearth of women in the ex-con's life, but he had fought with most of them, had beaten one severely, and had not taken any hint of rejection without seeking revenge—not on the women who'd refused him but on his victims. After each fight or breakup with a girlfriend, he had gone prowling, looking for a pretty woman on whom to vent his wrath.

Interesting, too, was the fact that most of the attacks had taken place in the same neighborhood where Mike Smith had grown up—one directly across the street from his former home. Since his release from prison, he had been on the move, living with one friend or another in the North End of Seattle.

Michael Smith was slated to go on trial for attacking the four young women in whose cases charges were filed in August 1975. When Smith was faced with the voluminous evidence that detectives Johnson, Fenkner, and Berg and prosecutors Bernstein and Yates had gathered against him, however, he changed his mind about going to trial. He was allowed to plead guilty to a charge of first-degree kidnapping and robbery in Lynn Rutledge's case.

The other charges were dropped. The kidnapping charge would mean a mandatory life sentence (which in the state of Washington means a thirteen-year, four-month minimum), and had he been convicted on the four other charges, it would have been highly unlikely that he would have received any more prison time.

Michael Smith is in his sixties now and should be safely behind bars for a long, long time. But the scars on his victims will not soon fade. One woman is afraid to walk the streets by herself even in the daytime and no longer feels safe living alone. Another has suffered from painful recurring migraine headaches.

And yet they were lucky: they escaped with their lives.

# "TAKE A LIFER HOME TO DINNER . . . WITH MURDER FOR DESSERT!"

**The hobbies, pastimes,** and avocations of man are many and as varied as the idiosyncrasies known to the human race. For one undersized resident of Washington State, the question regarding his preference of activity evokes a simple answer: escape. For over thirty years, he has pursued escape with a diligence that cannot be rivaled. He has become a wizard of the art of making himself scarce.

What continues to baffle law-abiding citizens in the state, and especially the officers who worked so hard to put this modern-day Houdini behind bars, is why "do-gooders" in prison reform chose to give such a pro a virtual key to freedom. The widow of the man he killed after his last escape wonders why, too, and her lawsuit against the state of Washington puts more than a little bite into her question.

The afternoon of Wednesday, May 3, 1972, was—by Northwest standards—a fine spring day: sixty-seven degrees and not a hint of rain. Lori Taylor, fifty, who, with her husband, Bob, fifty-four, ran Tacoma's Avenue Loans & Swap Store at 3017 Portland Avenue, glanced at the store's clock and noted gratefully that the 5:30 closing hour was near. The pawnshop was empty of customers; maybe she and Bob would be able to get away on time and enjoy a quiet dinner and a peaceful evening in their comfortable home on East 31st Street.

The Taylors were popular members of the Portland Avenue commercial community. They'd been there for years doling out loans on the guitars, stereos, silver sets, diamond rings from relationships that had soured—all the possessions that their customers could "hock" when they needed quick money.

Bob and Lori were fair, law-abiding, and happy in their small family business, even if it was not the safest way to make a living. They'd been ripped off with a regularity that would tend to make many store owners pack it all in.

But the Taylors weren't about to let small-time punks drive them out. Both of them wore holsters with loaded .38s. The Taylors figured that would show the next punk that they weren't going to stand still for another heist.

As Lori Taylor prepared to close up shop for the day, locking and checking the front entrance, a short middle-aged man suddenly burst through the unlocked rear door of the cement block building. The spunky woman shouted at him to get out.

"Shhh!" the intruder hissed. At that point, Mrs. Taylor

saw that the man held a pistol. She called her husband, whose back was turned. As Bob Taylor turned, the gunman fired twice, wounding him.

Still, Taylor fought back. He drew his .38 and fired at the holdup man. The gunman was hit and stumbled backward into a small bathroom. Lori Taylor drew her revolver and fired. The man slumped down onto the toilet seat, but he didn't stop shooting. Lori Taylor turned and ran for cover. She didn't make it; bullets thudded into her back and she fell.

Witnesses drawn toward the pawnshop by the repeated sound of gunshots saw a bloody figure emerge. He was a small man, but mighty determined to get away. He fell to his knees but scrambled upright again and made it to the driver's seat of a car parked nearby. He tried to start it, but the effect of his wounds was getting to him and his hand fell ineffectually away from the ignition switch.

Inside the shop, neighbors found Bob Taylor sprawled out on the floor. He was unresponsive to his friends' frantic efforts to help him. Lori Taylor sat nearby in a chair. She appeared to be in deep shock, and the chair beneath her was stained with blood.

While a few neighbors tried to staunch the blood from the Taylors' wounds, others put in a call for emergency help from Tacoma Police. Officers reached the store in a matter of minutes.

There would be no manhunt for the would-be robber. Police found him still sitting in his car, which was fast becoming as bloody as he was. Whatever threat he had posed minutes before was gone; the gunman and Lori Taylor were dispatched to Tacoma General Hospital—ironically, in the same ambulance.

But the little man obviously had a lot more to hide than his recent shooting spree. Even as the ambulance sped toward the hospital, he surreptitiously tried to straighten a reddish-brown wig, which had slipped over his forehead, and to tear up a temporary driver's license he carried. He flatly refused to identify himself or to talk with police.

Both Lori Taylor and the nameless gunman were admitted to the hospital in critical condition—the latter with ten bullet wounds in his body!

"Any guy with ten holes in him who's still trying to hide his identity has got to have more secrets than a pawnshop rip-off," a detective commented. "You recognize him?"

His partner shook his head. "If he won't talk, we can print him. I'll bet you two days off he's got a rap sheet that would choke a horse."

There was to be no speeding ambulance for Bob Taylor; he lay dead in his own store, his .38 still clutched in his hand. Lori Taylor fought for her life as surgeons probed for the .45 slugs that had slammed into her back.

Detectives began to process the suspect's car. They found a .45-caliber revolver, with six empty cartridges in its cylinder, beneath the gore-soaked front seat. There was another wig in the glove compartment. Efforts to trace ownership of the sedan were thwarted when the vehicle proved to have been sold recently without the property filing of transfer papers.

Attendants at Tacoma General who cut away the gunman's clothes found a pair of steel handcuffs in one of his pockets.

Mrs. Taylor's .38 was found on the floor of the store's bathroom. Although she could not remember doing so, she probably had thrown it at the gunman as it clicked harmlessly against an empty chamber.

As the wounded widow remained in critical condition, her assailant was wheeled into surgery early Thursday morning. After long hours of surgery, physicians had removed all but one of the bullets fired at him by the Taylors. They speculated cautiously that the mystery gunman might live if infection did not set in. Late Thursday afternoon, detectives were allowed to question him briefly, which drew no response at all; the patient appeared to be a confirmed cop-hater. Nevertheless, his uncooperative fingertips were rolled across an ink pad and placed firmly on a card.

It didn't take long to find out who he was. The answer brought some incredulous looks and not a few unprintable expletives from lawmen in the Northwest.

Arthur St. Peter. "St. Peter the Escaper." The same St. Peter who had once been quoted as saying that his main purpose in life, once he was "inside," was to start figuring out how he could get out, and he didn't mean through regular channels.

As far as the men who'd sent him up were concerned,

the five-foot-four escape artist should have been firmly locked inside the walls at the Washington State Penitentiary in Walla Walla. He'd been convicted in 1962 of first-degree assault, escape, armed robbery, auto theft, and of being a habitual criminal. The latter charge was what convicts called "The Big Bitch." He was sentenced to life.

Arthur St. Peter was born in Montreal, Quebec, Canada, in 1924. Two years later his family moved to Seattle, Washington. In 1941, two destructive events took place; the beginning of the Second World War and the beginning of Arthur St. Peter's criminal career. The war was over in four years; St. Peter never quit.

On April 18, 1941, young St. Peter was seventeen years old. His first fall was for petty larceny; he got two weeks in the Sunnyside, Washington, jail. Sent home to his parents, he kept his nose clean, presumably, for five whole months. At least, he didn't get caught.

On September 26, the novice crook was in Salt Lake City, Utah. Again, he dabbled in petty larceny. His time behind bars doubled. He got sixty days this time, thirty of them suspended. He served his thirty days. The idea of getting out—that is, without permission—had not occurred to St. Peter yet. Or if it had, he didn't know how to go about it. But it wouldn't be long.

By October 28, young Arthur had made his way up into Idaho. In Twin Falls, he was arrested for car theft and burglary. Six months in the county jail. He stayed in just short of four months, and he sure didn't stop to shake the sheriff's hand as he broke out on February 24, 1942. He didn't go back to that jail this time. He got two to five years in the Idaho State Penitentiary.

St. Peter played it cool while he was inside the walls, and he was out on parole and back in Seattle by the summer of 1943. But then he repeated himself and went to the Washington State Penitentiary in Walla Walla after conviction of auto theft and burglary on August 29, 1943.

St. Peter didn't like it much at Walla Walla, but he'd discovered a "hobby" that suited his talents amazingly well—the study of prison breakouts.

His first successful effort took place on May 9, 1944, but he was caught in one day. He tried it again on October 4 of the same year and upped his free time to five days. King County sheriff Don Sprinkle and Seattle Police detective Austin Seth found the wily St. Peter in a skid row restaurant in Seattle and escorted him to the county jail. The con-wise escapee smiled slightly as they locked him up; nobody had noticed the hacksaw blade he had hidden in the sole of his shoe. Alert guards, however, did notice him a day or so later as he was industriously cutting through the bars of his cell.

Back he went to the Washington State Pen.

Needless to say, Arthur St. Peter was fast falling far down on the list of favorites of the prison staff. Assistant Warden Chick Hardesty commented: "He's one of the toughest convicts at Walla Walla."

He probably should have said "in or out" of Walla

Walla. St. Peter took off again on July 20, 1949. His escape this time was given a special boost by his homemade nitroglycerine bomb—a bomb so effective it cost a prison guard an arm.

The crafty little con was free until May 19, 1950, when he was caught and sent back to Walla Walla. For more than seven years St. Peter and the Washington State public were separated by steel bars. The next time he got out, he walked out the main gate of the pen, paroled on October 25, 1957.

On February 11, 1958, he became a parole violator and fugitive when he committed a rather clumsy burglary. He was back inside in March. Paroled again in February, 1961, Arthur St. Peter was thirty-seven years old. He had little to show for his adult life but twenty years of crime and a lot of time behind bars, time marred by escape after escape. As Chick Hardesty commented, "Once he made it over. Once he was shot off the wall. Once he made a nitroglycerine bomb, and once he tied up two officers in an escape attempt."

Even the most optimistic rehabilitation expert would have hesitated to predict that St. Peter intended to tread the straight and narrow. St. Peter obviously had no intention of finding out what life was like for the working stiff. He was soon wanted in three counties for auto theft, robbery, and carrying a concealed weapon. By the early fall of 1961, the diminutive lawbreaker was once again a reluctant resident of the King County Jail.

The King County Jail was—and is—quite a challenge to inmates who would rather be elsewhere. It occupies the tenth floor of the courthouse and, even if a prisoner should get out of his cell and seek escape, he still finds himself ten floors from freedom.

But fate had placed St. Peter in the King County Jail at the same time as another prisoner: Thomas R. Fasenmeyer. Although Fasenmeyer had a lot more class than the little French Canadian, the two of them were as alike as Tweedledum and Tweedledee when it came to philosophy of escape. They both wanted out badly.

Fasenmeyer had been dubbed "the society burglar" by Seattle newsmen, and speculation was that his jewelry thefts in only eighteen months might total more than a million dollars. Arrested in Seattle on July 11, 1962, he had been charged with four counts involving gem thefts from some of the Queen City's wealthiest citizens. The brilliant scion of a wealthy Kansas City family, Fasenmeyer was wanted in eleven states when Seattle cops caught up with him. He told reporters that his criminal career began when he served a short hitch in the air force and looted a tavern. Since March 1960, he had escaped from a Florida road gang, a St. Louis jail hospital ward, and the Los Angeles County Jail.

He made one bid to escape from the King County Jail on October 7, 1961, but he was discovered trying to saw his way through a steel plate. Admittedly an expert on such things, the society burglar told his jailers that "except for the soft steel on your window bars, the county jail is the toughest, best, or worst jail—depending on how you look at it" to escape from. Despite the compliment, Fasenmeyer spent several days in solitary confinement.

The jewel thief summed up his philosophy on escape to his jailers, an outlook that St. Peter no doubt echoed: "I try to get out and you try to keep me from it. No hard feelings."

If there is a patron saint of jailbreakers, she must have arranged the meeting of Arthur St. Peter and Thomas Fasenmeyer, two kindred spirits among the jail's burgeoning inmate population of 650. Their mutual interest in escape drew them together at once. St. Peter was particularly interested in breaking out; he'd been convicted on September 1 of the robbery charge and of being a "habitual criminal," and he was sentenced to Walla Walla for the rest of his natural life. Fasenmeyer had fifteen years hanging over him.

October 22, 1961, was a Sunday. Fasenmeyer and St. Peter had a special project planned for that day, a project involving the use of hacksaw blades they'd had smuggled in to them. They were joined by seven fellow prisoners who had nothing but admiration for the masters.

The men began in the morning by sawing away at the bars of their cell. But the bars were of case-hardened steel and they made no progress. Next, they tried the ceiling. That didn't work, either. Then they tried tying the hacksaws to a broomstick and reaching across the corridor to saw at the outside window bars. The bars began to give, but it was tediously slow and they feared they'd be discovered before they made a big enough opening.

Later in the evening, after the 6:30 recreation period, a wad of cardboard skillfully placed in the cell's locking device kept it from clicking completely closed. Cooperative prisoners in a cell some distance away called to guards that a window was broken in their cell. As the guards left, St. Peter and Fasenmeyer dashed to the window and finished sawing through the soft steel.

It was 9:00 on a pitch-black, rainy Seattle evening. One by one, the seven prisoners eyed the skimpy rope made out of sheets that was supposed to support their weight and get them to the comparative safety of the ninth floor.

St. Peter was first, swinging out from the rough cement of the courthouse ten floors above the pavement. Then he was down and in a window on the floor below. Two more men followed safely. The fourth man, a twenty-five-year-old charged with burglary and rape, started down. He got halfway between floors and froze. He began to holler that he was slipping. Suddenly, he lost his tenuous grip and plunged, screaming, to his death.

Nobody but his fellow escapees heard him above the wind; they didn't stop to mourn him, but moved methodically down the sheet-rope.

Once the eight surviving escapees had climbed in through the unlocked window on the ninth floor, they broke up into smaller groups and sought a way out of the courthouse. St. Peter's group surprised a sheriff's elevator operator and forced him to take them to the second floor. There, they gagged and bound the man and two other courthouse employees and left them in a restroom. The elevator operator managed to free himself and sound the alarm.

Two of the prisoners were caught almost at once by Seattle policemen Steve Brozovich and Bernard Mayhle, who spotted them outside the courthouse. Two more didn't make it any farther than the railroad yard, where they were apprehended by railroad security officers.

Not surprisingly, none of the four caught right away was St. Peter or Fasenmeyer.

Sheriff's deputies found the broken body of the inmate who fell nine floors to the hard cement. Virtually every bone in his body had been broken in the impact.

On Monday, at 3:00 in the morning, units of the Washington State Patrol, King County Sheriff's Office, and Bellevue Police engaged in the high-speed chase of a vehicle racing east of Seattle in Factoria, Washington. The fleeing car suddenly went out of control and veered off the highway to crash into a bridge abutment. For a moment there was silence; then two figures crawled from the wreckage and started to run. The officers quickly seized the fugitives.

They fully expected to find that one of them was Arthur St. Peter, since the site of the crash was only two miles from the residence of the cunning breakout artist.

The men captured were members of the escape party all right, but neither was St. Peter. If he had been in the car, he had once again made a clean getaway.

With every passing hour, detectives knew that St. Peter and Fasenmeyer were probably putting more miles between themselves and jail. On Tuesday, the FBI joined the search for the missing duo. The men were reported to be here, there, and everywhere in the Northwest. But when officers arrived to check out tips, they were always gone.

And then, on Thursday, October 26, Thomas Fasenmeyer—a thoroughly chilled, sodden, and disheartened Fasenmeyer—was flushed out of the rain-soaked brush at the Canadian border near Blaine, Washington, by border patrolmen. The frozen fugitive seemed almost glad to be captured and complained that he'd never seen anything as disheartening as Washington's continuous rain.

Fasenmeyer had split from St. Peter immediately after the jailbreak. He'd stolen a Cadillac belonging to Ruby Chow, one of Seattle's most successful restaurateurs, and he intended to head south to Portland. But he became confused and headed north instead. He abandoned the Cadillac in Marysville when he figured it would be spotted. He continued to head north along back roads, looted a safe for thirteen dollars, bought a bus ticket to Bellingham, where he stole another car and drove to Blaine. He said he had planned to get a job and go straight if he made it into Canada.

"But I'd probably have stolen. The harder they look for you, the harder it is to go straight."

Fasenmeyer refused to say where the hacksaw blades had come from: "I can't tell you that. You know I can't."

Fasenmeyer may have been surprised by the unrelenting Washington weather, but St. Peter had known what to expect in his home state, and he obviously was faring better than his fellow escapee.

Just what St. Peter was planning came to light the next night.

King County deputies Frank Chase and Jim Harris were working a special detail in the north part of the county that Friday night. Shortly after 11:30 P.M., they headed toward home. They were just three blocks from Harris's house in Richmond Beach when the patrol car's radio blared an alert: "Closest patrol. Check Seattle Trust and Savings Bank, Aurora and 175th. Armored car noticed water on bank floor." Chase and Harris heard a reserve unit respond, "We are six blocks from bank. Will check it out."

The deputies decided to back up the reserves. As Harris recalled the events to this reporter, he said, "We were north of the bank. There's a two-block road behind the bank and we headed for that. We could hear that patrol car in front. As we cut down a side street, we spotted a reserve patrolman running toward us, and sensed there was something wrong."

Harris jumped from the car and quickly identified himself because the deputies' car was unmarked. The reserve officer called, "I just 'spooked' someone and he ran back behind the bank!"

Harris grabbed a shotgun and instructed, "Go around on Aurora. I'll cut between the buildings."

Harris had a slight advantage because he was a long-time resident of the area and knew his way around the buildings, even in the black of night. He heard a dog barking near the Brayton Food Lockers next to the bank and he crept around north of the locker building. Suddenly, a shot rang out. Harris felt it whistle inches from his ear and spotted a suspect crouching beneath the food locker where the building was supported by pilings. The man fired again and then ran up an embankment behind the locker and disappeared into the brush beyond.

Chase ran to the car and radioed, "Subject shooting—in the brush now." Then Chase placed his car in position so that his headlights would illuminate the brushy area where the suspect was hiding. Another unit arrived and flooded the field with light from the other end. Within minutes, eight sheriff's cars sped to the officers' aid.

Lieutenant Richard Christie, head of the patrol unit, came from the south end of the county. With a bullhorn, he commanded, "Come out or we'll come in—you're surrounded."

There was only silence in response.

Jim Harris had had only a glimpse of the fleeing figure. "I thought it was a kid. He was so short."

Christie, Harris, and Chase volunteered to undertake a

foot-by-foot search of the brush. In the glare of floodlights, they inched, three abreast, across the field. At one point they prepared to step across a drainage ditch, which was almost hidden with blackberry vines. Chase felt an eerie chill as he looked down. Someone was crouched there, holding a .45!

Harris put a shotgun next to the suspect's head and barked, "One arm up at a time!"

The man was handcuffed and dragged from the ditch. The deputies checked the .45 and found a third round jammed in the chamber.

The suspect kept his face determinedly turned away from his captors until Jim Harris said, "I want to see who was shooting at me."

The "kid" turned. It was Arthur St. Peter.

In the light of day the next morning, detectives discovered why the bank had "water on the floor." St. Peter (and probably cohorts who were never captured) had been working nights to cut through the roof of the bank. A fused dynamite charge was found on the roof. When Harris found St. Peter beneath the food lockers, he had apparently been on his way to a nearby service station to steal a battery to set off the fuse!

The bank heist had been carefully planned. An electric drill was found between the ruptured roof and the top of the bank's vault. Wires led from the fused dynamite into the bank itself. Several bags of sand had been strategically placed to muffle the sound of the blast. The would-be bank robbers had also made a hole in the ceiling of the men's restroom so that they could use the bank's own electric power to run their drill.

But their plans had gone awry when water standing on the bank's flat roof had run down in the hole and caused the plaster ceiling first to bulge, and then to leak into the floor. Were it not for the alert armored truck drivers, who wondered about the puddle of water, St. Peter would have had a healthy stake to finance his getaway.

Back like a yo-yo to his home away from home—the King County Jail—St. Peter was asked if he thought he'd be caught.

He shrugged his shoulders. "Oh, eventually."

Arthur St. Peter went back to Walla Walla, this time for life. Well, almost.

On November 22, 1964, St. Peter and a new crew of admirers who shared his penchant for wide-open spaces crawled to freedom through a tunnel they'd painstakingly dug beneath the prison. They kidnaped a Walla Walla couple and then appropriated their car and drove to Oregon. St. Peter couldn't seem to stay away from Washington, however. A Whitman County deputy sheriff spotted a truck parked beside a road near Colfax seventeen miles from the Idaho border. Checking it out, he found a short, bewhiskered man asleep in the front seat. A loaded gun rested on the seat next to the sleeping man. The deputy picked up the gun before he shook the man awake.

It was a most thoughtful precaution; the man was Arthur St. Peter.

Before the start of St. Peter's trial this time, U.S. District Court Judge William Goodwin learned that St. Peter would have a homemade handcuff key hidden under his tongue when he appeared in the courtroom! Goodwin arranged for St. Peter to be shackled throughout the trial with a special set of handcuffs.

This, then, was the man who had gunned to death pawnshop owner Bob Taylor and critically wounded his wife, Lori. The reader might ask, "How did St. Peter escape from prison the last time?"

He didn't. Nor was he paroled. Arthur St. Peter left the walls of Walla Walla as a dinner guest! St. Peter was chosen to participate in a program designed to help convicts readjust to civilian life. The program's name is self-explanatory: "Take a Lifer to Dinner!"

Lawmen who had spent the prior thirty years chasing St. Peter and returning him to prison felt that taking him home to dinner was akin to inviting Jack the Ripper to a sorority picnic.

Actually, you have to give him credit. St. Peter didn't run away the first time he was taken to dinner at the home of a prison employee. He waited until the second invitation. He ate the meal, complimented the cook, and asked if he might use the bathroom. There, he kicked out the window and took off.

He escaped on April 21. It was eleven whole days before he killed anyone.

Arthur St. Peter was not eligible for parole consideration

until March 1988. Even then, if he did win parole, he would have to be held on a detainer for the federal charge of kidnapping. Judge Goodwin had sentenced him to thirty-five years on that charge.

In point of fact, St. Peter was not eligible for the "Take a Lifer to Dinner" program at all, but fellow prisoners had gone to bat for him and persuaded prison authorities to "give Art a chance."

It won't help Bob Taylor much now, but the "Take a Lifer to Dinner" program has been canceled.

St. Peter's latest crime has only served to heighten disputes between Washington law enforcement personnel and prison reform crusaders. In effect, both sides are losing. So are prisoners who sincerely hope to have a straight life on the outside.

Washington State has seen the introduction of several programs to help an ex-con rejoin society in a productive manner. Officers do not quarrel with the basic philosophy behind these plans; what they do quarrel with is the haphazard selection of the prisoners and parolees who benefit. Prisoners themselves have been critical of selection, which places unfit and dangerous men back in society. Every time such a man breaks faith with a program, scores of conscientious men back in prison lose their chance to participate.

The Junior Chamber of Commerce's program "A Piece of the Action," meant to help parolees readjust, received a severe blow in 1970 when parolee John Reece, whom they had "adopted," repaid their generosity by stabbing the wife of an East Wenatchee member. The woman survived, but her unborn child died. Reece was also the prime suspect in the knife slaying of an elderly Wenatchee widow.

In February 1972, Trooper Frank Noble of the Washington State Patrol, was shot in the back and killed by Robert Clark in Zillah, Washington. As far as local officers knew, Clark was supposed to be behind bars in Walla Walla. He wasn't; he was on "furlough" from the prison to help him readjust to life outside the walls!

Arthur St. Peter survived the ten bullets that had pierced his body. He did not face the death penalty; it was outlawed in Washington State only weeks before it was declared unconstitutional nationwide. Whether his wounds have diminished his enthusiasm for escape remains to be seen.

One waggish newsman upon reading of his latest escape, commented, "You know, I just had a thought . . . naw, it's too bizarre. The public would never go for such a program. It's called 'Take a Cop Home to Dinner.'"

# Acknowledgments

With deep appreciation for the contributions of: Anne Jaeger, Detective Bob Regimbal, Kerrie Regimbal, Robyn Light, Detective Gil Schultz, Detective Paul Motard, former Limestone County District Attorney James Fry, Larry Clemons, Tracy Clemons, Amanda Jones, Kathy Pecore Taylor, "Dana Rose," Detective Mark Plumberg, Detective Laura Price, Deputy Leif Haugen, Patrol Lieutenant Evan Tingstad, Island County District Attorney Eric Ohme, Jenna Knutsen Detective Phil Farr, Detective Ed Wallace, Lead Forensic Scientist for the Washington State Patrol Crime Lab Mary Wilson, Forensic Anthropologist Katherine Taylor, Washington State Patrol Crime Lab specialist Kathy Geil, Washington State Ferry Security Officer Helmut Steele, Deputy Dan Burns, Lori Snider, Jami Hill, Highway Patrol Trooper Terry Uhrich, Lori Nemitz, Susan Nemitz, Susan Stewart, Shirley Hickman, and Detective Wayne Dorman.

Thanks to the following for their love and support:

# ACKNOWLEDGMENTS

Donna Anders, Joan and Joseph Foley, Barb Thompson, Kate Jewell, Florence Scott, Cindy Tyler Wilkinson, Machell Sherles, Kristin Ballew, and Terri Charon.

Thanks to Abe Miller of Mr. Happy Computer, who has rescued my files more than once.

Thanks to my publishers Louise Burke and Jen Bergstrom, my patient editor Mitchell Ivers, Natasha Simons, Jean Anne Rose, Joel Breuklander, Lisa Litwack, Susan Rella, Liz Psaltis, and the whole Gallery and Pocket Books team.

Last but not least, special thanks to Leslie Rule.